Selfish or Caring? America's Choice

Social Character, Leadership, and the Presidential Elections

THOMAS S. LANGNER, PH.D.

Retired, Formerly Professor
of Public Health
and Psychiatry
Columbia University
New York, New York

iUniverse, Inc.
New York   Bloomington

iUniverse books may be ordered through booksellers or by contacting:

iUniverse
1663 Liberty Drive
Bloomington, IN 47403
www.iuniverse.com
1-800-Authors (1-800-288-4677)

Because of the dynamic nature of the Internet, any Web addresses or links contained in this book may have changed since publication and may no longer be valid. The views expressed in this work are solely those of the author and do not necessarily reflect the views of the publisher, and the publisher hereby disclaims any responsibility for them.

ISBN: 978-1-4401-9015-5 (sc)
ISBN: 978-1-4401-9016-2 (ebook)
ISBN: 978-1-4401-9017-9 (dj)

Printed in the United States of America

iUniverse rev. date: 1/19/2009

Contents

List of Tables

Preface

"I'm mad as hell, and I'm not going to take this any more." So spoke Howard Beale in the film *Network* (1976). That's how many of us felt after George W. Bush stole the presidential election in 2000 with the help of the Supreme Court. We got even angrier and incredulous when, after four years of malign neglect of his electorate, a majority of our citizens, including a large portion of the poor and minorities, voted for him once again.

Right after the 2004 election I decided to write this book. Aside from coping with my anger by intellectualization, I hoped that I could help to explain what seemed a complex puzzle. Why do people so often fail to act in their own best interests? Self-destructive behavior has been examined in numerous case histories and news reports of examples such as outright suicides, bulimia, sky-diving, and road rage. By comparison, the slow death by poor political choice and passivity has been slighted by psychology and psychiatry.

In 2004 I reached the age of eighty. They say "Old soldiers never die, they just fade away," but I couldn't do that, given the disastrous downward spiral of the Bush/Cheney years. I grew up during Franklin Roosevelt's tenure. Then we had a president who, despite his patrician upbringing, cared for the common man. He knew that a good leader would provide a safety net for the less fortunate. Barack Obama is also a good leader, who may be able to provide a safety net despite the financial meltdown handed to him by the previous administration.

Over the past thirty years, our civil liberties have been trampled on, and our working and middle classes have lost financial security in the maw of a gigantic kleptocracy. Perhaps you have felt as helpless to change the direction our country was heading as I have. I made sporadic attempts. On November 15, 1964, my first wife and I took our teenagers to join the 250,000 protesters marching against the Vietnam War in Washington, D.C. While this helped, it did not stop the "military–industrial complex" Eisenhower warned us about. We still have troops in Iraq and Afghanistan, and elsewhere throughout the world.

During the Nixon years, I was called to Washington by John Dean to a meeting with Daniel Moynihan in the White House basement. They wanted me to say that we should get mothers off Welfare, since my study of one thousand Welfare and one thousand non-Welfare families showed that Welfare mothers who worked had children with better mental health. Their answer was, "Get them off Welfare." With the help of two high-level advisors in the National Institute of Mental Health, I was able to tell the Nixon team, to their chagrin, that only the healthier Welfare mothers were *able* to get jobs, and thus their children were mentally healthier to begin with. They had it backwards, to suit their political objectives. Of course, Moynihan coined the term "benign neglect," which had its Bush equivalent in "compassionate conservatism."

In the 1970s I testified for eight hours in the New York State Supreme Court, coached by two civil rights lawyers. I tried to show with my research data that children in New York City public schools had far greater special needs in the mental and physical health areas than did children upstate and in the suburbs. New York State was spending much less per capita on city children's education. We won a better apportionment of funds, but this same underfunding of the city schools goes on to this day.

I served in the U.S. Army in World War II, moving from Private to First Lieutenant. I spent a year in the Philippines. My father served in World War I. These were wars of necessity. We and our allies had been attacked. The wars of Vietnam, North Korea, and

Iraq were preemptive wars, wars of choice. Are we helpless to stop war; to curb global warming; to rescue our economy from the greed of the banks, insurance companies, hedge funds, and bailed-out corporate CEOs still traveling in private jet planes?

Can Barack Obama, our bright new hope, guide us back to solvency when his economic team has Larry Summers and Tim Geithner on it, men who were supposedly in charge of regulation when the credit default swaps and subprime mortgages were being promoted?

One new answer to the question of why people vote against their self-interest came to me as a gift. At that time I was going through a divorce from my first wife, and sought help from a psychotherapist. I asked him why people often choose marital or sexual partners who have the personality characteristics of the parent who gave them the least affection, or even neglected or abused them. He said, "They are choosing the person with whom they hope to resolve the unresolved conflicts with their 'bad' parent." Freud treated this as part of "repetition compulsion," and its modern version is called "imago theory."

So it occurred to me that if you had a cold, punitive, or labile (changeable) parent, you might also vote for an uncaring president. (It is no accident that George Washington is called the *father* of our country. In contrast with George Bush, he was a *caring* parental figure.) A search of the literature confirmed my hypothesis. Case histories of patients and leaders in the works of Alice Miller and Arno Gruen provided further insights.

Loss of parental affection is not the only loss we suffer. Recently, in our society, losses have become more prevalent, such as loss of physical and financial security and an accompanying loss of self-esteem, loss of identity, loss of love and affection, loss of social supports, loss of control over life events, and exposure to rapid social change. These cumulative losses act as stressors and produce a state of mind wherein we choose or tolerate uncaring leaders. We get depressed, anxious, and even fearful. Fear was even intentionally stoked by warnings of "weapons of mass destruction" and repeated colored alerts.

Why do we defeat ourselves? Why don't we fight back? Various reasons have been suggested, and they all may contribute to the explanation. The social isolation of individuals in our society may lead to political passivity. Fear of punishment for civil disobedience is another deterrent to protest. In a time of financial depression, you don't want to lose your job, your health insurance, and your home. Lack of power is a factor that can't be overlooked. In this book I review some of the hypotheses about why people vote for an incompetent and uncaring president. I emphasize that the psychology of submission and helpless resentment (related to depression), much of it stemming from uncaring parenting, plays a major role.

For those who are interested in my qualifications, I majored in Social Relations as an undergraduate at Harvard. I earned a doctorate in sociology at Columbia University. My doctoral dissertation was based on a study of the mental health and friendship patterns of six hundred children in the town of Ignacio, Colorado, populated by Ute, Navajo, Hispanic, and Mormon families. The "Tri-Ethnic" study was conducted by the University of Colorado. I worked in the research department of The Anti-Defamation League studying racial prejudice. Later I analyzed propaganda from foreign countries for the U.S. State Department's *Voice of America*.

The fact that women in the United States generally reported more psychophysiological symptoms than men prompted me to do a study in Mexico. I compared the women and men in Tehuantepec, a town in rural Mexico, with women and men in Mexico City. The Tehuanas (the women) were well known for their independence and assertiveness. They reported significantly fewer symptoms compared with their men (such as headaches, upset stomach, poor appetite, trouble sleeping, in low spirits, feel weak all over, can't get going) than did women in Mexico City and in the United States. This result supported the hypothesis that positive self-esteem reduces symptomatology.

I was a partner in two major epidemiological studies of mental health and disorder. One study was of five hundred subjects older than sixty years of age. Another, the Midtown Manhattan Study of sixteen hundred and sixty subjects in New

York City, was a pioneering effort in the field of social psychiatry. After that, as principal investigator, I conducted a longitudinal study of approximately one thousand Welfare families and one thousand families in a random sample of Manhattan, focusing on one child's mental health or disorder in each family. During my career I have been a Professor of Public Health and Psychiatry at Cornell University (New York Hospital), New York University (Bellevue Hospital), and Columbia University. I have had training in anthropology and psychology, and extensive contact with people of many countries.

I hope that my training has helped me to make some small contribution to political psychology. In addition, I hope that this book will have some influence on the future funding of education. There is a crying need to train teens for parenting. They need hands-on experience, such as tutoring or acting as assigned "older brother or sister" to children of lower grades. This exposure to younger children can be supplemented with a course on child-care and parenting. We cannot grow a nation of clear-thinking autonomous citizens who vote with their heads, if we don't address parenting in the schools. If we can't end the days of "tough love," severe physical punishment, and narcissistic parenting, we are in danger of losing our democracy. We came very close to that in 2000–2008.

Acknowledgments

My wife, Susan Kassirer, deserves my highest praise and thanks for her many hours of editing the manuscript. She often caught errors and contradictions that crept into my writing. Her words of advice were always on target.

Several people made detailed comments on early drafts. My daughter, Lisa Langner, MSSW, made many helpful suggestions based on her experience as a psychotherapist. Joseph Jaffe, M.D., made numerous comments in the margins, and posed questions that helped me make the results of the multiple regression analysis more understandable. John Orton, Ph.D., and his wife, Elizabeth, both responded usefully to my early drafts.

Several friends aided me in formulating my ideas through many conversations about the elections of 2000 and 2004, the war in Iraq, 9/11, and the sorry state of our union. Some of these were Theo Skolnik, M.A., Robert Rieber, Ph.D., Andrew Lazarus, Robin Winkler, and Karen Kassirer, Theresa Kornak, who edited my previous book, *Choices for Living: Coping with Fear of Dying*, has done another excellent job of polishing this text. Her suggestions for changes or additions of content were always right on the mark.

I wish to thank my wife and children for their patience and support, as well as all the abovementioned colleagues and friends. With the exception of citations, the ideas and opinions in this book are my own, and I take sole responsibility for them.

Introduction
Why People Don't Vote in Their Self-Interest

These are some hypotheses that suggest the possible factors causing the apparent lack of economic and general self-interest in the 40% of people with household incomes of $50,000 or less who voted for George W. Bush, in 2004, and rather consistently voted Republican over a 50-year period. This same percentage of voters with incomes below $50,000 voted for McCain in 2008. I think they voted a second time against their best interests. These factors and hypotheses also help explain why there was a significant shift to the Democrats in 2008, which brought Barack Obama to the presidency.

I chose these hypotheses and possible causal factors first because of my estimate of their potential causal power, and second because of the interest in some relatively unexplored areas of political research. Examples of the latter are no. 1. Parental Practices; no. 4, The Stubborn Mule and Shock; and no. 10, Physiological or Genetic Basis of the Conservatism-Liberalism (or GOP–DEM) split.

The first hypothesis is, I think, my original contribution to political theory. It applies the dynamics of denial of parental rejection found in individual case histories to the massive denial (in 2004) of rejection by an uncaring parent (G.W. Bush).

Possible Factors Influencing U.S. Voters to Vote against Their Self-interest, in Approximate Order of Estimated Power and Interest (nos. 1–10; nos. 11 and 12 are hypotheses about the future direction of political persuasion. They could not have affected the 2004 election.)

1. Parental Practices Create Anger and the Selfish Social Character.
2. Race
3. The Smokescreen or Head-Feint Effect (GOP Propaganda)
4. The Stubborn Mule Hypothesis: Getting the Working and Middle Class to Focus Attention on Their Self-Interest Through Economic Disaster (Shock)
5. Conservative Policies and Propaganda Created Stresses that in Turn Produced an Increase in Mental Disorder
6. Rapid Social Change
7. Working Class Swayed to Vote GOP by Per Capita Income Increases in Pre-election Year, with Weight on Fourth Quarter
8. Election Fraud Favored the GOP.
9. The United States Has Become Too Middle Class to Vote Democratic.
10. The GOP–DEM Split May Have Some Physiological or Genetic Basis.
11. The Growth of Minorities, Especially Hispanics, Will Tend to Favor the Democrats.
12. The United States Is a Very Conservative Nation, and We Should Not Expect Any Sweeping Change in the Very Close Split Between the Right and Left Any Time Soon.

---

1. *PARENTAL PRACTICES CREATE ANGER AND THE SELFISH SOCIAL CHARACTER.*

Poor parental practices are essentially selfish and narcissistic. Coldness, punitiveness, lability, and neglect create anger and subordination of the child's self to the parents' well-being, leading to a loss of the child's true identity. This anger and the selfish parental model create a selfish social character in the children of these parents. Social character is not a mental disorder. It describes the character structure of a group of people. If it is a negative character, it is called a socially patterned defect. Since it is widely shared and may permeate a culture or subculture, it does not isolate the selfish individual from his society. Surrounded by others like himself, he does not suffer ostracism. His behavior is socially acceptable and even approved and rewarded. An historic example is the authoritarian social character of the majority in Nazi Germany. (See Erich Fromm, 1941 and Richard Brickner, 1943.)

I use two terms for political "ideal types," the "GOPS" and the "DEMS." They stand for Republican/conservatives and Democrat /liberals. They are abstractions, of course. The GOPS exhibit a relatively selfish, rigid, and authoritarian character, as opposed to the DEMS, who are somewhat more caring, flexible, and open-minded. These traits are discussed in Chapter One. (A striking example of rigidity and selfishness is the attitude of the GOP toward the rescue of the Big Three auto makers in Detroit in November and December of 2008. If General Motors, followed by Chrysler and Ford, collapse, then several million workers, including those who make auto parts, will be out of work and unemployable due to the recession. The GOP argument seems Darwinian; survival of the fittest corporations is natural selection. The market selects, and government should not interfere. The fate of millions of families is of little or no concern. The Democrats, in contrast, struggled to get a cash infusion for Detroit, as Treasury Secretary Henry Paulson did for the financial industry (of which he is a member).

From 1952 to 2004, involving fourteen terms, there have been only four Democratic presidents in five terms (Kennedy, Johnson, Carter, and Clinton [two terms]) versus five Republican presidents in nine terms (Eisenhower, two terms; Nixon, two terms; Reagan, two terms; G.H.W. Bush, one term; and G.W. Bush two terms.) Republicans have dominated in this period 65% of the time. This is a period of fifty-six years. The country has been rather consistently conservative.

The GOP social character seems prone to ridicule those less fortunate (see Paul Krugman quote later), to be more prejudiced against minorities (including homosexuals), to view human nature as imperfectible (infant damnation?), and to favor faith over science, among many other characteristics.

In particular, the GOPS have inveighed against "permissive" parental practices. They tend to believe in "Spare the rod and spoil the child." The liberal "elitists" are criticized as being too permissive.

The psychodynamics of harsh and uncaring parenting are discussed in Chapter Three. Cold, punitive, and labile parenting is prone to result in a "false self," which leads to anger in the child and later anger as an adult. That anger is expressed in prejudice and violence against minorities, immigrants, and the "anti-Americans" so labeled by Sarah Palin, the 2008 GOP vice-presidential candidate.

Due to preselection, these selfish authoritarians have drifted to the right over many generations. They tend to be poor, less educated, rural, male, and white Protestant. They have been left behind as the economy and wages improved over the years. They comprise the "bitter" folks who "cling to their guns and religion," as Barack Obama unfortunately (but accurately) said in a private fundraising speech in California. This "bitter" group has been overlooked by both parties, but this white working-class segment directs most of its anger against the liberals. This is partly explained by the effects of a barrage of propaganda that the GOP peppered them with (as in *What's the Matter with Kansas*, by Thomas Frank, 2004) and partly by the social character of some Virginians, described in *Deer Hunting with Jesus* (Bageant, 2007).

"The Scots-Irish working class culture...often comes down to this: Drink, pray, fight and fuck."

Bageant traces this social character to the Calvinist/Scotch Presbyterian history of these immigrants who, unlike the New England Puritans who sought religious freedom, came here because they sought to escape oppression from the British and absentee landlords. He cites Lynndie England, who tortured an Iraqi prisoner, as an example of the "left behind" Appalachian, a high-school graduate who was plucking chickens in a factory. She left to join the Army, which was a step up from low pay and a dead-end job. Sergeant Graner was able with little effort to induct her into torturing naked Iraqi prisoners and also managed to get her pregnant.

I had a cousin who was raised Catholic, the product of my (Jewish) father's illegitimate half-brother and a former nun (sic!). He told me that on Saturday night he and his buddies would leave the Presidio, and after a few drinks would go looking for Mexicans in zoot suits. Then they would beat their victims with their two-and-a quarter inch wide Sam Browne belts, which had huge brass buckles. This was during World War II, which shows what a long-standing tradition we have for beating up minorities.

This penchant for hate crimes is an American legacy, starting with the Native Americans, then the slaves, homosexuals, and any handy minority target, such as Muslims or Latino immigrant workers. In 2008, seven Long Island teens beat and stabbed to death an Ecuadorian, Marcello Lucero, who worked at a dry cleaner's. The suspects were Jeffrey Conroy, Kevin Shea, Jose Pacheco, Anthony Hartford, Mick Hausch and Jordan Dasch, all 17, and Chris Overton, 16. These high-school students wanted to do some "beaner jumping" (slang for beating Mexican immigrants who pick beans). The survivor of the attack, who fled, said the youths yelled racial epithets. Conroy allegedly stabbed Lucero in the chest. Conroy is a lacrosse and wrestling star, and has a swastika tattoo on his thigh. Note that the names of at least four of the seven teens are of the Scots-Irish "Borderers" background described by Bageant. However, they live in Long Island, not in Virginia.

These examples show how far this angry-fighting-religious ethos has permeated our country. Look at the thousands of Hollywood Westerns, war, and gangster movies, where the hero has a hair-trigger temper. The mantra is "Knock this chip off my shoulder" (and I'll kill you), or in the classic novel, *The Virginian*, "Smile when you say that!"

This rather extreme picture of the resentful and "bitter" working class whites, especially males, may become more extreme since the movement of some Independents and moderate Republicans to the Democrats during the 2008 primaries and the final election.

Those who shifted significantly toward Obama from 2004 were women (56 %), 18-to 29-year-olds (66%), Hispanics (67%), and the unmarried (65%). Despite these shifts, it should be emphasized that about half the nation (47%) has voted Republican on average over 60 years (since 1952). More details on presidential election shares are given later.

Again, the consistency of the demographic distribution of conservative (and liberal) voting is striking. For example, in the 2008 election, 65% of white Protestants voted for McCain, 55% of whites, 53% of those with income between $10,000 and $50,000, and 40% with household income under $50,000. The 40% certainly do not fit the *homo economicus* model: a logical pursuit of economic self-interest.

The split between conservatives and progressives has been exacerbated by the eight years of Bush/Cheney right-wing radicalism. The preemption of the Iraq war, the shift of power to the Executive branch, the curtailment of civil rights and invasion of privacy, the packing of the Supreme Court with conservatives, and the lack of concern for a safety net for the needy (and now for the middle class) has pushed the two camps far apart.

The DEMS, in my view, are more concerned with the safety net than are the GOPS. Interestingly, a distinguishing characteristic of people likely to believe that global warming is real, and to do something about it, are "highly attuned to inequality among people." A survey concluded that the green-oriented people were "more concerned with social justice." It is noteworthy that the value of "caring for others" seems to underlie much of the DEMS' ethos. In addition, the positive worldview is more DEM than GOP. Perhaps the Calvinist history of the extreme right wing encourages a Hobbesian view of man's life as short, savage, and brutal, even beyond a state of nature.

The role of parental practices in political affiliation and social character is complicated by the fact that since the start of the twentieth century, there has been a shift in permissiveness (toilet training, weaning, punishment) across social class lines. Early on, the middle and upper classes were strict, and the working class breast fed longer and toilet trained later. That changed over time, and with the advent of Dr. Benjamin Spock, the middle class became more permissive. In contrast, working class mothers with jobs cut toilet training and breast feeding short, in order to earn a living. While data on parental practices and voting behavior over time are hard to correlate, this shift to harsher practices in the working class would tend to result in more conservative generations in that class. The middle class shift to permissiveness would tend to favor more caring and empathetic offspring over time.

"Spare the rod and spoil the child" is still the mantra of a large portion of the poor and working class. The widespread child abuse and neglect in the United States is reviewed in Chapter Three. There are also plenty of examples of wealthy abusers and uncaring parents, including Joan Crawford, Henry Fonda, and Bing Crosby. There have also been periods in which the middle class was caught up in abusive fads, such as Ferberizing, when a child was left to "cry it out" without comforting.

The work of Alice Miller and Arno Gruen suggests how narcissistic parents create psychopathology in their children, and how this is related to political persuasion and activity (Chapter Three).

2.   RACE

Due to various preselection factors, the selfish authoritarians have drifted to the Right over time, and to the GOP, as social conservatism fits with the Republican platform, though *fiscal* conservatism (a Scots specialty?) was abandoned by George W. Bush. The Grand Old Party reached out to its "base," the evangelicals. This was the perfect marriage. The "Southern strategy" clearly turned the solid Democratic South into Republicans, due to racial fear and hatred. This shift came after Johnson, a Democrat, signed the Civil Rights Act of 1964.

Self-esteem is an explanatory variable hidden within the race hypothesis. Identification upward can be seen as a defense against being on the bottom. Fear of being on the lowest rung of society breeds racism (years of anti-black and anti-Catholic rhetoric and activism, and recently anti-immigrant sentiment and violence). This defense of self-image was exploited by the GOP recently, and by the Southern Democrats historically. Being a Republican signifies that you are middle class, or even a small-time CEO. The attempt by Bush and Cheney to privatize Social Security had a not-too-well hidden purpose: to make little Republican stockholders out of the masses, and thus get them to identify with the millionaires. There was no concern for market risk and its danger to the tiny nest eggs of the working and middle class. Fierce white racial pride, so evident in small-town Virginia, can be seen as a boost to the self-image of those "bitter" and left behind.

3. *THE SMOKESCREEN HEAD-FEINT EFFECT*
   (GOP PROPAGANDA)
   (SEE APPENDIX TWO)

Thomas Frank, in *What's the Matter with Kansas?* (2004), suggested that the religious and family values propaganda blinded the working class to its own self-interest. Bread-and-butter issues were trumped by hot-button issues such as abortion, gay marriage, and creationism. He also noted that the Democratic Party moved to the center, as when Clinton abolished "Welfare as we know it." So he did not overlook the economic effect of the Democrats being less helpful to the working class over time

Joe Bageant's *Deer Hunting with Jesus* (2007) is similar to Frank's thesis; a mixture of the Smokescreen/Propaganda hypothesis and the "left-behind" economic explanation. It is more relevant to the Southern states, and looks in detail at Winchester, Virginia. The focus on Scots-Irish makes it no less relevant to other ethnic or religious groups who have at some time been anti-minority (working class Italians, black and Mormon rejection of gays, the rise of black anti-Semitism [Louis Farrakhan], the defection of Jews from their former leadership in the Black Civil Rights Movement, the 1935 Harlem riots, and so on and on).

The techniques of propaganda used by Bush/Cheney/Rove, and in 2008 by McCain/Palin, are discussed in Chapter Three, Section II (The Techniques: Fear, Hope and Lying, Camouflage, Euphemisms, Appeal to Violence, and Character Assassination).

4. THE STUBBORN MULE HYPOTHESIS: GETTING THE WORKING AND MIDDLE CLASS TO FOCUS ATTENTION ON THEIR SELF-INTEREST THROUGH ECONOMIC DISASTER (SHOCK)

The "left behind" mule is a hard worker, but he is stubborn and "clings to his usual behavior: religion, guns" (to quote Obama) and various antipathies to other groups. I use the mule as a proxy for the "bitter" working class white.

What makes people drop their reliance on religion, racism, or anti-immigrant sentiment and "family values" to deal with their low socioeconomic status, and turn to bread-and-butter issues instead? None other than Abe Lincoln, one of the great minds of our country, had the answer. He told the story of a farmer who bought a mule from a salesman, who told him that if he treated the mule nicely and spoke to him politely the mule would do any task. When the mule refused to plow the farmer's field, the farmer called the salesman and complained. The salesman took a two-by-four and hit the mule in the head, and then whispered in his ear, "Plow!." The mule got up and started to pull the plow. The farmer asked "Why did you hit my mule with a two-by-four?" "First you have to get his attention," replied the salesman.

It seems that the shock of a major economic depression has gotten the attention of some of the "bitter" Pennsylvanians, the evangelical right wing, and some independent voters. Getting hit on the head with a financial meltdown, job losses, the failure of the Detroit automobile industry, the millions of foreclosures, and the obliteration of some life savings, a substantial proportion of voters decided that the Democrats cared more about their welfare than the Republicans did. This is not to minimize the excellence of the Obama campaign, and the boomerang effect of the "pit bull" attacks of the McCain/Palin campaign.

When do people say "Enough is enough?" There has to be some point at which the stresses and losses incurred by the less fortunate lead to action, rather than to tilting at windmill targets such as terrorists, other races, immigrants, abortionists, and same-sex marriages. The skills of people like Dick Cheney, Lee Atwater, and Karl Rove must also be taken into account. Without their continuous barrage of lies and disinformation, many of the "bitter" class would have voted for Dukakis and Kerry.

There is a larger question. How does emotion relate to severe deprivation? At what point do the lack of security, the lack of food and shelter, and the general stress created by poverty cause a change in outlook, even a restructuring of the brain? When does oppression lead to withdrawal, and when does it give birth to social change? This discussion could take up a whole book. In brief, the initiators of revolutions have often been members of the middle class, as in Russia. Many of the 9/11 hijackers, particularly the Saudis, were of the middle class. Two medical doctors were involved in a recent London bombing. The American Revolution was started by a group of wealthy British colonials who were sick and tired of the high taxes, especially on tea imports. If you are so severely deprived that you are ill and malnourished, you don't have the energy to fight back, even if you are angry. This state has been called *ressentiment*, and is evidenced by grumbling rather than action. Education is also crucial to social change. Leaders have to be able to organize others, and often have had military training. The bitter left-behinds are not likely to have much clout, due to decades of poverty, poor health, and less education.

Several related concepts are involved in the stubborn mule metaphor. One of these, cognitive dissonance (Leon Festinger), occurs when a person feels uncomfortable or even distressed due to holding two incompatible ideas or opinions at the same time. The conflict between these opposing ideas must be reduced in order to restore comfort to the sufferer. Some examples exhibit the wide applicability of this theory. In the Gilbert and Sullivan operetta, H.M.S. *Pinafore*, Josephine loves a lowly sailor, Ralph Rackstraw, but is engaged by her father to Sir Joseph Porter, K.C.B. Her life with Ralph would be one of poverty but love; with Sir Joseph, wealth and boredom. Filial duty and *economic self-interest* call her to Sir Joseph. She sings "Oh god of love and god of reason say... which shall my poor heart obey?" Of course it isn't her heart that's distressed—it's her brain. Gilbert resolves her dissonance by Little

Buttercup's revelation that Ralph is not a lowly tar (sailor) after all but of noble birth.

To reduce dissonance, you may change one of the dissonant beliefs or behaviors. If you are in conflict over being a meat eater because you are an animal rights advocate, then you can stop eating meat and resolve the conflict. You can acquire new beliefs or behaviors. You can rationalize the conflict. When Judeo-Christian ethics call for loving your neighbor, and you hate your neighbor, the dissonance is often resolved by "animalization" (Langner, 2002) or "enmification" (Rieber, 1997). If your neighbor becomes a pig or a *Schweinhund* (pig-dog), you can slaughter him with impunity.

When members of the "bitter" working class feel torn between the frightening reality of poverty and the fear of losing their self-esteem, they often resolve the dissonance by identification upward with the GOP. They then consider themselves better than the successful elitists whom they envy, and bolster their identity with guns, religion, and resentment of minorities and immigrants, as Obama put it.

Paul Lazarsfeld studied the influence of "cross-pressures" on voting behavior and opinion. He noted the mixed feelings of U.S. Catholics during the war between the Spanish Republican Army, which was supported by Communist Russia, and Franco, a fascist dictator. How could Catholics support Communists/atheists, and at the same time side with the underdog International Brigade who were democratic compared with the Falangists? Even John McCain has said that "Robert Jordan (the hero of Hemingway's novel, *For Whom the Bell Tolls*) was everything I ever wanted to be." Is there any dissonance here for a conservative presidential candidate to choose a Communist hero as a role model? A frequent resolution of the dissonance (if there is any) is to forget or repress one of the conflicting ideas, opinions, or membership groups—that is, forget Jordan was fighting for the Communists.

Another way to look at the Democratic victory in 2008 is to view the move of independents and moderate Republicans and some of the bitter working class away from the Bush/Cheney base as an example of the "tipping point" (Malcolm Gladwell, 2002). The concept comes from epidemiology, the study of the origins of disease. It is the "moment in an epidemic when a virus reaches a critical mass." Gladwell feels that ideas often spread like a virus. While the emphasis is on sudden explosions of illness or behavior, the term is also applicable to more gradual phenomena.

Think of the cognitive dissonance or cross-pressures on the white, bitter, working-class, left-behind males. They are part of the Republican base, which gives them their identity. As part of the 40% of Republicans with household incomes below $50,000, they voted for George W. Bush not once, but twice—in 2000 and 2004—against their economic best interests. They can see and feel that they are economically "left behind," yet they cling to the GOP identity. Suddenly (starting in 2006 as some turned to the Democrats) and more precipitously in the fourth quarter of 2008, when they were hit with the full impact of job loss, home foreclosures, credit collapse, and catastrophic financial chaos, the tipping point was reached for a rather large portion of the "bitters." They helped elect Obama, despite their right-wing allegiance. It is as if two dissonant tendencies, their GOP self-image and their pocketbooks, were fighting for dominance, and the pocketbooks finally won. Pundits said the class war came back and replaced the culture war.

As a teen-ager I hiked all over the Presidential Range with two college friends. When we reached the summit of Mount Washington, the last step brought a tremendous vista into view. This was a tipping point, or "trip reaction," and like that last step, a whole new worldview comes into being as people cross the political divide. This is a conversion, like changing religions. Except for a small group of permanent undecideds and independents, the vast majority are committed to one party or ideology. Yet it is the converts and moderates who are the target of the spinmeisters. It is also the large key (contested and thus undecided) states that win the electoral vote.

The "stubborn mule" hypothesis seems compatible with the noteworthy (if not astonishing) change from right to left in the 2008 election. But getting hit on the head may set you up for turning *either* right or left, depending on many factors, including who is in power. Rahm Emanuel, Obama's Chief of Staff, said

"Never allow a crisis to go to waste." He suggests that the financial crisis and economic shock can help to usher in social change of a more liberal persuasion. Naomi Klein, in contrast, emphasizes how crisis or shock can be an opportunity to usher in arch-conservative change.

> For 35 years, what has animated (Milton) Friedman's counter-revolution is an attraction to a kind of freedom available only in times of cataclysmic change—when people, with their stubborn habits and insistent demands, are blasted out of the way—moments when democracy seems a practical impossibility. Believers in the shock doctrine are convinced that only a great rupture—a flood, a war, a terrorist attack—can generate the kind of vast, clean canvases they crave. It is in these malleable moments, when we are psychologically unmoored and physically uprooted, that these artists of the real plunge in their hands and begin their work of remaking the world. (Klein, 2007)

Of course, the shock of 9/11, Iraq, and Katrina paved the way for rampant capitalism, but the 2007–08 recession paved the way for Obama and a swing to the center-left. What is common to these shocks and the mule's headache is the confusion and disorientation of the public. A study of preschoolers (ages 1–5) who had a very frightening experience *before* they were exposed to the 9/11 World Trade Center attack (lived near or went to school nearby) showed they tended to suffer from depression, emotional outbursts, or poor sleep three years later. Those children without the prior trauma did not show much emotional upset after 9/11. The reporter summed up the explanation: "A truly frightening experience appears to heighten baseline activity in circuits involving the amygdala, a subcortical area that registers threat, and makes it harder for higher areas of the brain (*frontal cortex)* to inhibit amygdala response. If the system is hit again by another trauma, it can become chronically over-reactive, research suggests" (italics mine).

It has been common knowledge for centuries that emotions tend to trump logical thought (cognition), but controlled studies had to come later. Alexander R. Luria early on did a study of Russian students who were about to take an exam that would determine whether they would go on to higher education or become part of the working-class masses. This was an extremely stressful situation, and their cognitive (and motor) abilities were severely limited, as shown by various tests.

Alexander Leighton (1959) listed "rapid social change" as one of the major causal factors in mental illness. The trauma of war and catastrophic inflation paved the way for Hitler to win over Germans to the Nazi movement. This confusion, this "state of shock," overlaps with depression and severe anxiety. That brings us to the possible creation or exacerbation of mental disorder by conscious GOP policies and propaganda. As Naomi Klein suggests, this was a deliberate program of Cheney and Rove, to take advantage of the state of shock to promote their own brand of imperial presidency and the privatization of everything.

I would like to think that the shock of the 2007–08 recession paved the way for better cognition on the part of those who switched to Obama and the Democrats. Perhaps an initial relinquishing of old right wing party ties and *emotional* hot-button family values due to the recession shock, followed by a shift to *cognitive* dominance as bread and butter issues prevailed, is a better explanation of the moderates, Hispanics, and youths who brought us Obama. One thing is certain; shock does not always produce conservatism or Fascism. It opens the way for *change*, which was the Democrats' mantra on 2008.

I cherish the idea that autonomous individuals, raised to "think for themselves," can actually make informed political choices. That is, they should be able to vote for the candidate(s) who will best serve their needs. This may be wishful thinking on my part. Cognitive dominance may be a fantasy, according to the report of a recent study ("A Shocker: Partisan Thought Is Unconscious," Carey, 2006). Dr. Drew Westen, a psychologist, led a study of thirty adult men, half self-described Bush and half Kerry supporters. They were given MRI (magnetic resonance imaging) scans of the brain as they considered statements attributed to the two candidates that were congruent (Bush supports Kenneth Lay of Enron, and

Kerry supports keeping Social Security intact). Then the subjects were exposed to "doctored" statements by the candidates, in which they expressed views opposite to those previously considered.

> Each group let its own candidate off the hook.... After the participants read the contradictory comment, the researchers measured increased activity in several areas of the brain. They included a region involved in regulating negative emotions, and another called the cingulate, which activates when the brain makes judgments about forgiveness, among other things. Also a spike appeared in several other areas known to be active when people feel relieved or rewarded. *The 'cold reasoning' regions of the cortex were relatively quiet*" (italics mine).

While this is just one experiment on a limited sample, it calls into question whether there is much cognition involved in political judgments at all. Perhaps because these subjects were chosen for left or right partisanship, they exhibited less cortical activity. (They didn't need to think about their favored candidates. Emotions dominated.) A sample of self-designated moderates or independents might have shown more activity in the frontal cortex and less in the emotional subcortical areas.

5. *CONSERVATIVE POLICIES AND PROPAGANDA CREATED STRESSES THAT IN TURN PRODUCED AN INCREASE IN MENTAL DISORDER.*
   (SEE ALSO APPENDICES ONE AND TWO, "TERROR MANAGEMENT.")

People who are anxious and depressed are more easily swayed by propaganda such as "family values," and by the terror of "weapons of mass destruction" (WMDs). Many Americans believed that they would be "nuked." A high level of fear was reinforced after the 9/11 attacks by constant color alerts, false reports of discoveries of chemical weapons labs, and forged reports of the sale of 500 tons of yellowcake uranium to Saddam Hussein. This ended in a revelation of Vice President Dick Cheney's role in promoting the Iraq invasion. His chief-of-staff, I. "Scooter" Libby, was sentenced to two-and-a-half years in prison for lying about his role in "outing" the CIA agent

Valerie Plame. This was meant to punish her husband, Ambassador Joseph Wilson, for revealing the uranium hoax. President Bush commuted Libby's sentence. (At the end of his second term, Bush refused to pardon Libby, which infuriated Cheney.)

Anxiety and depression were also stoked by the lack of GOP concern for Main Street and the common man over eight years. In 2003 a World Health Organization (WHO) survey found that the United States had the highest prevalence of mental disorder, 26.4% (primarily anxiety and depression), among 14 nations surveyed (Kessler, 2004, see Chapter Six). Because of this anxiety and depression, they could more easily be swayed by hot-button "values" issues, which took their attention away from bread-and-butter issues. Numerous studies have shown that anxiety and depression interfere with cognition (for example, making judgments about issues). The amygdala and the medulla oblongata usually overrule the frontal cortex—or in other words, emotions preempt logical thought. Fear of WMDs, racial fears, and sexual fears were played upon more easily due to this preexisting level of anxiety and depression.

The mental disorder hypothesis is a corollary of the "stubborn mule" and the "shock doctrine" hypotheses. It gives the shock and confusion a psychiatric label.

6. RAPID SOCIAL CHANGE

In times of rapid social change, economic retrenchment, and conflict over values, such as occurred in Weimar Germany and in 2000–2008 in the United States, people looked to an authoritarian leader who promised to solve all their problems with simple oft-repeated promises. Leighton (1959), as mentioned before, saw rapid social change as an important factor in differential rates of mental disorder in selected communities in Nova Scotia.

A related social change factor is the ever-growing complexity of a "society." This was evident in Germany just before the rise of Hitler, and in the United States for several decades. Since 1900, we changed from an agricultural to a manufacturing to a service-oriented society. Sexual mores have changed dramatically, with some acceptance of homosexuality and premarital sex. Attitudes toward race and minorities are changing, to the degree that we have elected an African American president. Faced with various confusing changes, many people long for community (homogeneity of race and values), strong authority in a leader, and a religious orientation, all hallmarks of the two Bush terms. The "imperial presidency" grew in power during those terms, weakening the Judicial and the Legislative branches. A return to the "Community" (labeled *Gemeinschaft* by Ferdinand Toennies, 1887, 1963; see Chapter Three) is supposed to solve all the problems of modern "Society" (*Gesellschaft*).

It is interesting to see how in her speeches, Sarah Palin emphasized the small town as the "real America." The towns she visited on her campaign tour were heavily white. Perhaps she was chosen because she represented the *Gemeinschaft*. She is from a small Alaskan town, Wasilla. Its population of 5,469 is 85% white. It is homogeneous by race, and presumably by religion and values. Palin spoke for "community" over "society" when she said: "We believe that the best of America is in these small towns that we get to visit, and in these wonderful little pockets of what I call the real America, being here with all of you hard-working, very patriotic, very pro-America areas of this great nation." (Translation: Democrats are lazy, unpatriotic, and anti-American.)

7.   *Working Class Swayed to Vote GOP by Per Capita Income Increases in Pre-Election Year, with Weight on Fourth Quarter*

Lane Kenworthy, in "Bread, Peace and the 2008 Election" (2008), failed to predict that Obama would win. He used a model proposed by Douglas Hibbs, (2000), in which pre election fourth quarter per capita income increases seemed to predict election outcomes ("bread"), and favored the incumbent president. This would seem to refute the idea that poor people consistently voted against their economic best interests.

Thomas Frank, while emphasizing that millions of citizens voted against their best economic interests because they suffered from a "carefully cultivated derangement" (the Cheney/Rove smokescreen), also noted that the Democratic Party had moved to the center, so it became less of a spokesman for the poor and left-behind. So he also invoked the "bread" argument (or economic self-interest) but as secondary to the effect of the GOP propaganda "values" blitz.

Kenworthy (in February 2008) predicted a GOP win, but suggested that the model might not be working this time for several reasons. The "incumbent," McCain (acting as a *proxy-incumbent*, since he followed the Bush policies closely, especially as the campaign progressed) would be hurt by U.S. casualties in Iraq. However, the war took a back seat as soon as the economic recession exploded. Thus "income growth in the pre-election fourth quarter" did not help the GOP. On the contrary, *loss* of income probably created the very margin Obama needed for victory by pushing moderate Republicans and the undecided toward the left. This supports the role of "bread" in the model, but instead of continuing the Republican domination of 50 years, it broke the GOP's winning streak. (The "mule's attention" hypothesis would emphasize the enormity of the hammer-blow of the 2008 recession which became undeniable just before the election. By this reasoning, loss of "bread" had to be cataclysmic to overcome the smokescreen of family values.) Kenworthy also notes that per capita personal income is no longer a good measure of "bread." "Since the mid-seventies per capita income has continued to do so (rise) but median family income has been relatively flat." The average per capita income is skewed upward by the rapid income increase in the wealthiest 1% to 5%.

Kenworthy essentially is saying that the decline in working-class support for Democrats started in the mid-seventies, before the rise of the family-values issues (guns, religion, abortion, evolution). The outsourcing of jobs, the decline of the unions, and the stagnation of wages made the Democrats seem of little help to them. "Beginning in the mid-to-late 1970s there was increasing reason for working-class whites to question whether the Democrats were still better than the Republicans at promoting their material well-being."

Kenworthy's thesis does not contradict Frank's emphasis on the family-values propaganda blitz. It simply claims than an earlier shift to the right by the white working-class left-behinds preceded the values-blitz, and suggests that values carried on, or even exacerbated, their shift to the right.

I find it implausible that the factor of race is given minimal prominence in this analysis. After the Civil Rights Act of 1964, the "solid South" turned against the Democrats, and became split, but heavily in favor of the GOP. The grip of the Democrats on Congress from 1930 to 1960 was broken.

8. ELECTION FRAUD FAVORED THE GOP.
   (SEE APPENDIX TWO)

While there is strong evidence of election fraud, especially by the Republicans, I personally doubt that it was a major contributor to the GOP win in 2004. In 2000, however, the scandal over "chads" in Florida, the blatant partisanship of Katherine Harris, the Florida Secretary of State, and the 7–2 vote by the U.S. Supreme Court stopping the recount, gave Bush a small majority, and thus gave Florida's electoral votes to Bush. This small majority (537 votes) was tiny compared to the 173,000 "scrub list" of assorted "felons" who were denied a vote by Harris. Since they were primarily black, as is most of our prison population, those who had served their sentences would have voted heavily for Gore, changing the course of the next eight years, the Iraq war, and progress on environmental issues.

In 2004, Bush did get a small majority of the popular vote. There certainly was hanky-panky in Ohio and Florida and other states, but nothing as gross as in 2000. Many types of fraud are possible, and have been documented. The Diebold Corporation's internal memos suggest that thousands of votes in Florida were lost by machine errors. Touch screens can be rigged. Votes can be switched by programming. Minorities can be disenfranchised by demanding voter picture-I.D. cards, items that minorities and the poor tend not to have, because they often don't have cars and driver's licenses. Voting booths can be scarce in poor neighborhoods, creating long lines and travel expenses for the poor. The creation of poorly designed voting forms, such as the one with the famous "chads" that had to be punched out, led to more "hanging," or improperly punched out chads by the poor and uneducated, and perhaps the elderly. This in turn probably favored the GOP.

There is no way of telling the exact impact of voter fraud on the outcome of elections. Until we get paper ballots to back up the machines, we must remain in the dark about the "true" popular vote.

9. *The United States Has Become too Middle Class to Vote Democratic.*
   (See Appendix Two)

Did economic issues become less important to voters, particularly in the 2000 and 2004 elections, as the country got richer? This might be true for the "Reagan Democrats." It might also be true for the previously well-compensated workers in the UAW, the United Auto Workers union. But there was already trouble on the horizon for Detroit. Wages had been slipping, there were layoffs, and Detroit was losing ground to foreign cars. Then in late 2008 came the virtual collapse of the Big Three: G.M., Ford, and Chrysler. The government (mainly Democrats) has tried to bail them out, but many on the right, who bailed out their own buddies in the financial sector (for example, Henry Paulson, Secretary of the Treasury) held that the auto makers brought about their own demise, and should be left to twist slowly in the wind. The Republican Senators refused to give General Motors and Chrysler fifteen billion to avoid bankruptcy. They argued that the United Auto Workers get $75 per hour, much more than the auto workers in Japan or other foreign countries. The difference is due to the fact that foreign car makers don't pay for medical insurance. A universal health care program would solve this wage differential. The right wing has little regard for the three million workers who are involved in auto assembly or in manufacturing and transporting parts, and whose financial security is in doubt. The actual wages of $35 per hour and medical and retirement benefits of the auto workers are now going down the proverbial "tubes." To tide Detroit over, the Democrats have offered a temporary bailout, until the auto companies restructure.

I discuss this "too middle class" hypothesis in Appendix Two, and come to the conclusion that it does not hold water. In fact, for the immediate future, we know that the country as a whole is seeing sharp declines in income and well-being. When even the middle-class is really hurting financially, the working-class cannot be "too satisfied with its economic lot to vote Democratic."

10. THE GOP–DEM SPLIT MAY HAVE SOME PHYSIOLOGICAL OR GENETIC BASIS.

There is a possibility that the difference between the authoritarian social character of the conservatives and the less martial and more empathic character of the liberals is based on physiological or genetic differences between these two groups. It may be the most controversial area of political research, for it raises hackles among conservatives, and because most of the academics who do the studies are liberals, the results, or at least the interpretations of the results, are open to bias.

For example, could hormone levels be different for conservatives and liberals? It is true that young men, with relatively high levels of testosterone, are most likely to commit (conservative) hate crimes. However, they could just as well be involved in violence of the left wing, and have been in such protests as the riots against the Vietnam War. This hypothesis doesn't seem to fit with the fact that 66% of 18-to-29-year-olds voted for Obama. Men, however, were split almost evenly (49% for Obama). And we know that white men have voted heavily Republican. If male hormones are not the primary influence, then there are many studies of genetic effects, one example of which should be sufficient to show the design.

Genetics

A Minnesota study of heritability (Bouchard et al., 2003) analyzed a subset of fifty-four pairs of monozygotic (MZ or "identical") and forty-six pairs of dizygotic (DZ or "fraternal") twins, *all reared apart*. A conservatism scale showed a difference between the MZs and DZs equivalent to a correlation of 0.56, showing a large genetic influence. This would suggest that genetics, or the difference between the one-egg and two-egg twins, accounts for about 30% of the variance in conservatism. For example, one egg ("identical") twins are much more likely to *both* be conservative or *both* be liberal than two-egg twins or siblings.

Personality Differences Between the Blue and Red States Suggest Physiological Differences

Personality variables in the United States seem to be distributed in accordance with the Blue State (Democratic) and Red State (Republican) map. This striking finding suggests some selection for the coasts by the more open-minded, the influence of immigration on coastal heterogeneity and acceptance of multiculturalism, and the larger coastal cities and colleges as magnets for intellectuals and the adventuresome. People are drawn to others like themselves, and this may result in selective migration, with the Blue DEMS on the coasts, and the Red GOPS in the Midwest.

A study by Rentfrow et al. (2008) looked at more than 600,000 on-line responses to the "Big Five" personality test items, and then looked at how these five personality factors were distributed by states that voted Republican or Democratic in the last three presidential elections.

The five factors were:

O = Openness to Experience. People high on "openness" are imaginative rather than practical, prefer variety to routine, and are independent rather than conforming. People low on "openness" are practical, down-to-earth, and enjoy simple routine.

C = Conscientiousness. Are you organized or disorganized? Disciplined and careful, or careless and impulsive?

E = Extraversion. Are you sociable and fun-loving, or serious and reserved? Warmer or cooler toward strangers?

A = Agreeableness. Are you a liberal softy or a hard-hearted, ruthless person? Are you trusting or suspicious?

N = Neuroticism. Are you an anxious sort, or pretty calm? Do you feel insecure or secure?

When the states whose subjects rated themselves high on openness (imaginative, independent) were mapped, they corresponded strikingly with the Blue states in the Red/Blue maps. The Blue Republican states scored low on openness, but high on conscientiousness (disciplined, careful, traditional, organized, dependable and responsible.)

The Blue states (Democratic) subjects tended to rate themselves "more talkative, enthusiastic, energetic, and sociable," while the Red states showed more inhibition and reserve.

The states that voted heavily for John Kerry in 2004 scored high on neuroticism. This seems to fit with the anxiety and depression that has been shown to be prevalent in middle and high socioeconomic groups, while character disorders and psychoses are more common in less educated and lower income levels.

The openness of the Blue/DEMS, especially the seeking of variety and new experience, seems to contrast with the findings that the Reds are more close-minded and suspicious. This supports our GOP/DEM character dichotomy. Research described below found that conservatives were more reactive to external threats than liberals, as shown by physiological responses. (That the Blues were more likely to say they were anxious seems like a contradiction, but it may be a function of the greater introspectiveness of the Blues, while the Reds deny their fear and project it outward onto minorities, the Muslim enemy, WMDs and the Iraq war.)

Laura Bush said that "George is not an overly introspective person. He has good instincts, and he goes with them. He doesn't need to evaluate and reevaluate a decision. He doesn't try to overthink. He likes action." In 2000 and 2004, we got a president who seems to typify the Red/conservative personality type. His amygdala probably dominates his cerebral cortex, as Laura's quote suggests, but he denies the fear that he felt all his life, as the son of a president, brother of a favored son, and a failure for the first decades of his life. How well G.W. fits the Red profile! He is practical, down-to-earth, careful, sociable, ruthless, and suspicious. He's not outwardly anxious, and would never say so on a questionnaire, because he is out of touch with his anxiety. As Laura puts it, he is "not overly introspective," the understatement of the century!

John McCain shows a psychological profile somewhat similar to George Bush's. Details of his early life and adult behavior (see main text) support this similarity. In brief, he was a breath-holder as a child (suggesting autonomic dysfunction), confrontational in school, known as "McNasty" for fighting, graduated fifth from the bottom of his Naval Academy class, known for a quick temper and impulsivity, and a risk taker (life-long gambler). He is not as careful as Bush, but he is similarly sociable and affable. He is extroverted, in contrast to John Kerry, Jimmy Carter, or Adlai Stevenson. His exposure to wartime captivity and torture has probably exacerbated some tendencies that were already there. As the son and grandson of admirals, he had a lot to live up to, just as George Bush, the son of a president and war hero, did.

A characteristic related to introspection is "locus of control." People tend to believe either that they control life events, or that events are controlled by external forces (fate, God, people in power). George Bush, when asked if he consulted his father about the decision to invade Iraq, invoked a higher authority: "You know, he is the wrong father to appeal to in terms of strength. There is a higher father that I appeal to." And again: "Events aren't moved by blind change and chance," but by "the hand of a just and faithful God" (Fifty-first National Prayer Breakfast, held February 2003 in Washington D.C.).

This is in sharp contrast to the unnamed associate of the Cheney/Rove workshop who told Ron Suskind that "we create our own reality." Whom are we to believe; George W. with his external locus of control, or the Cheney/Rove types with their self-assured internal locus of control, verging on hubris? Do we have a new president, Obama, whose religious background and emphasis on the "audacity of hope" seem to place him somewhat more on the external locus side, as opposed to his cabinet picks, most of whom seem strongly on the internal locus side (striving, competitive, controlling)? Liberals were concerned as 2009 approached that the president-elect had gathered too many of the "old Democratic hands" around him to effect the change that he promised during the campaign. Let's hope they are wrong. In Obama's books, his character seems at odds with most of his picks for his cabinet and advisers.

The association of religiosity and faith with external locus of control is a no-brainer. Just how conscience or superego is externalized is a topic too extensive for this book. Lack of introspection does not always increase with religiosity, since prayer and concern with morality are often important and involve insight. But wrestling with angels and devils or God versus Satan may not help with internal conflicts, since these are personifications of the warring emotions, and shield the individual from confronting his own feelings. In addition, the confessional offers forgiveness at the pleasure of the church, so the locus of control is again external. In the movie *House of Games* (David Mamet, 1987), a psychiatrist who has been cheated out of her money by a con man who became her lover shoots him to death. She meets with her old training analyst, and asks "What should you do when you've done something unforgivable?" The old lady replies, "You forgive yourself." Part of Mamet's message seems to be that we are all potential psychopaths, but psychoanalysis teaches us to forgive *ourselves* (internal locus of control). This is in sharp contrast to the confessional, where the church must forgive you.

Are we becoming two warring tribes, one conservative, the other liberal, with radically different brains and physiology? Is selective migration and selective mating producing a Blue and a Red nation? Are the Reds retreating to gated communities, or suburbs, and the blues flocking to the cities in such numbers that they will form two new racial groups? Because I'm a liberal, I would call them the new Red Neanderthals, and the new Blue Cro-Magnons.

Steven Pinker (2009) discusses a form of balancing selection, where two opposing groups alternately gain power over time, such as hawks and doves, or liberals and conservatives.

> Selfish people prosper (*reproduce more?*) in a world of nice guys, until they become so common that they start to swindle one another (*for example, Bernard Madoff?*), whereupon nice guys who cooperate get the upper hand, until there are enough of them for the swindlers to exploit, and so on. The same balancing act can favor rebels in a world of conformists and vice-versa, or doves in a world of hawks. (Pinker, ibid., italics mine.)

It is tempting to say (as Pinker does not) that after eight years with selfish people in charge of our government they started to swindle each other, by creating a gigantic economic collapse due to unlimited deregulation. The "nice guys" (the Democrats?) did band together and did in fact get the upper hand.

There are at least two problems with this scenario. (1) The time span for genetic effects is probably thousands of years. (2) The nice guys, in my opinion and that of many liberals, are too nice, and are going to allow a lot of the civil rights losses to stand. This is due to pressure from the CIA (and the right wing) saying that they will not be able to fight terrorism if the Patriot Act is overturned. Will the nice guys be able to reproduce more than the selfish ones, since they have lost millions of jobs, while the CEOs are only "down to the last yacht?" I doubt it.

Balancing selection supports the maintenance of a number of competing personality types over time. It has two forms that are most relevant to personality characteristics. The form discussed above is called negative frequency-dependent selection. The "payoff of each strategy decreases as its frequency increases, relative to the other strategies in the population" (John et al., 2008). A second form is temporal or spatial variation in selection pressure. An example (op cit.) is the selection of adventuresome individuals during times of famine, who dare to search new areas for food, while the timid starve. In times of plenty, the timid souls are favored, while the adventuresome will be exposed to predators (like Bernie Madoff, Wall Street, aggressive subprime lenders, and "securitizers?")

Differences in Physiological Response between Liberals and Conservatives

Studying differences in physiological responses to threat between liberals and conservatives suggested that conservatives are more sensitive to threat, "and are more likely to be supportive of public policies that deal with (larger) threats." (Oxley, Smith et al. 2008). While the sample is small (forty-six persons), the subjects were selected for strong political beliefs, right or left. They were subjected to sudden noises and frightening visual images (a bloodied face, a maggot-filled wound). Their heart rates, sweating, and blinking were measured. These are all involuntary reactions, controlled by the sympathetic nervous system. When exposed to these threats, the conservatives had faster heart rates, sweated more, and had stronger blinks than the liberals.

> ...individuals with measurably lower physical sensitivities to sudden noises and threatening visual images were more likely to support foreign aid, liberal immigration policies, pacifism, and gun control, whereas individuals displaying measurably higher physiological reactions to those same stimuli were more likely to favor defense spending, capital punishment, patriotism, and the Iraq war. (ibid.)

Since the Minnesota twin study already implies that political persuasion is in part genetically determined, it is not inconceivable that the Oxley/Smith study has discovered physiological reactions to threat that are genetically linked. The startle reflex clearly has a survival value, and individuals with a *reasonable* response to threat will probably survive and out-reproduce those with no reaction to loud noises or the sight of their own or others' blood. But hypervigilance can be debilitating, so that either extreme sympathetic response or lack of response can be deadly. Hypervigilance is usually observed in posttraumatic stress disorder (PTSD) patients. The upper range of adult vigilance is no doubt connected to trauma in childhood as well as in war. One must be constantly alert when raised by abusive, punitive, or especially by labile parents (who can hit soon after a hug; see Chapter Three, VI).

Various organs and functions are governed by the sympathetic system: heart rate, blood pressure, respiration, size of the pupil, sweating, and urination. The early studies by Walter Cannon led to the "fight or flight response" hypothesis. These organ responses are needed for survival, but can also result in hypertension, hyperventilation, frequent urination, sleeplessness, and other symptoms associated with hypervigilance.

The sum of these studies, which represent only a tiny fraction of the work already done, indicates that conservatives are genetically and physiologically different from liberals. Their fears are probably more in the unconscious than those of liberals, since both are exposed to war, poverty, disease, and finally death, but conservatives are less introspective , as Laura Bush said of George. Conservatives may react to threat more by sympathetic responses, which are unconscious. Liberals may react more by overt anxiety and depression, as shown by the elevated "neurotic" scores of those who voted for Kerry in the Rentfrow study.

Further discussion of differential response to threat is undertaken in Appendices One and Two. Subjects who were reminded of their mortality rated Bush more favorably ("mortality salience" and "terror management" theory).

In these Appendices, an interesting connection between fear of death or dying and narcissism is explored. Christopher Lasch, in *The Culture of Narcissism* (1979), noted the excessive death fear of narcissists. While he chose to criticize narcissists of the left, the narcissists of the right could just as well have been blamed for the seventies' "crisis of confidence" (the term used in Jimmy Carter's speech, based on a visit with Lasch). The narcissistic personality (or social character) has these central traits: grandiosity, focus on success and fame, a feeling of uniqueness, the need for excessive admiration, feelings of entitlement, using others (instrumental values), lack of empathy, and fragile self-esteem. In pathological narcissism, fear of death and dying is common. It is striking that many of these traits seem to parallel the social character of the GOPS in Table 2, Chapter One. This suggests that the fear of death is stronger in conservatives, who may also tend more toward narcissism, and who have exhibited stronger physiological reactions to threat (death).

Since the extreme concern with self and lack of empathy for others (especially those who are different from you and your kin) is a conservative hallmark (see a *New York Times* October 5, 2007 Op-Ed column by Paul Krugman) and conservatives react to death threat (blood, maggots, etc.) with stronger physiological response than liberals, the common thread is fear of dying. I never made the connection between death-fear and conservatism in my book, *Choices for Living: Coping with the Fear of Dying* (2002), except in the case of Nazi Germany. There were no studies of genetics or physiological responses to link death threat directly to U.S. political persuasion, but in retrospect the connection is almost self-evident.

Neurobiology

While I don't know of a study connecting brain structure directly to political persuasion, there is a suggestion that a diminished empathy in conservatives (again see the Krugman Op-Ed remarks) could be related to a smaller volume of spindle and mirror cells. Parr, Waller, and Fugate (2005) state that: "empathy, or emotional awareness, might have a neural basis in specialized cells in the neocortex, that is, spindle cells that have been associated with self-conscious emotions, and mirror neurons that have recently been shown to activate in response to communicative facial gesture."

The reasoning behind this connection between spindle cells and empathy is that autistic individuals have a reduced volume of spindle cells where they are usually located (the anterior cingulate cortex). Since one of the main characteristics of autism is severe lack of social communication and ability to "read" other people's feelings (especially through facial expression), the spindle cells may be necessary for empathy.

I would not be surprised if, in a few years, a neurologist finds out that Republicans have fewer spindle and mirror cells. Barbara Bush's "Marie Antoinette" remarks about the survivors of Hurricane Katrina being better off after the storm are a case in point. Her son George's anger over the guilt feelings of his rich Yale schoolmates when confronted with other people's poverty is another bull's eye. Not to be left out, John McCain, during his 1986 Senate campaign, referred to Sun City's Leisure World retirement villages as "Seizure World," and he angered Valley senior citizens when he failed to make a timely apology.

11. THE GROWTH OF MINORITIES, ESPECIALLY HISPANICS, WILL TEND TO FAVOR THE DEMOCRATS.

This is truer now since the Democrats were more acceptant of immigrants during Bush's second term, while the GOP was busy putting up border fencing and arresting illegals. Hispanics favored Obama heavily in 2008 (67%, versus 31% for McCain). Hispanics comprised 9% of the voters in that election.

This Hispanic population growth helps explain the shift to the Democrats in 2008, but does not help us to understand why Hispanics voted for Bush in 2000 and 2004. Florida's Cuban population favored the GOP because of its strong anti-Castro stand. Bush's support for more liberal immigration policy may have earned him some votes, but the GOP in the Southwest border states was actively anti-immigrant, no doubt contributing to the Hispanic tilt to Obama.

12. *THE UNITED STATES IS A VERY CONSERVATIVE NATION, AND WE SHOULD NOT EXPECT ANY SWEEPING CHANGE IN THE VERY CLOSE SPLIT BETWEEN THE RIGHT AND LEFT ANYTIME SOON.*

It is remarkable that there has been a difference of only a few percentage points between the two parties in the average popular vote over fifty years or more. A look at a table of the percentage of popular vote for president from 1944 to 2008 shows an average of 49% voting for the GOP from 1952 to the present. So at least half the country is conservative. (An apocryphal tale claims that the president of the American Statistical Association once said in an opening speech that "many a six foot man has drowned in a river that averaged three feet deep." So much for averages?)

While this closeness in the vote split is striking, it hides the fact that there were four big landslides since 1952, three of which went to the Republicans. Looking at the sixth column in Table 1 showing the percentage difference (d) between winner and loser, you can see the landslides marked by an asterisk. They were, in order of magnitude:

1972	Nixon vs. McGovern	60%/37%*	$d = 23.2\%$
1964	Johnson vs. Goldwater	61%/38%	$d = 22.6\%$
1984	Reagan vs. Mondale	58%/40%	$d = 18.2\%$
1956	Eisenhower vs. Stevenson	57%/42%	$d = 15.4\%$

*Percentages were rounded; differences were not.

TABLE 1: PRESIDENTIAL ELECTIONS 1944-2008, POPULAR VOTE						
YEAR	GOP	%	DEM	%	DIF %	
2008	McCAIN	46.1	**OBAMA**	52.6	6	
2004	**GW BUSH**	50.7	KERRY	48.3	2	
2000	**GW BUSH**	47.9	GORE	48.4	-0.5	**
1996	DOLE	40.7	**CLINTON**	49.2	9	#
1992	GHW BUSH	37.7	**CLINTON**	43	6	*
1988	**GHW BUSH**	53.4	DUKAKIS	45.6	8	
1984	**REAGAN**	58.8	MONDALE	40.6	**18**	
1980	**REAGAN**	50.7	CARTER	41	9	
1976	FORD	48	**CARTER**	**50.1**	2	
1972	**NIXON**	60.7	McGOVERN	37.5	**23**	
1968	**NIXON**	43.4	HUMPHREY	42.7	0.7	
1964	GOLDWATER	38.5	**JOHNSON**	61.1	**22.6**	
1060	NIXON	49.6	**KENNEDY**	49.7	0.1	
1956	**EISENHOWER**	58.4	STEVENSON	42	**15.4**	
1952	**EISENHOWER**	**55.2**	STEVENSON	44.3	10.9	
1948	DEWEY	45.1	**TRUMAN**	**49.6**	4.5	
1944	DEWEY	45.9	**ROOSEVELT**	53.4	7.5 s	

PEROT 10.1%
*PEROT 18.6%
** Electoral vote beat popular vote
Winners are in bold
Landslide percentages are in bold
Source: Presidential Elections 1789-2008, infoplease.com, with minor revisions and rounding of percentages.

Since we are trying to review hypotheses about why George W. Bush won twice with the support of people who were voting against their economic best interests, and why such a large proportion (about half) of the American electorate has consistently voted this way, we have looked at the popular vote rather than the electoral vote. The only recent election where the electoral vote trumped the popular vote was in 2000, where Gore won the popular vote by 543,895 votes (0.5% of all votes), but lost the election by 266 electoral votes to George Bush's 271. This was, of course, due to the Supreme Court's 5–4 decision to stop the recount, which gave Florida's twenty-five electoral votes to Bush. There have been other times when electoral votes trumped the popular vote, such as 1824 and 1888, but they do not really inform this inquiry.

Since 1952, the GOP has won nine of fifteen presidential elections, to the Democrats' six. More striking, since 1976, a third of a century, only Carter (1976) and Clinton (1992, 1996) have won for the Democrats. It took eight more years of the catastrophic Bush/Cheney presidency (and the 2008 recession) until another Democrat came to power. (This supports the hypothesis of "getting the stubborn mule's attention" through the pre-election economic disaster.)

While Obama's 6% lead in the popular vote might seem small, and anything but a landslide, it should be considered a major victory. An African American with no military experience was running against a white war hero, John McCain, during (Iraq) wartime, which would favor the survivor of a Vietnamese prison and torture. Racism would favor McCain. Terrorism would favor McCain. Obama thus won against great odds, with a strong campaign, great oratory, and help from the recession and the gaffes of Sarah Palin (who could "see Russia from Alaska" as evidence of her foreign policy expertise).

The conservative strength in the United States is shown by the fact that in the seventeen presidential elections since 1952 the GOP has received less than 40% of the popular vote only twice. In 1992 G.H.W. Bush got 37.7% vs. Clinton's 43.0%. (Ross Perot's 8.9% of the popular vote has been blamed for Bush's defeat by Clinton, but that has been questioned.) Also in 1964, Goldwater only got 38.5% of the poplar vote versus Johnson.

This consistent conservative strength, through good times and bad, suggests to me that a pervasive social character is at work keeping the working class and the middle class from pursuing their best interests. These interests include not just "bread" but all that money can buy: universal health care, nutritious and adequate food, good public schools and colleges, affordable housing, stable jobs, decent wages, protection of civil liberties, and diplomacy that buys peace in our time. (See hypothesis no. 1 re parental practices and how they relate to social character.)

Most of these hypotheses and factors are referred to in the main text of this book. However, some of them (nos. 7 and 9) are given short shrift (a brief penance given to a person [or a hypothesis] condemned to death, so that absolution can be granted before execution).

Chapter One
The Puzzle of 2004, GOP and DEM
Core Beliefs, and Social Character

I.   THE PUZZLE

After George W. Bush stole the election in 2000—with the help of the Supreme Court—I was angry, but certain that he would last only four years in office. When he won again in 2004, I became frightened. How did he manage to persuade slightly more than half the voting public that he would look after their best interests? After all, he had curtailed their civil liberties with the Patriot Act, he had cut back on education, health care, and housing, and more jobs had been lost during his first term than during the first term of any other president. What's more, he had managed to create the largest deficit in our history, following a large surplus during the Clinton administration, by giving a huge tax cut to the wealthy and starting a war of choice in Iraq to find nonexistent "weapons of mass destruction." Here was a great mystery: why did the poor, the working class, and the middle class vote in such large numbers for Bush, when it was clearly against their economic self-interest? My conclusion is that there is a hierarchy of self-interest, and that the preservation of self-esteem (psychological well-being and equilibrium) trumps economic self-interest. Not only Americans, but also millions in many cultures before them, have placed the preservation of their self-image above the preservation of their bread-and-butter needs (health, housing, and jobs)—even above the preservation of their lives!

I think that this overweening need for status and self-esteem and a loss of autonomy (ability to think and act independently) are two of the main reasons why Bush won again in 2004, despite his record of *un*compassionate conservatism. I am convinced that these problems arise from the widespread experience of poor and uncaring parenting in the childhood of the voting public. This will be my main thesis. Later on I will discuss it in detail. I will also try to look at possible explanations of why this need for maintaining status and self-esteem is so important or "salient." I think it comes from a certain social character, which develops when there is childhood experience ranging from uncaring parenting all the way to physical abuse.

II. REPUBLICAN VERSUS DEMOCRAT CORE BELIEFS

It is a habit of humans to classify others into two types. A sociological joke says that "There are two types of people; those who classify people into two types, and those who don't." I feel it is better at this point to be a "lumper" and squeeze the numerous variants of political ideology into two camps. Later on, I discuss some of the variants, as in *Beyond Red and Blue*, the report of the Pew Research Center (Kohut, 2005). The splitter looks at the details, the lumper tries to get an overview. Both are necessary.

Two political camps are now at war. Maybe they have been since time immemorial. In the United States, they have been a product of what is essentially a two-party system. Third parties have not prospered in the United States, while parties proliferate in many countries. What makes a clarification of the difference between our parties important is that the Bush administration, though promising to be bipartisan before both the 2000 and 2004 elections, has been anything but. Paul Krugman argued for a continued partisan effort by the Democrats to reverse the inroads in personal liberty and economic and physical security produced by six years of GOP rule. Once the Democrats had a majority in the House and Senate, he felt that they should confront the White House on all these issues, including the war in Iraq.

> ...Barack Obama recently lamented the fact that 'politics has become so bitter and partisan'—which it certainly has....But politicians who try to push forward the elements of a new New Deal, especially universal health care, are sure to face the hatred of a large bloc on the right—and they should welcome that hatred (in the words of Franklin Roosevelt), not fear it. (parentheses mine) (Krugman, *New York Times*, January 26, 2007).

I think that the main division between the current GOP ethos and that of the Democrats is between selfishness and caring. Another name for this dichotomy could be greed versus empathy. Remember that the use of "ideal types," as described by Max Weber, necessarily ignores the myriad individual differences in the real world.

This dichotomy, selfish versus caring, applies to more than the two-party system in America. They are attributes of societies and of individuals the world over. Any anthropologist can tell you of hunter-gatherer tribes or fishing villages that share their catch. They can also cite the Ik tribe (Colin Turnbull, 1972), who, according to this British anthropologist, not only don't share, but are a tribe of adulterers, wife-beaters, plundering psychopaths, and are heartless to their children.

I am going to apply some adjectives to these two ideal types, and then try to link these qualities to the U.S. two-party system, as it seems to me today, in 2009. This may be painful to some readers. There are many selfish Democrats and caring Republicans. My apologies to caring Republicans. I am also lumping fiscal conservatives, social conservatives, libertarians, and fundamentalist Christians. I am also ignoring the differences between Reagan Democrats, Dixiecrats, Midwest populists, and Eastern liberals. The predominant impression I get of the parties is that the GOPS represent the rich and their values, along with their white working class Evangelist base, and the DEMS represent most of the rest of us.

TABLE 2	
GOP AND DEM SOCIAL CHARACTER:	A GENERAL DESCRIPTION
GOPS	DEMS
Authoritarian	Permissive
Selfish, greedy	Caring
Bellicose	Peaceful;
Unsympathetic, averse	Empathic
Extroverted	Introverted
Imperceptive, not insightful about their own motives and feelings, insensitive	Perceptive, "emotional intelligence," good at deconstruction
Anti-intraceptive, dislike of subjectivity and imagination	Intraceptive; feelings, imagination, and fantasy predominate
External locus of control; see events controlled by fate, God, powerful leaders	Internal locus of control; see events controlled by the self
Rigid, strict, literal	Flexible, easy-going
Closed mind	Open mind
Sincerity	Authenticity
Conformity, other-directed	Autonomy, inner-directed
Hate cynicism or irony	Cynicism and irony accepted as criticism of the establishment
Instrumental values; friendship as networking, art for resale	Intrinsic values, friendship for mutual warmth, art for enjoyment
Pragmatism	Idealism
Intolerance of ambiguity	Tolerance of ambiguity and nuance

Most of these characteristics fall into the authoritarian vs. permissive/tolerant personality types. Few individuals on the right or left would exhibit all of these traits. Those who did might easily pass for monsters or be candidates for sainthood. Given the medulla oblongata and our evolutionary history, we may very well breed many more monsters than saints, but most of us lie somewhere in between. Hitler and Mother Teresa are both rare birds. However, when it comes to leaders, as I will show in a following section, there seems to be a preselection for monsters.

I am not alone in thinking that these two personality types are distributed unevenly between the two political parties. Paul Krugman (*New York Times*, October 5, 2007), previously quoted, said "What happens, presumably, is that modern movement conservatism attracts a certain personality type. If you identify with the downtrodden, even a little, you don't belong. If you think ridicule is an appropriate response to other peoples' woes, you fit right in."

Before moving to the issues promoted and/or actually funded by the GOPS and DEMS, a brief review of the above character traits is needed. Some of the words may seem mysterious to those not steeped in the jargon of the social sciences and the therapeutic community.

III. GOP AND DEM SOCIAL CHARACTER

I was loath to use the word "permissive" to describe the DEMS, since this has been used as a buzz word to slander the left. The conservative distortion of this word has made it over into the image of parents who never set limits for their children, and thus are actually uncaring. A possible substitute for "permissive" might be "anti-authoritarian" but it doesn't seem correct, although the term has been used in some research. In a famous study of group atmospheres, Kurt Lewin used the words "authoritarian," democratic," and "laissez-faire" to describe the way teachers handled groups of children. The democratic teachers listened to what the children said, and praised their productions (masks, art work) but the laissez-faire teachers (saying" That's O.K." about the children's productions) seemed as uncaring as the authoritarian teachers. The democratic group was the most productive of the three.

A more technical word for selfish and greedy would be "narcissistic." While this is the label for a personality disorder, it is also a name for a character disorder. When such a social character is widespread in a culture, it is termed a "socially patterned defect." (See *The Culture of Narcissism*, Christopher Lasch, 1991.) The narcissistic personality has three main characteristics; grandiosity, a strong need for admiration, and a lack of *empathy*. This lack of empathy is seen in Barbara Bush, in George W. Bush, and in John McCain, as noted previously. Bob Herbert said: "I wanted to see him (G.W. Bush) slip the surly bonds of narcissism and at least acknowledge the human wreckage that is the sum and substance of his sustained folly. (Bob Herbert, "Long on Rhetoric, Short on Sorrow," 2007.)

The authoritarian and the narcissist are unaware of their own motives. They generally don't want to discuss their feelings or the feelings of others. They are extroverted and imperceptive. Being in touch with one's feelings (especially the "bad" ones like sex and aggression) is the product of good parenting, which includes permission to express those feelings in a protective frame. You can say how you feel, without fear of being punished.

The rigidity of the GOPS is seen in George Bush's statements, "I'm the decider," and his refusal to admit a mistake or to change his mind. The strict interpretation of the Constitution in the right wing of the Supreme Court, and the literal interpretation of the Bible by the evangelicals, are other reflections of this rigidity, or coarctation (narrowing, as in cardiology). Flexibility in John Kerry, the Democratic presidential candidate in 2004, was labeled "waffling" by the GOP, and seen as weakness.

The "closed mind" (Rokeach, 1960) is not open to other people's ideas. This is partly a defense, since opening up to other people's ideas may undermine your own weak self-esteem. This is linked to the protective grandiosity of the narcissist, which compensates for the poor self-esteem created by a narcissistic injury in childhood.

Sincerity means being true to oneself in order to be true to others. (This is the advice Polonius gives to Hamlet; which Hamlet scorns: "This above all: to thine own self be true, and it must follow as the night the day, thou canst not then be false to any man" [I, iii, 75].) Authenticity means being true to yourself no matter what society demands (see Lionel Trilling for this distinction).This is related to the other-directed/inner-directed dichotomy (Riesman, 1961). Politicians try to present themselves as authentic, but they are by nature of their profession bound to respond to the demands of the electorate, thus making them more sincere than authentic.

The autonomous person is inner-directed and authentic. We expect this social character to be more liberal, and to be able to make decisions based on the issues rather than on group belongingness (ascriptive identity). Yet when autonomy is extreme, there is no concern for others in the society. The extreme form of authenticity/autonomy is espoused by some of the libertarians. In a review of the work of Charles Fried, Gary Rosen (2006) says that the "autonomy and self-sufficiency of the sovereign individual" goes too far. This exaggerated position is taken by Ayn Rand, one of whose book titles is *The Virtue of Selfishness*.

A couple of examples of Ayn Rand's plots help us to understand the GOP philosophy, and give us a picture of autonomy at its extreme. I choose her work because it is easier to see the selfish worldview in its exaggerated form. It should also not be forgotten that Alan Greenspan, the former head of the Federal Reserve Board and one of the most influential men in America, was a co-founder of Rand's Objectivist movement, and her disciple. (Greenspan in 2008 admitted that his model of laissez-faire conservatism and avoidance of regulation of the "free-market" needs rethinking, and contributed directly to the current financial meltdown.) Two of Rand's novels were best sellers, and one was made into a movie. John Galt of *Atlas Shrugged* is an inventor and creative industrialist.

> Rand upheld the industrialist as one of the most admirable members of any society and fiercely opposed the popular resentment accorded to industrialists. This led her to envision a novel wherein the industrialists of America go on strike and retreat to a mountainous hideaway. The American economy and its society in general slowly start to collapse. The government responds by increasing the already stifling controls on industrial concerns." (Rand, 1957)

Her earlier novel, *The Fountainhead* (Rand, 1943), had a similar message. Howard Roark is a typical Rand superhero. He is a brilliant architect who designs an entire village, only to destroy it when it is not built to his specifications by inferior beings (construction workers and contractors being all too human). He is an extreme narcissist, more devoted to his self-esteem than to the welfare of an entire community. In the 1949 movie, Gary Cooper played Roark and Patricia Neal played his girlfriend.

These heroes exhibit extremes of autonomy. They appear to be above and independent of society. They are arch-conservatives. This seems to contradict my conviction that the Democratic or the liberal voter is generally more autonomous. He (or she) is more inclined to think about issues, and to hear both sides of an argument. Hence the appeal of a John Kerry (the "waffler," as opposed to George W. Bush, "the decider").

I think this can be explained by the fact that autonomy, carried to its extreme, sees the individual entirely independent of, and above, society. The independent voter is not hostile to society. She takes it into account, and she is a product of her society. Of course, she does not vote in lockstep with her family, city, religion, or ethnic background. Autonomy must be taken with a grain of salt.

In a later section I discuss the worldview of Hobbes versus that of Rousseau, and how Freud and Durkheim were essentially Hobbesian. They both saw society as necessary to curb the demons of our nature. For Freud, "man is a wolf to man." Civilization is necessary, but it has its "discontents." Durkheim saw a state of societal "anomie" when human nature was not properly regulated by society; for example, higher suicide rates. Thomas Sowell (1987) reworked this dichotomous view of human nature, labeling one view the "constrained vision" (humans are flawed, and not perfectible; the conservative view) versus the "unconstrained vision" (man is perfectible, inherently good; the liberal view).

If you believe that man is an incurable "wolf," then you will be less apt to spend money on social programs to improve him or even to ameliorate his condition. Thus the GOP lack of concern for the safety net and the conscious goal of "starving the beast" (big government) so that little discretionary money will be left over for social programs once the military and the wars are financed.

I think it is necessary to take one step backward to find the origins of political ideology. One's worldview certainly is a major factor in determining conservatism or liberalism. But what determines the worldview? And why would a person with a negative view of mankind tend to be more selfish? If you view man as brutish and bestial, selfish in his deepest soul, you may then be projecting your own feelings of selfishness onto mankind. In addition, if all men are selfish, then your own selfishness is partly justified. "Everyone does it" is the common excuse for all sorts of antisocial behavior.

This suggests that one's view of human nature is not the wellspring of political behavior. Rather, early experiences affecting attachment and self-esteem that derive from warm and supportive parental practices and family atmosphere, *create* the view of mankind as similarly supportive and perfectible. The lack of early warmth and support leads to a view of mankind as basically flawed.

Generosity flows from the generosity of love experienced in childhood. Selfishness flows from the experience of selfish, narcissistic, cold, or even openly abusive parenting. Your parents are your model of mankind. This tends to be a reiterative process, with worldviews passed on from generation to generation, creating a more or less stable social character. Think of the Athenians, with their relatively permissive upbringing, contrasted with the Spartan militaristic child-rearing.

How stable are these worldviews and party affiliations that seem to accompany them? While there are surges in the proportion of independent voters, it is estimated that 80% of the U.S. voting public vote as their parents and reference groups (ethnic, religious) vote. I think this is due to cross-generational modeling and identification. In the Introduction (Factor 10) I wrote about the possible genetic and physiological factors influencing political persuasion. It is possible that cross-generational modeling and selective mating eventually affect brain structure and the dominance of one part of the brain over the other. Cerebral cortical activity (logical thinking) might then dominate in one group, while subcortical activity (the emotions of the amygdala and medulla oblongata) could dominate in another group. In the future, we could have Athenians and Spartans right here in America.

That is not to say that major shifts in voting do not occur. It has often been noted that as long as southern Democratic politicians supported white supremacy, the South remained the "solid" (Democratic) South. As soon as Lyndon Johnson, with the Civil Rights Act of 1964, moved the Democratic Party toward equal rights, the Southern states moved heavily to the GOP. The view of human nature (and of African Americans) in the White Supremacist portion of the population probably did not shift.

9

Rather, their party allegiance shifted to remain compatible with their strongly held worldview and racist fears.

The intensity of feelings associated with the basic conflict between generosity and selfishness cannot be exaggerated. It almost seems to stem from the instinct for survival, as if giving up something like money or food will threaten the life of the giver. Again we can look to Ayn Rand as the prophet of selfishness. Note the paranoid ideation that one is "sacrificed" by altruism!

> Do not hide behind such superficialities as whether you should or should not give a dime to a beggar. That is not the issue. The issue is whether you do or do not have the right to exist without giving him that dime. The issue is whether you must keep buying your life dime by dime, from any beggar who might choose to approach you. The issue is whether the need of others is the first mortgage on your life and the moral purpose of your existence. The issue is whether man is to be regarded as a sacrificial animal. Any man of self-esteem will answer "No." Altruism says "Yes." (Rand, 1960)

Rand criticizes Immanuel Kant's advocacy of altruism. She blames him for a revival of altruism which she brands as mysticism. She asks what the logic is behind altruism, and cannot find any logic in giving up part of one's possessions or sacrificing for one's family or society. Today the selfish gene theorists would say that altruism, especially toward one's children or one's siblings, is a logical (not mystical) way to protect one's gene pool. From behind the elaborate smokescreen of Rand's philosophy there peeps a familiar conservative face: "It is Kant's version of altruism that's working whenever people are afraid to admit the pursuit of any personal pleasure or gain or motive—whenever businessmen are afraid to say that they are making profits ..." (ibid).

Self-reliance is as American as apple pie. Margaret Mead (1942) pointed this out, quoting the adage, "Trust in God, but keep your powder dry." This seems to be an offshoot of the Protestant ethic. Gaining the possibility of salvation through hard work and productivity meant that you had to rely on your own muscle. Importantly, God would not let you know that you had achieved a state of grace. This probably led to the accumulation of wealth as a sign that you deserved a state of grace. The lack of a cap on accumulation in turn produced the "anomie" (see Durkheim) that has had such devastating consequences for our social character. It is responsible for the rising income disparity in our country, which has reached astronomic levels. What Max Weber called "worldly asceticism" (the sacrifice of worldly pleasures in pursuit of salvation) has now turned into the pursuit of worldly pleasure itself, at least in the United States. Veblen's "conspicuous consumption" fails to describe the extremes of hedge-fund and CEO salaries, Wall Street bonuses, the seven homes of John and Cindy McCain, and the private planes, yachts, islands, and gated communities of the wealthy.

When the GOP railed against "Welfare dependency," they were in part speaking from their strong value of self-reliance. Bill Clinton's promise to end "Welfare as we know it" was a move to capture the middle vote, and was the end product of the GOP's and Moynihan's "benign neglect."(Daniel Patrick Moynihan suggested this course to Nixon in 1970.) The DEMS, in contrast, tend to accept dependency, especially in children and the elderly.

The GOPS are more likely to believe in absolute truths. This is shown in the strict interpretation of the Constitution by the conservative members of the Supreme Court, and in the belief in "intelligent design" and a literal interpretation of the Bible by the right wing of the evangelicals. Relativism is more acceptable to the DEMS, although the line is often drawn at sexual or aggressive behavior. The more liberal judges try to look at the Constitution in the light of current societal values, and especially those that are worldwide, as opposed to local U.S. values. Until quite recently, psychiatry listed homosexuality as a mental illness. Even the medical profession is capable of change. DEMS are somewhat less likely to be moralistic, while the GOPS have led the attack on gay marriage and abortion.

The GOP, under Bush, and again in the campaigns of McCain and Palin, has sold itself as the party of faith, and branded the DEMS as those of little faith. It is doubtful that Cheney, Rove, and Rumsfeld are highly religious. Much of their reference to God, faith, and family values is part of their rhetoric, not their belief. Bush is more of a true believer, but has phased in and out of that role, and into his Joe Six-Pack frat-boy persona at times. This is not to say that the DEMS don't use religion to attract votes and to take people's minds off bread-and-butter issues, but there is less of the evangelical cast to their rhetoric.

The GOPS seem to favor particularism; they favor their own family or tribe over the "others." This stance is seen in the treatment of the Hurricane Katrina victims. The DEMS, though by no means all, are likely to have universalistic values. They think multiculturalism is fine and that minorities, ethnic groups, the poor, the young, and the elderly are to be accepted under one tent. In contrast, multiculturalism is anathema to the GOPS. It seems to invoke in them fears of invasion by hordes of people they see as outsiders: blacks, immigrants, Muslims, Mexican "wet-backs," and anybody who does not belong to their in-group. There is a "them versus us" tone to much of the rhetoric, a black-and-white Manichaean worldview. They are more apt to like a homogeneous society, hence the gated community and the isolation of much of our leadership from 2000 to 2008.

The ideal type GOP hates cynicism and irony because a rosy picture is necessarily maintained in the face of reality. The continual denial of the chaos in Iraq is a dramatic example. The DEMS, in contrast, tend to accept cynicism and irony, since it is used so frequently to criticize the establishment. Much of the humor on late-night TV is cynical and uses irony. The humor tends to make fun of Republicans more than Democrats. (In particular, Jay Leno, David Letterman, Jon Stewart, Lewis Black, and Bill Maher lean toward the Democrats.) Perhaps it is because the Bush administration was so bizarre that it lends itself to satire. While Joe Biden sometimes misspeaks, the gaffes of George W. and Sarah Palin have been countless.

The GOPS seem to favor instrumental values, such as ambition, persistence, courage, and politeness. They are the means to achieving goals or ends. They are not the goals in themselves. My examples are the cultivation of friendship only to gain money or power or services through networking, or the purchase of art not for its intrinsic value and enjoyment, but as an investment and as a hedge against inflation. The DEMS are more apt to favor intrinsic values. Friendship or art would be sought "for its own sake," and for the warmth and enjoyment that they offer.

Conrad M. Black, former chairman of Hollinger International, a global publishing empire, was indicted in November 2005 on charges of cheating shareholders and tax evasion (including mail and wire fraud, racketeering and money laundering). Interviewed in 1989, Lord Black said "The essence of social life is to make your contacts as interesting as they can be. Many people are intellectually stimulating. Some are not, but they happen to be important. So there is some utility in knowing them" (Thomas, 2007). There could hardly be a clearer example of instrumental values as they operate in the social whirl that mixes "high society" with big business.

The GOPS are more apt to be practical. The DEMS, especially the liberals, tend to be more idealistic. However, at the extreme religious right, there is a great deal of idealism, sometimes misdirected, but sometimes of great concern for others, as in the evangelical aid to the victims of genocide in Darfur. The Catholic support of immigrants in the Southwest is another example of charity in the face of angry opposition.

The GOPS seem to abhor ambiguity, while the DEMS are more likely to tolerate it. This split became clear during the GOP attack on John Kerry as a "waffler." They appealed directly to those on the right who fear nuance, and who want simple answers to complex problems. Adlai Stevenson, like John Kerry, was obviously a man who studied all sides of an issue. George Bush, on the other hand, "shoots from the hip." He called himself "the decider." There is nothing hesitant about him. McCain, as I discuss later, would have made a very impulsive president, judging by his past behavior. Obama seems to exhibit a good balance of cerebral control and emotional expression. He restrained himself visibly when being attacked by Hillary Clinton, but in his rebuttals was mostly calm, organized and eloquent. His former career as a law professor suggests strong frontal cortical dominance. He will need that, since he was already being attacked by the GOP for imagined connections to the "sale" of a senatorial seat by Governor Rod Blagojevich (December, 2008).

I think we are talking about very profound differences here. The forces that split America into the Red and the Blue are somewhat of a mystery to me. Perhaps there has always been a divide between the "tough love" and the more easy-going types. Maybe the Bush administration brought out the extremes. The expectation was that once the Obama team took over on January 20, 2009, there would be more talk across the aisle, since there is a common threat that often brings people together (as in the months after 9/11). Despite Obama's numerous attempts to close the gap, the Republicans have shown no interest in bipartisanship.

I have painted the GOP as the party of selfishness, while the Democrats came out as relatively caring. Make no mistake; the differences between the parties have been very slim at times. The Bush administration, however, with the expert guidance of Dick Cheney and Karl Rove, in eight years made for a much wider gap than usual in the behavior and goals of the two parties. The traits of the two "ideal types," the selfish versus caring (or authoritarian versus permissive), apply worldwide in addition to the GOPS and DEMS. They form a dichotomous "social character" that includes a range of opinions and favors one side or the other of current issues.

I have listed some of the personality traits more commonly found among the GOPS and the DEMS. The issues they espouse closely reflect these traits. Let's look at how the issues, values, and opinions play out and differ between the two parties as they *presently* stand. (Remember that Lincoln was a Republican. His views on minorities would fall more to the current Democratic side. How the parties have switched positions!)

TABLE 3
GOPS AND DEMS ON ISSUES

GOPS	DEMS
"Sink or swim." The individual is responsible for his own welfare. Self-reliance value is dominant here, but may be a cover for greed.	A safety net is needed for those less able to care for themselves.
Protestant Ethic. Secular asceticism; hard work and possessions as proof of worth and salvation.	Catholic and New Testament emphasis on "caritas," helping the poor. Rich men "cannot enter heaven."
Freedom defined as freedom from government regulation	Freedom defined as equal opportunity.
Taxes seen as unfair redistribution of hard-earned fruits of one's labor.	Taxes defined as small redistribution of wealth to help those of lesser ability or opportunity.
"Tort reform" is a disguise for the deregulation of industry. "Laissez faire" means "Let business do what it wants."	Generally support use of tort law when used in class action law-suits against corporations.
"Government is the problem." Spending on war while cutting taxes for the wealthy is a deliberate campaign to "starve the beast." This leaves little discretionary money for the safety net of social programs	Government should be the main provider of the safety net; Social Security, Medicare, Medicaid, Housing, Food Stamps, national emergencies such as Hurricane Katrina or 9/11.
Market forces, the "invisible hand" of Adam Smith, will take care of everyone's needs. Dislocations due to market crashes, outsourcing, globalization, global warming, are a problem for the individual, not the government.	Adam Smith is replaced by John Keynes. The government must intervene when rapid change threatens the well-being of the populace.

GOPS	DEMS
"Family values" are essentially a set of social controls over sexuality. This includes eliminating contraception, abortion and stem-cell research. Parental consent and "partial-birth abortion" ban are approaches to a complete ban.	Often a centrist view of contraception as a way of reducing abortion. More liberal stance is that women must have free "choice" over their reproduction, and that government can not regulate it.
Anti-contraception and anti-gay activism, "girlie men." Strict definition of marriage	Support of gay rights but not gay marriage. Favor stem cell research.
Environmental laws seen as a restraint on business; mining, lumber and oil. Global warming viewed as voodoo science	Environmental laws are needed to protect the public health and public land, and to avoid future economic collapse due to global warming
Religion should be the central ethos of our country. Separation of church and state is an imposition on the faithful by those of little or no faith. Support school prayer, parochial schools, magnet schools.	Strict separation of church and state generally supported.
Race and minority prejudice strong but covert. Buzzwords ("bussing," "special treatment,")	Much covert prejudice, but it is mitigated by pro-diversity and multicultural values. Support for racial and ethnic minorities.

GOPS	DEMS
College quotas seen as "reverse discrimination."	Racial disparity in opportunity recognized, and should be corrected.
Generally anti-immigration, but it is supported by large corporations that need cheap labor.	Mixed support; strong support by wealthy liberals who need nannies, but fought by minorities who fear job loss.
Basically anti-science as it threatens faith, or promotes government regulation . But very pro-science when it creates profits or protects health.	Generally pro-science. It is seen to be in the public interest.
Evolution diminishes man. Descent from monkeys and mice intolerable. Global warming, pollution and drug-side effect studies cut profits. "Intelligent design" takes social intervention out of our hands and places it in God's lap. Fatalism?	Evolution seen as culminating in mankind. Evolution as continuity, suggesting faith in man's perfectibility (hence intervention). Pro-scientific support for pollution and warming control, testing of prescription drugs (including post-market).
Foreign policy: goal of war and American hegemony. Pre-emptive war is O.K. Support for unilateral intervention. A Manichaean worldview; either enemy or friend.	Support for war only with backing of allies and United Nations. No pre-emptive war. Current view, Congress must pre-approve president's war, and limit his war powers through funding.

GOPS	DEMS
Belief in biological determinism; nature over nurture. If intelligence and ability are in "their" genes, then why bother to fund social intervention programs? Neurology and brain studies are replacing social psychology and social psychiatry. Minorities are seen as genetically inferior (Jensen 1969, Herrnstein 1994).	Belief in the power of the socio-cultural environment; nurture over nature. Faith in the efficacy of social intervention. Poverty and racism seen as causal factors in mental and physical illness, and in the minority achievement gap. The *interaction* of genes and the environment is emphasized. "Good genes are expressed in a supportive environment."
Fatalism, determinism; in extreme form it is apocalyptic. Related to Calvinism, original sin, and intelligent design. Man's nature is seen as Hobbesian, animalistic, and immutable.	Hopefulness, the illusion of free will, and an internal locus of control are all opposed to fatalism. Belief in the (partial) perfectibility of man, and the eventual amelioration of the human condition.
Strict construction of rules (the Constitution, the Bible). A literal interpretation of laws and sacred texts. Examples of Piaget's "moral realism." Results in conservative decisions in the courts, schools, hospitals, families, etc.	Flexible approach to societal rules. Ability to change rules when appropriate. Examples of Piaget's "moral relevance." Belief that laws should be updated to conform to changing national values and accepted behavior.

Most of the issues, positions, and opinions discussed in Table 3 are self-evident. A few need some further discussion.

When Republicans say "Government is the problem," they mean "big government"—that is, spending on social problems. The Bush administration didn't mind spending billions on the war in Iraq. There is also an amusing oxymoron involved: How can you say that "government is the problem" when you *are* the government? Then *you* are the problem! This sacred bromide was first spoken by Ronald Reagan during his inaugural address on January 20th, 1981: "Government is not the solution to our problem; government *is* the problem."

"Starve the beast" as a deliberate program was first brought to my attention in a brilliant column by Paul Krugman in the *New York Times* (December 23, 2005). Not only has the "beast" been starved, but the cost of two simultaneous wars (Iraq and Afghanistan) and the lack of financial oversight coupled with rampant deregulation has brought about the worst recession since World War II, perhaps since the crash of 1929. The "beast" has almost been killed.

Some Democrats have tried to create "bridge values" in an attempt to get more votes from the center. In appealing to the right of center they say that abortion is often painful for women, both physically and psychologically, and that they see contraception as a way to reduce the number of abortions. The Obama administration had to move a bit to the center, since it doesn't have a filibuster-proof majority of sixty in the Senate, and will have difficulty passing the more liberal parts of its agenda (health care, low income housing, extended unemployment insurance). Attempts to move "across the aisle" have been rebuffed by the Republicans. For example, after Obama tried to cajole House Republicans, they voted unanimously against his economic rescue plan on January 29, 2009. The bill passed due to the Democratic majority.

A strict definition of marriage as limited to the union of only a man and a woman is part of the "moral realism" mentioned later. This is an early stage in moral development (Piaget), in which the established rules of the game can never be changed.

The centrality of homosexuality and abortion in attacks upon the "liberal elite" makes one wonder if the GOP "doth protest too much." Recent revelations of right-wingers' homosexuality among those most vociferously against gays suggests projection of their own tendencies. Ted Haggard had a three-year affair with a male prostitute. As head of the National Association of Evangelicals, he was getting his epiphanies in a manner hardly approved by his vociferous fellow-anti-gays. Republican Congressman Mark Foley resigned in 2006 when questioned about his liaisons with Congressional pages under age eighteen. The "macho" stance of Bush is discussed in a later chapter. Governor Arnold Schwarzenegger's characterization of Democrats as "girlie men" only called his own body-builder persona into question.

In discussing the division of the GOPS and DEMS on evolution, I mention that DEMS are more likely to see mankind as perfectible. The animalistic view (man is a wolf to man) leads to conservatism. This may be a major axis on which people the world over differ.

In a comparison of the GOP tendency to favor biological determinism and the DEM preference for sociocultural influences, I should mention the writings of Stephen Jay Gould (1981). He has pointed out that the shift to genetic explanations and to the current emphasis on neurology rather than psychiatry has coincided with a strong shift to the right in politics and public opinion. I will later discuss some of this shift when talking about Sally Satel, a resident scholar at the American Enterprise Institute, the premier right-wing think tank. A major change in attitudes toward mental illness is taking place among both professionals and the public, and this is a change for the worse, toward behaviorism, (the "practical" approach, which derides insight as a mere excuse for patients to avoid change). This approach suggests the hard-headed, practical, extroverted clinician, the signature belief in "tough love," and the denigration of insight. These are more likely to be conservative traits.

Fatalism is a hallmark of an external locus of control. The more hopeful DEMS may tend to an internal locus of control. People who feel that they are controlled by forces outside themselves (other people, luck, fate) have an external locus of control. Based on a long series of experiments, those who felt they were more or less in control of events were shown to be quite different in their behavior and physiological responses. There may be an association between external locus of control and depression. The concept of locus of control is related to Riesman's inner-directed/other-directed dichotomy, and to the distinction between authenticity and sincerity, discussed previously. It may be easier to visualize these dichotomies as axes of personality that can be rotated in space to form larger groupings.

It is interesting to speculate that the "moral realism" stage mentioned in the section on "strict construction of rules" is an early and lower level of moral development than that of "moral relevance." Piaget found that younger Swiss children could not conceive of knocking marbles out of a square. It had to be a circle, just like the game daddy taught them. By age eleven or so, they were willing to substitute a square for the traditional circle, as long as their friends agreed (moral relevance). By this token, the DEMS are at a higher stage of moral development than the GOPS. I doubt that the right wing of the Supreme Court would agree with this interpretation, but strict construction of the Constitution, without relevance to modern conditions and changes in the culture, can result in thirty thousand handgun deaths per year. For example, the Second Amendment that states: "A well regulated Militia, being necessary to the security of a free State, the right of the people to keep and bear Arms, shall not be infringed." was written at a time when America was young, and law enforcement was weak. The focus was on a militia to protect the country. With the current standing Army, Navy, Air Force, and National Guard, we have no need for a militia with muskets to protect us. (Or maybe we do, since most of our muskets are in Iraq and Afghanistan.)

The rest of Table 3 is self-explanatory. It is certainly not exhaustive. A complete book could be written about our political parties' differences. I have tried to create a *typology* called GOPS and DEMS. Again, there is no living Democrat or Republican, conservative or liberal, who exhibits all of the characteristics on either side of the ledger. In making an abstraction, I have slighted the individual differences out of necessity.

As you look at these two tables, with their binary view of the world, you may notice something that struck me as remarkable. The general characteristics of authoritarian GOPS and permissive

DEMS fit closely with the positions of the two parties on issues. For example, being averse to "safety nets" fits in with the GOP and Protestant ethic value of independence. This is seen in extreme form in the stance of libertarians, who would rather do away with government if it creates dependency. Remember the big issue of "Welfare dependency." Note that Peter Edelman quit the Clinton administration as Assistant Secretary of Health and Human Services when it moved to the center and abolished "Welfare as we know it." He would be the idealist, well to the left of the average Democratic liberal. Another example is the style of Dubya Bush ("the decider," never admits a mistake, rigid, with a closed mind), compared to John Kerry, who was flexible, not dogmatic, looked at all sides of an issue, and was thus labeled a "waffler." This label damaged Kerry with the more authoritarian folk, who believe in a strict construction of the constitution and a literal interpretation of the Bible. There is a yearning for the strict rules, the old ways, and a simpler way of life which I discuss later in a section on *Gemeinschaft* (community) versus *Gesellschaft* (society).

Later on I will also go into some of the GOP versus DEM differences in more detail, but this can rapidly become a disquisition in philosophy, at which I am far from an expert. Suffice it to say that a remarkable consonance exists between Bush's character structure, the character structure of a large portion of the electorate, and the ethos and policies of the Republican Party. Again, I repeat that the core of that value system is selfishness and greed. The slogan "compassionate conservatism" of the first G.W. Bush term is reminiscent of Daniel Patrick Moynihan's advice to Nixon that "the issue of race could benefit from a period of "benign neglect." And this from a "Democrat!"

Chapter Two
Selfishness and Leader Preselection: Bellicose and Authoritarian versus Peaceful

That "politicians are all crooked and ambitious" is a common stereotype. It is true that it takes a supreme effort to campaign (often for years), raise money, and give speeches in order to get elected. Why are some people ready to sacrifice a normal life in order to get into positions of power? Is it because they want a better world, and think they can make changes in the current society? Certainly some leaders are altruistic. I think you will agree with me that by far the majority of our politicians are motivated by ambition, a desire for power, and worldly goods. Leaders in general are basically narcissistic and self-centered, but by the process of helping themselves, many of them help their countrymen. Some, like Lincoln or Lyndon Johnson, and at times Bill Clinton, empathized with the poor due to their own early experience with poverty. Many, particularly those in the Bush administration, showed little or no empathy with those less fortunate. It was as if the White House was a gated community, with little contact with the reality of the lives of the general populace.

While wondering how we could have elected such a group of self-seeking people to power a *second* time, since four years of uncompassionate conservatism had shown us their true colors, I became interested in the character of Bush, Cheney, and Rove. How did they get selected to lead this nation? How is Bush different from or similar to other leaders in the past?

Aside from the loss of many of our civil liberties, damage to the economy, the huge burden of our national debt, and the blot on our moral leadership in the world, one of the biggest issues has been the war in Iraq. How did we get into it? How did we elect a president who was so militant? Are leaders preselected to be bellicose and authoritarian? What makes for a relatively peaceful leader?

In order to understand what has happened to our country since the year 2000, and the character traits that got us into wars in Afghanistan and Iraq, with threats of war against Iran and North Korea, it might be helpful to look at the character and early experience of some other bellicose leaders other than "bring 'em on" Bush and his advisors.

Nicholas D. Kristof's *New York Times* Op-Ed column of February 4, 2007, "Under Bush's Pillow," reviews readers' comments on the literary or historical parallels to the Bush administration and its war in Iraq. He says: "...frankly, it's difficult to find great literature that encourages rulers to invade foreign lands, to escalate when battles go badly, to scorn critics, to be cocksure in the face of adversity."

Kristof mentioned that Alexander the Great used to sleep with the *Iliad* under his pillow. This made me think, "Why not look at the early history of some of the most famous (or infamous) leaders? Might there not be some special preselection process for leadership, which favored aggressive, stubborn, and hubristic types? The result was surprisingly consistent. Each of the leaders who came to mind had experienced a traumatic childhood, and presumably had to compensate for the psychological injury incurred. Although the documentation of the lives of these early leaders is somewhat thin, the extreme experiences of their young lives as reported either by historians or in legend support my argument. It is very likely that immense anger was probably the common spur to these martial achievements.

Most of the early great leaders were also military men. There were few peaceful leaders to choose from, until the likes of Mahatma Gandhi. Yet even in our times, there has been a predominance of world leaders with military backgrounds. Recently there has been a civilian president (G.W.B.) who was more bellicose than those with military careers, such as Eisenhower.

I. THE CHILDHOOD OF SOME FAMOUS LEADERS

Alexander the Great

Let's take a look at Alexander (356–323 B.C.). His father, King Philip II of Macedonia, had two wives with no male heir before he married Olympias, Alexander's mother. She was the dominant figure in her son's early life.

> She may also have tried to turn him against his father, especially criticizing Philip's moral shortcomings. This indoctrination likely contributed to the dislike that developed between father and son, while Alexander always held his mother in the deepest respect, despite knowledge of her less scrupulous actions. Moreover, the dynamics of these relationships likely contributed to the sexual reluctance or restraint apparent in Alexander's later years (Alexander, URL).

Alexander was known for holding grudges and for never forgetting an injury. He rarely failed to carry out his vengeance. He was also known for his temper tantrums.

One of them took place at a feast held to celebrate his father's marriage to his final wife. The bride's uncle, Attalus, toasted the couple, saying that he hoped his niece would give birth to a legitimate heir to the throne. "What about me? Am I a bastard?" Alexander shouted, hurling his goblet at Attalus.

A brawl between father and son with drawn swords followed. Fortunately, Philip fell down drunk, preventing a combined regicide and patricide. Since Philip married three times more after his marriage to Olympias, Alexander rightly feared that his father would appoint another male heir to the throne (Alexander, URL).

This insecurity about his biological father ("Am I a bastard?"), the constant fear of betrayal by his father, and the domineering and malicious character of his mother might well have contributed to Alexander's compulsive drive to prove himself and conquer the world (which he almost did).

Genghis Khan

The history of this fierce warrior (1165–1227) is filled with violence and loss early in life.

> Born to the noble family of Yesugei and Ho'elun, Genghis Khan was first called Temuchin. At an early age, he was betrothed to Borte who belonged to another tribe. After leaving Temuchin with Borte's family, Yesugei (his father) was returning to his own camp when he was poisoned by Tatars. After his father died, Temuchin returned to his family, still a boy. (Genghis Khan, URL)

According to the primary source of information on Temuchin's life, *The Secret History of the Mongols*, he endured many hardships, including the kidnapping of his wife Borte, but slowly recruited supporters and assumed a mantle of leadership among the Mongols" (Genghis Khan, URL).

At the age of nine Khan lost his father, and was subjected to treatment that anyone would consider traumatic.

> When Temuchin (Khan) was nine, rival tribal members killed his father, forcing the family into exile. They barely survived the harsh winter, and their situation became even more tenuous when another tribe raided their camp and took Temuchin prisoner, placing a heavy wooden collar around his neck to prevent escape. He freed himself, and by his early teens gained a reputation as a furious warrior. (Genghis Khan, URL)

Napoleon Bonaparte

Napoleon (1769–1821) seems at first glance to have had a less stressful early life. Since he was born into a wealthy family of noble lineage, you might think that life was easy for him. But deprivation is relative to those with whom you compare yourself (your "reference group").

> The Buonapartes were a wealthy family from the Corsican nobility, although when compared to the great aristocracies of France Napoleon's kin were poor and pretentious. A combination of (his father) Carlo's social climbing (and his mother) Letizia's adultery with the Comte de Marbeuf—Corsica's French military governor..." probably made for a special sensitivity to status differences, and a feeling of inferiority. In addition, there were two other factors that probably contributed to inferiority feelings on his part; being short, and being Corsican (Italian) in an elite French setting. (Napoleon, URL)

> Napoleon was known as the little Corsican because of his height of 5 feet 2 inches. When Napoleon was nine, his father sent him to a French military academy at Brienne-le-Chateau, near Troyes. Then in 1784, Napoleon was selected for the elite École Militaire in Paris. While there, he was constantly teased by the French students. At the age of 16, he joined the French army. (Napoleon, ibid.)

Napoleon despised the French. He thought they were oppressors of his native land. His father was a lawyer, and was also anti-French (Napoleon, ibid.).

Being born into a family with an adulterous mother was not good soil for the growth of a loving and outgoing character structure. Napoleon was known as a misogynist. He was a compulsive worker, often impatient, and a risk-taker. It is not too simplistic to guess that his short stature and comparatively deprived social status (compared with the French nobility in Paris), the ridicule he was subjected to, and having to seek promotion in a country that he and his father hated (France) all conspired to produce anger, and an overwhelming need to compensate. He eventually came to dominate not only France, but all of Europe. Able was he, 'ere he saw Elba.

Adolf Hitler

Because he is the very model of a martial and destructive leader, we should take a look at Adolf Hitler. This man, driven by his pathological anger and hatred, killed six million Jews and started a war that killed many more millions. World War II caused the greatest loss of life and material destruction of any war in history, killing twenty-five million military personnel and thirty million civilians. Elsewhere I have given some details of Hitler's childhood as told by Alice Miller. A few more aspects of his early years are reviewed here. He is the archetypical destructive monomaniac, driven by early trauma and humiliation, to dominate and kill others. He was no military genius, like Napoleon, Alexander, or Genghis Khan, yet he conquered Europe and gave the Allied Forces a hard fought war with terrible civilian and military casualties on both sides. It was the largest war in the history of the world

Hitler's father, Alois Hitler, was an Austrian customs official. He married Klara Pölzl, his second cousin. Adolf was the third son and fourth child of six, but only he and his sister Paula survived into adulthood. Alois was born illegitimate, and used his mother's surname, Schicklgruber, until he was forty. Then he used his stepfather's surname, Hiedler. A history of severe abuse by Adolf's father is well documented.

> As a boy, Adolf was whipped almost daily by his father. Years later he told his secretary, "I then resolved never again to cry when my father whipped me. A few days later I had the opportunity of putting my will to the test. My mother, frightened, took refuge in the front of the door. As for me, I counted silently the blows of the stick which lashed my rear end." (Hitler, URL)

The origins of his virulent anti-Semitism may have been in his concern about his own Aryan blood lines, and the fact that his father was of uncertain paternity. "There were rumors that Hitler was one-quarter Jewish and that his paternal grandmother, Maria Schicklgruber, became pregnant while working as a servant in a Jewish household" (Hitler, URL).

Adolf's sister, Paula, remembered in detail the brutality of her father in his daily abuse of her brother.

> Adolf challenged my father to extreme harshness and got his sound thrashing every day. He was a scrubby little rogue, and all attempts of his father to thrash him for his rudeness and to cause him to love the profession of an official of the state were in vain. How often on the other hand did my mother caress him and try to obtain with her kindness where the father could not succeed with harshness.... (Hitler, Paula, URL).

The severity of Alois' beatings of Adolf were such that Adolf's mother tried to intervene bodily between father and son. A diary discovered in 2005, written by Paula, gives us a picture of a demented alcoholic father and a desperate mother trying to protect her son from extreme physical injury.

> Fearing that the father could no longer control himself in his unbridled rage, she decides to put an end to the beating...She goes up to the attic, covers Adolf who is lying on the floor, but cannot deflect the father's final blow. Without a sound she absorbs it (Hitler, Paula, URL).

Paula, by these comments, seemed to show empathy for her brother. That this was not returned in kind is suggested by another entry about his bullying her during their teens. "Once again I feel my brother's loose hand across my face" (Hitler, Paula , URL).

II   A FEW OTHER LEADERS

Joseph Stalin

Having picked three martial and destructive leaders, all of whom happened to have traumatic or abusive early lives, I feared that I had cherry-picked a few who would support my hypothesis. Why not try Joseph Stalin? He was martial. He killed millions by execution, by starvation, and in the Gulag. (He also managed to bring Hitler to his knees, but at a terrible price in casualties.) Sure enough, the early story is repeated. Stalin was beaten severely by his father, a cobbler. His mother was a serf. His three other siblings had died early on. His father went bankrupt, and was forced to work in a shoe factory, which may have accounted for his heavy drinking and the angry beatings.

> Rarely seeing his family and drinking heavily, Vissarion often beat his wife and small son. One of Stalin's friends from childhood wrote, 'Those undeserved and fearful beatings made the boy as hard and heartless as his father.' The same friend also wrote that he never saw him cry. Another of his childhood friends, Iremshvili, felt that the beatings by Stalin's father gave him the hatred of authority. He also said that anyone with power over others reminded Stalin of his father's cruelty (Stalin, URL).

Stalin's father abandoned the family and left them destitute. Joseph went to school at age eight. Here he and his Georgian friends were ridiculed. This seems a replay of the snobbery of the French students toward the "little Corsican," Bonaparte. It is also reminiscent of the humiliation of Hitler by his father (see the "little toga boy" story related by Alice Miller).

> When attending school in Gori, "Soso" was among a very diverse group of students. Joseph and most of his classmates were Georgian and spoke mostly Georgian. However, at school they were forced to use Russian. Even when speaking in Russian, their Russian teachers mocked Joseph and his classmates because of their Georgian accents. His peers were mostly the sons of affluent priests, officials, and merchants. (Stalin, URL)

Beatings, father–son conflict, uncertain paternity, severe economic deprivation or deprivation relative to higher social classes, and a façade of early toughness adopted to preserve self-esteem seem common to these leaders. What of some of our own native sons? It could be of interest to look at a leader, who, despite a traumatic childhood, never initiated a preemptive war, and was not a destructive martial person.

William J. Clinton

Several of the themes in the lives of the previous leaders are repeated in the early life of Bill Clinton: a search for identity due to a loss of a father figure, a struggle with an abusive father figure (his stepfather), an early separation from his mother, and relative poverty.

> I never met my father. He was killed in a car wreck on a rainy road three months before I was born...After that, my mother had to support us, so we lived with my grandparents while she went back to Louisiana to study nursing. I can still see her clearly tonight through the eyes of a three-year-old, kneeling at the railroad station and weeping as she put me back on the train to Arkansas with my grandmother (Clinton, URL).

The search for identity is a spur to power in these histories, but in Clinton's case, that power was used benignly, compared to the previously discussed leaders: "I think the fact that I was born without a father, and that I spent a lifetime trying to put together a picture of one also had a lot to do with how I turned out... Good and not so good" (Clinton, URL).

I do not know if an abusive or domineering father or step-father is a common history among leaders, martial or peaceful. In Clinton's case, the abuse must have led to anger, but it may have been redirected into political striving and sexual activity.

> Roger was an alcoholic and a gambler, often losing the family's money, including Virginia's earnings as a nurse-anesthetist. He cursed and sometimes beat his wife and verbally abused Bill and Bill's younger brother, Roger, Jr....Bill was especially close to his mother and sometimes stood up to his stepfather to protect her (Clinton, URL).

The violence in Clinton's family was not your typical middle-class squabble or dish-throwing. Bill had to intervene to protect his mother from injury. This Oedipal struggle was almost on a par with that of Philip and Alexander, but with fists, not drawn swords. Virginia (Bill's mother) couldn't tame Roger Clinton or stop him from attacking her with his fists, a pair of scissors, and even shooting his gun at her.

> This sounds crazy but I never hated my stepfather, Roger Clinton. Even after he pulled the trigger in here, when he was drunk, even after he beat my mother—even after I got big enough to stop him from beating my mother, I had some understanding that he was a good man and couldn't whip his drinking problem. And that he was full of demons that he couldn't control it and he took it out in destructive, hateful ways. I hated what he did, but I never hated him (Clinton with Dan Rather, URL).

The repression of anger toward Clinton's vicious stepfather is one of the typical ways in which abused children handle these feelings. This serves to maintain a good image of the abusing parent, despite the physical and emotional injuries suffered by the child. Clinton talks of going to school the day after a violent confrontation and not saying anything to anybody—keeping his family and school lives separate. This leads to "compartmentalization," an ego-saving skill that Clinton perfected. The excuses for the abuser are evidence of the pitiful need to preserve some semblance of a caring parent, despite all evidence to the contrary. This massive denial of the parent as "bad," often accompanied by self-blame, is repeatedly seen in the case histories of multiple personality disorder (discussed in detail later). A second coping mode is to assume a "tough" persona that can take the beatings in stride. In the case of Stalin, this was most evident.

John F. Kennedy

While John Kennedy is not in the same bellicose league as Alexander, Genghis Khan, Napoleon, or Stalin, he did initiate the Bay of Pigs invasion of Cuba, which he always regretted. He faced down Nikita Khrushchev, who had built nuclear missile launchers in Cuba in 1962, and the launching sites were removed. He showed some of the conditions that might have produced striving for leadership. The primary motivation might have been to compete with his older brother, Joe Jr., who was the first born and "golden boy" of the family. After Joe Jr. was killed in a plane explosion in World War II, the presidential mantle fell on Jack. His father, a self-made multi-millionaire, was determined to have a president in the family.

Jack was a sickly child. At 14, he weighed only around 100 pounds! He contracted every possible childhood disease. Then at college he ruptured a spinal disk while playing football. He suffered a painful back for the rest of his life, often taking painkillers to relieve his suffering, and for a while receiving illegal injections from a quack doctor (Jacobson). During the sinking of his PT boat during World War II, he reinjured his back, though still rescuing his men.

Much of the motivation for high office came from his father. He also suffered from being a Catholic in a predominantly Protestant private school, Choate. In Boston, the Brahmins looked down on Catholics, even if they were millionaires. (This is reminiscent of Napoleon; though of noble birth, he was no match for the rich French nobility.)

Kennedy, a Democrat, was generally on the side of civil rights, and concern for the common man. His father, though a Democrat by membership, was strongly pro-German until World War II, and had shady dealings during his meteoric rise in the business world. He was "living through" his sons, which is one hallmark of the narcissistic parent.

The similarities between Kennedy and Clinton, though one was originally wealthy and the other poor, one sickly, the other relatively robust, are in the areas of striving for power, a charismatic personality, and sexual hyperactivity.

> What we have come to know posthumously about the personal conduct of many of history's most extraordinary political leaders suggests that a combination of charismatic personality, a drive to attain power, and

> sexual compulsivity is a common pattern among heads
> of state. How might we understand the psychological
> connection between sexual addiction, charisma, and the
> quest for power?" (Bloland, 2000)

Bloland points out that both Clinton and Kennedy, as compulsive womanizers, "risked their political careers (if not the welfare of the country) in the addictive pursuit of sexual gratification." She also states that Mao Zedong, Gandhi, and Martin Luther King "qualify as sexual addicts." To my mind, sexual addiction is not necessarily part of the leadership preselection complex. There have been plenty of leaders, martial or not, who were not sexual addicts.

My guess is that many women are attracted to men who have enough charisma to get into positions of great power. The availability of these women doesn't turn these leaders into sexual addicts. They may be merely sexually hyperactive, and taking advantage of their position. This could happen with a college professor and his female students, or a male psychotherapist and his women patients, any situation where there is a large difference in status and prestige. These relationships are generally frowned upon, specifically because of the disparity in power between the partners.

III. BUSH AND HIS HANDLERS: THE PROTOTYPE MARTIAL LEADER: EARLY AND LATER LIFE

My motivation for writing this book was George W. Bush's re-election in 2004. I could understand how about half of the electorate voted for him in 2000 (even though the Supreme Court really made the decision in his favor). What I could not comprehend was that a small majority re-elected him in 2004, despite the fact that he had a record of four years of failure in so many areas of government. Moreover, his policies had strongly favored the wealthiest 1% of the nation. Yet (as I show later on) about 40% of voters with household incomes below $50,000 voted for him. A large section of this book is devoted to finding an explanation for the fact that a series of issues ("family values," fear of terrorists, racial prejudice, etc.)

trumped economic and social-safety-net issues (jobs, education, housing and health).

It is quite clear from ancient and recent history that with some notable exceptions, leaders are preselected for personality characteristics which fall into a range between compulsively driven, narcissistic men who are often authoritarians and full-blown psychopaths. This is a worldwide phenomenon, and we tend to accept the negative traits that accompany charisma. If a man shouts "I say unto you!" or lays claim to higher authority, we know from experience that he may have his downsides, but we tend to downplay these negative qualities as we bargain for a "vision" and for the magnetism and charm of the leader.

The history of mankind is punctuated by wars, thousands of them: civil wars, religious wars, ethnic cleansing wars, and world wars. There has been a steady escalation in the armaments and fire power, from the club or stone axe, bow and arrow, crossbow, sword, rifle, machine gun, high explosive, poison gas, atomic bomb, to the hydrogen bomb. The number of casualties, both civilian and military, has risen almost steadily (although the proportion of the population killed has not grown as fast). There had to be a large number of aggressive and pugnacious leaders involved in these wars. There also had to be a populace that supported these leaders into positions of power (with the exception of kings and emperors in earlier times who ruled by virtue of divine right or raw power).

The fact that people in countries considered to be democracies, such as Germany and Italy, could vote into power dictators like Hitler and Mussolini is astounding. Historians are still trying to understand the pathways to fascism. A recent book, *Hitler's Beneficiaries* (Götz, 2007), suggests that the Germans kept Hitler in power because they got free cash, clothing, and household objects that had belonged to Jews or people from occupied countries. While this doesn't explain how he got into power, it shows that the view that World War I reparations, anti-Semitism, and Hitler's charisma are not the only explanations for his popularity.

As you might guess, this discussion of preselection for leadership is aimed at trying to understand how voters in the United States could bring into office once again (in 2004) a president who so obviously cared little for the public and the common man. Immediately, it occurs to you that no American thinks of himself as the "common man." Most identify themselves as middle class and some as working class. Nobody is "lower class." If nobody is "common" then everybody is a self-appointed crypto-CEO. This is surely one, but only one of many, factors contributing to Bush's re-election.

With George W. Bush, we cannot consider his rise to power without looking at his handlers, Dick Cheney and Karl Rove. We are not discussing a self-made warrior such as Alexander, Khan, or Napoleon. We are dealing with a man who avoided active duty (unlike his father) but nevertheless presented himself as a tough guy in the John Wayne tradition. I discuss his persona later in "The Five Faces of George W. Bush." The public didn't vote for Cheney and Rove. They voted for the front man, Bush, as he was presented to them. He was tough, he got his guidance from a higher authority, he was a failure who was born again, and he was a "good fella." Even more important, to my way of thinking, is that he was an uncaring parent—a leader out of touch with the electorate, from a sheltered patrician background. He showed that he cared not a whit for the social safety net, nor for that bane of the GOP, "social engineering." This right wing mantra of "tough love" was recoined as "compassionate conservatism." It proved to be anything but compassionate.

While the path Bush took to the presidency was paved with privilege (high-level jobs, and later on campaign money, through his family connections) it cannot be denied that he had charismatic appeal. The question I have posed is how that appeal and the propaganda that his spinmeisters spewed out was able to overcome the dismal self-evident record of lack of empathy. This inquiry into the ability of the populace to overlook the glaring hard-heartedness of an American leader (as evidenced by his actions, not his speeches) should shed light on the acquisition of power by uncaring and dictatorial leaders in other countries and other times.

Does "Dubya" Bush fit the profile of the leader abused in childhood? We want to know, since we are curious as to how someone can grow to be so uncaring. As far as we know, he was certainly not abused in the way Genghis Khan or Hitler was abused. He may have been humiliated, however, in the way that Napoleon was by the French military students, and by his stature, considerably shorter than that of his father or brother. (Interesting word, "stature," since it means physical height and also social standing.) There is evidence that Mao Zedong, like Hitler, was beaten and also humiliated by his father, who called him "lazy and useless" in front of assembled guests

Is that lack of empathy for the downtrodden, the poor, and the unemployed simply a matter of cross-generational transmission of the GOP *Weltanschauung*? Has Bush just internalized the aristocratic attitudes of his parents? Certainly Barbara Bush's "Marie Antoinette" moment in New Orleans, mentioned before, suggests a condescending attitude toward the masses. In her view, Hurricane Katrina benefited the poor people, since it forced them to flee to new places with new opportunities! In a more egregious example, Barbara Bush had an interview with Diane Sawyer on ABC-TV just before the U.S. invasion of Iraq. She said "Why should we hear about body bags and deaths and how many, what day's it gonna happen? It's not relevant. So why should I waste my beautiful mind on something like that?" Deaths of U.S. soldiers are irrelevant? Over and above this possible modeling on his parents' attitudes, we might consider George W.'s lack of empathy to be overdetermined. This is to say that elements of his early experience may have blocked out his potential empathy.

The information on George Bush's early life and family environment is sparse. I have tried to piece together several reports garnered from websites, including those based on books, such as *Bush on the Couch*, by Dr Justin Frank.

Dr. Frank diagnosed the president as a "paranoid megalomaniac" and "untreated alcoholic" whose "lifelong streak of sadism," ranging from childhood pranks (using firecrackers to explode frogs) to insulting journalists, gloating over state executions, and pumping his hand gleefully before the bombing of Baghdad showcase Bush's instabilities. Other clinicians have backed up Dr. Frank's impressions: "Dr. Frank's conclusions have been praised by other prominent psychiatrists, including Dr. James Grotstein, Professor at UCLA Medical Center, and Dr. Irvin Yalom, M.D., Professor Emeritus at Stanford University Medical School" (Thompson, 2005, URL). This same source reported that Bush's mood swings were "drastic," and that he is an "angry obscenity-spouting man who berates staff."

Bush is the only U.S. president to have worn a military uniform during a public appearance, on the deck of the aircraft carrier U.S.S. *Abraham Lincoln*. He was wearing a green flight suit. A sign behind him said "Mission Accomplished," but the war troubles in Iraq had just begun. Years later, there is still chaos in Iraq, but little accomplishment. (The "surge" has been touted by the GOP as having turned chaos into "victory.") In December of 2008 Muntader al-Zaidi, a correspondent for Al Baghdadia, an Iraqi-owned television station based in Cairo, threw his two shoes at Bush's head during a Baghdad news conference. This is the supreme insult in the Arab world, signifying that the shoe recipient is as low as the dirt under the shoe. He shouted in Arabic "This is a farewell kiss, you dog!" Bush ducked, made a wisecrack about the shoes being "size 10," and went on to say that the war is "on its way to being won." George W. certainly perfected the art of sticking to his delusions. The GOP has truly "created its own reality."

What were the childhood experiences that might have helped to produce such an extreme personality?

Oliver James, a British psychologist, has pieced together a believable story of Bush's life up to age forty, when he became born again, "fell to his knees and implored God to help him." Being the son of a prep school and college star athlete, and a decorated war hero, was not an easy role. Dad's success inevitably made him feel a failure. He had botched several jobs, in the oil business and a baseball ownership, despite the financial backing of his family and family friends. At age twenty-five he had a DWI arrest after he crashed a car (see James, 2003).

George's father was away much of the time, and his mother, Barbara, ran the home and provided discipline. Jeb Bush described the home atmosphere.

> A kind of matriarchy... when we were growing up, dad wasn't at home. Mom was the one to hand out the goodies and the discipline.

> Every mother has her own style. Mine was a little like an army drill sergeant's...my mother's always been a very outspoken person who vents very well...she'll just let rip if she's got something on her mind (Bush, G.W., Jeb, uncle, URL).

There is further testimony that the abuse was not just verbal:

> According to his uncle, the "letting rip" often included slaps and hits. Countless studies show that boys with such mothers are at much higher risk of becoming wild, alcoholic or antisocial (ibid.).

In later discussions of uncaring and abusive parenting, the disconnect between the parents' behavioral demands and the child's own inclinations and needs are a primary focus. According to Miller (1981) and Gruen (1992), this results in the child giving up the "true self" and adopting a "false self." This sacrifice creates rage, which is then directed against the self or others.

Bush probably had a "false self" until his teens, an age when it is often safe to rebel. Then he was able to develop into the rebellious hard-drinking frat boy, which lasted to about age forty.

The second "false self" that Bush adopted was his Christian fundamentalist "born again" persona. His conversion (with the help of Billy Graham) made him into an extreme version of what his parents were and wanted him to be. The rigidity of his routines—his daily exercise, three-mile run, and his five-minute appointment blocks—are part of the general coarctation or constriction needed to hold the frat-boy in check. The strict interpretation of the Bible, the black-and-white or Manichaean worldview (you are either his enemy or friend) and the reliance on faith or given truths are all part of this protection against a return to the former drinker-wastrel-failure.

Bush showed other important characteristics: extreme extroversion and imperception. He does not look into his inner motivations. He loathes "people who feel guilty about their lot in life because others were suffering" (James, 2003). His basic empathy is lacking. There is no concern for the safety net. He probably sees social engineering as a weakness, and thus done only out of political pressure, not compassion. His messages came not from inside, but from "a higher authority" (and that authority was *not* his father, as he publicly stated).This suggests external locus of control, mentioned previously. Not looking under your own hood to see how the motor is doing is a way of protecting yourself from the past injury you suffered, and from awareness of the sacrifice of the self that you made. If you alternately present yourself as a tough guy and a good fella, you can fool most of the people most of the time about your real feelings. Those feelings wouldn't sit well with your family, nor with the electorate.

Bush's authoritarian personality grew out of the values and behavior of his parents, and out of his attempts to deal with the explicit demands for success, performance, and discipline they made. This character structure is bellicose, and seeks legitimate targets for its anger. When the Saudis destroyed the twin towers on 9/11, Bush and his handlers had their big chance to go to war. Cheney and Rumsfeld, Karl Rove, Douglas Feith, Paul Wolfowitz, Richard Perle, Elliot Abrams, I. Lewis Libby, and David Wurmser were some of the neo—and not so neo—conservatives in the White House who prepared the public and most of Congress to accept the unilateral and preemptive war in Iraq. Bush, because of his character structure, fitted in with their plans, which had been brewing for some ten years. Given Bush's anger and belligerent nature, Cheney and Rove probably knew they could count on him not only to go along with the neo-conservative war plans, but also to be the primary spokesman for the invasion. The shifting rationales for going to war—WMDs (weapons of mass destruction), regime change, establishing a new middle-East democracy, and defense against terror—came from his mouth, but initially sprung from the laptops of the neo-cons.

Other neo-cons outside the White House helped to provide the rationales for going to war, but Bush was the willing and enthusiastic bellicose front-man. As president, he had the bully pulpit and the trumped-up evidence to convince a good portion of the public, and Congress as well, that we should start a unilateral war, without necessarily getting approval from the United Nations. His character and the neo-con agenda fitted like a glove.

George W. Bush did not rise to power and fame through his own military skills, like Alexander, Genghis Khan and Napoleon. He had the help of his influential family, as did Alexander and Napoleon, but relied more heavily than they did on their connections. He didn't have the fanatical drive of Adolf Hitler or Mussolini or Stalin, who rose from the ground up on their own power. He had a great deal of charisma, as is evident from the adulation he received until the end of his sixth year in office. His early history is similar to that of the martial leaders in many respects. He suffered rejection and coldness at home, along with verbal and mild physical abuse. He exhibited major conflict with his father, though not the open swordfights of Alexander and Philip, or the physical abuse of Adolf by Alois. He may have had some mild form of neurological damage from birth or from excessive drinking, which could account for his numerous neologisms and mangling of the English language (Manglish?)

Early neurological damage seems supported by two facts. First, Bush's father, George Herbert Walker Bush, often made slips of the tongue, but these were mild compared with those of his son George Jr. This suggests that heredity may play a part in Dubya's word mangling. Second, George W.'s brother Neil is the CEO of "Ignite! Learning," a company that created and sells a "Curriculum on Wheels" that comes in a small box.

> Mr. (Neil) Bush said he began the business with no experience in pedagogy or software development. His only real experience, he said, was as a boy with dyslexia. Teachers once told his mother that Neil, then in the seventh grade, would probably not graduate from St. Albans, the Washington prep school that he did, ultimately, complete.(Schemo, 2007).

Given this revelation about his brother, it is not unreasonable to think that George W. also inherited this deficit.

W. was shorter than his younger brother Jeb (a favored son?) and his college-athlete war-hero father. At Yale he found himself in the midst of Eastern liberal "elites" while he was from Midland Texas, similar to Napoleon's experience in Paris. When he stopped heavy drinking and partying, he may have given up the frequent expressions of the sex drive that kept Bill Clinton and Jack Kennedy more on the side of "love, not war."

In the United States extramarital affairs have been like a third rail for politicians. The attack on Bill Clinton, financed by the billionaire Richard Mellon Scaife, almost resulted in impeachment. Gary Hart's dalliance with Donna Rice destroyed his chances at a presidential nomination. In Europe many politicians have survived revelations of their bedside trysts with impunity. Our country seems to have been more puritanical by punishing the miscreants with dismissal. As in the Clinton and Profumo affairs, the politician who denies his dalliance eventually gets charged with perjury.

Despite his early history, Bush has never been accused or suspected of marital infidelity. At the point of his epiphany, he apparently swore off any boozing or womanizing he had done earlier. Being born again implies that you have come "trailing clouds of glory," as Wordsworth put it. You are not the nasty brute struggling with sexual and aggressive instincts that Freud posited. You are as clean as a Botticelli cherub. It is just a conjecture that if George W. had slipped off the straight and narrow path just once after his conversion, he might not have taken us into war in Iraq.

IV. TEN QUESTIONS TO POSE ABOUT THE 2004, 2006, AND 2008 ELECTIONS: THE INDIVIDUAL AND SOCIAL FACTORS LEADING TO AUTHORITARIAN OR TOTALITARIAN GOVERNMENTS AND LEADERS.

Having laid some of the theoretical groundwork for the selection of presidential timber and leaders in general, and looked at the contribution that their early experience may have made to their character development, it is time to pose the following questions, among many others:

1. How did Bush get re-elected in 2004? A large majority of the electorate voted against what could be called their economic self-interest.
2. What techniques helped the GOP win the 2004 election?
3. What is the evidence for the influence of parental practices on political behavior and choice? What is the prevalence of various types of abuse and neglect?
4. What is the role of mental disorder in political affiliation ?
5. What factors in general contribute to the rise of authoritarian governments and leaders, and to the authoritarian character of the population that support them?
6. What subgroups are most likely to vote against their bread-and-butter interests, and to vote in terms of "family values," religious, sexual, and aggressive issues (race, war, terror)?
7. How did Bush and his handlers present him to the public? Was there a hidden "face" of Bush that appealed to voters who were abused, abandoned, neglected, or subjected to uncaring parents during childhood?
8. What is the role of authenticity and sincerity in winning elections?
9. How should the Democratic Party have acted to win in the 2008 elections? What policies should it endorse to present itself as a caring parent? (These questions are moot, since Barack Obama won the primaries and the election in 2008. It may have some historical interest, since Obama and Hillary Clinton were not clones, by any means.)
10. What are the competing theories on why the GOP won in 2004? How valid are these theories? What are their relative contributions? (This was reviewed in the Introduction, but some theories are discussed in more detail in later chapters.)

Chapter Three
Why Did Many People Vote Against Their Self-Interest in the 2004 Presidential Election?

Before looking at the relationship of self-interest and 2004 voting, or the social character of the voters and the influence of parental practices and mental disorder on voting, we should review the more mundane subject of the various techniques used by Bush & Co. to persuade, threaten, and trick people into voting for him once again. Most of this is common knowledge, but it must not be overlooked, since it played a large part in his re-election.

I. THE TECHNIQUES

Before going into the psychodynamics, social forces, and history that can help us understand the 2004 election, I will review here the standard techniques of propaganda that the Republicans have used with great effectiveness. This is an attempt to answer question 2, "What techniques helped the GOP win the 2004 election?" While these are well known, they must not be disregarded.

As I read various columnists and watched commentators on television trying to explain how Bush managed to win a second term, it seemed that there were some recurring themes. (I discount some of these explanations, including those that blamed Kerry for a poor campaign, "waffling," or dull personality, or blamed the Democrats for lack of effort, or lack of clear policies and goals. I do, however, give credence to the possibility that the Republicans cheated at the polls, rigged the voting machines in Ohio, and prevented many in poor neighborhoods from voting due to a lack of voting machines and biased disqualifying procedures that targeted blacks.)

1. Fear

First, Bush instilled fear after the 9/11 bombing of the World Trade Center by repeated color-coded alerts. Here in New York City, we were perpetually in Code Orange. He used fear to try to change Social Security. He told the public that they should fear "Big Government," while he *was* the embodiment of big government.

Through the use of *fear*, Bush furthered his goal of *privatization*. He focused on the privatization of Social Security, hoping to frighten people, especially younger people, into believing that the program was in a financial crisis, when in fact it can operate without further change up to around year 2050. There are attempts to privatize the public schools (always a Republican target) but these have failed to show better results than the current system. By starving the public schools, he kept them in a state of crisis. In New York City, the public schools lack not only science and math teachers, but also books and even toilet paper! (see Bob Herbert, *New York Times*, 2004). Bush's father preferred the "thousand points of light" (more euphemisms) over government social supports. George W.'s regime continued to favor private giving over government social programs.

For a more detailed discussion of the role of fear in Bush's re-election, see Appendix One: Fear and Terror Management.

2. Hope and Lying

Then Bush also promised *hope* but didn't deliver, by underfunding "No Child Left Behind" and foreign aid, especially for Africa. Promises for many programs went unfulfilled, such as his AIDS initiative and the Millennium Challenge program

(*New York Times* editorial, February 2, 2005). The prescription program for Medicare carefully protected the drug companies, by forbidding the importation of less expensive drugs from Canada and other countries. Discount cards turned out to be a confusing failure.

These unkept promises are just a form of *lying*. Bush lied about finding weapons of mass destruction (WMDs) in Iraq, and when none were found in Iraq, he changed the purpose of our preemptive invasion to "spreading democracy and freedom in the Middle East." All the while, our desperate need for oil was the primary reason for starting a war. We consume one fourth of all the oil that is produced, yet we are only one nation among 150 or more. He lied that tax cuts would go to the poor and middle class, but they went instead to the very rich. He lied about the deficit. In 2004, Bush promised to cut the deficit in half by 2009. Yet the budget projections left out the cost of the continuing wars in Afghanistan and Iraq, and the billions needed to rebuild New Orleans and repair the damage done by Hurricane Katrina. Just for 2005, the government asked for eighty-one billion dollars in addition to the normal military budget. We might still be in Iraq for several more years. The current date for all U.S. troops to be withdrawn is the end of 2011, and combat troops are projected to be withdrawn by August 2010. The government also admits that it needs to borrow 774 billion dollars in the next decade for Social Security payments for people sixty-five or older in 2005 (see Anon., 2005). There was no way these costs, excluded from the 2005 budget, would fail to put this country much further in the red. The 2008 recession will push our national debt into the trillions. For voluminous details of the Bushies' lying, see Al Franken's excellent book, *Lies, and the Lying Liars Who Tell Them* (Franken, 2003).

3. Camouflage (Disguise, Deception, Trick, Feint, Shell Game)

Bush appealed to a broad swath of voters by harping on the *family values* theme. This was a deliberate *smokescreen*, to draw people's attention away from health, education, and their own welfare by ranting about highly charged hot button issues such as abortion, gay marriage, and stem-cell research. (This is not just my opinion. See the quote from John A. Lawrence, *New York Times* letters to the editor, January 25, 2005. It is also the main theme of Frank's book, *What's the Matter with Kansas?*). His aides promoted school vouchers and the teaching of "intelligent design" rather than evolution in the schools.

Bush and his handlers, especially Karl Rove and Dick Cheney, made an all-out effort to convince targeted segments of the public that their programs would benefit them. To do this, government funds were given to conservative commentators to praise and promote Bush programs such as "No Child Left Behind." At least three cases have been uncovered: those of commentator Armstrong Williams ($240,000 contract), writer Maggie Gallagher ($21,500), and Michael McManus ($10,000). These contracts and arrangements were highly illegal (*New York Times*, January 29. 2005).

4. Euphemisms

This is a special form of disguise, using language. It has probably been used since the beginning of civilization, when kings and dictators needed to persuade the masses that what they were stealing or demanding was in the people's own interest. Our own country changed the name of the War Department to the Department of Defense. Well, it has lately been the Department of Offense, with a policy of "preemptive war."

George Carlin, comedian and acidulous social critic (who died in 2008), pointed out the renaming of the slums as the mild "inner city," and the disguising of World War I "shell shock" with the watered down "posttraumatic stress syndrome."

"Compassionate conservatism," a slogan of Bush's first years in office, turned out to be flim-flam. His first term proved to be anything but bipartisan, (reneging on his campaign promise) and his compassion is belied by the tremendous cuts in services to the poor and middle class. Compassion only for your buddies is not in the spirit of true Christian brotherly love. It is self-love, love of your in-group.

Looking back to Bush Sr., Operation Desert Storm was a slick piece of marketing. It was a war, not a storm or an "operation." The motto "shock and awe," which was supposed to win over or cow the resisting Iraqis, instead turned out to be a "catastrophic success." It was labeled a victory too quickly won! Sunni resistance grew, and was joined by terrorists from other countries, especially Syria.

The "thousand points of light," via speechwriter Peggy Noonan, was a way of encouraging private charity, while cutting government supports for the indigent.

Bob Herbert (2005) discusses "extraordinary rendition," which consists of kidnapping suspected terrorists and transporting them by plane, often under sedation, to countries like Syria and Egypt, where they can be tortured, presumably to confess. This is done without any due process, and is meant to circumvent our laws, which demand due process, representation by counsel, and the ability to contact relatives. This is certainly extraordinary, and it is also highly illegal both under our laws and international law.

A most flagrant example comes from the Bush war on the environment, opening national forests to mining and oil exploration. He and his vice president, Cheney, have both been in the oil business, and Bush's family has had connections to Saudi oil interests for several generations. Just before the end of his presidency, Bush opened up more than one million acres of land adjacent to the Grand Canyon National Park for mining of uranium. The runoff of this mining is highly toxic. John McCain, in October 2008, announced that he approved of this giveaway to the mining interests, showing he was joined to Bush at the hip all along. He also led the chorus of "Drill, baby, drill!" in response to the temporary increase in gas and oil prices.

Under the "Clear Skies" plan, an oxymoron of Guinness Record quality, Bush released forty-two million tons of additional pollutants. This is but one more example of the use of euphemisms to disguise the real intent of Bush-government programs.

A shift in the language used to describe the stock-market investment accounts that the Bushies were furiously promoting to eventually destroy the Social Security system was forced by the public's reaction to the verbiage. At first this portion of Social

Security payments was to be used to buy "private investment accounts." The word "private" told the true story of the privatization of the one program that guarantees some security in our old age, without risk of the volatility of the stock market. The language was quickly changed to "personal investment accounts." The White House had been playing a shell game, or Three Card Monte, with the public. Now you see it, now you don't. They cut off the "private" parts!

And don't forget the "Ownership Society." This was an attempt to make a nation of Lilliputian Republicans who own a few shares of stock believe they are fat cats and CEOs, while the Bushies cut their social supports out from under them. (I owe my use of the term "Bushies" to Maureen Dowd, whose columns, along with those of Paul Krugman and Bob Herbert in the New York Times, have castigated the Bush administration, and aided me tremendously in my thinking about our national situation.)

5. Appeal to Violence

The Bushies are strong advocates of *law and order.* They favor the death penalty. During Bush's governorship of Texas, there were more executions than in any other state in any other time, except in war. The Department of Justice punished even the medicinal use of marijuana, which helps to ease the pain of terminal cancer. The Republicans have consistently supported the National Rifle Association and gun manufacturers. The police, who might ordinarily be prone to favor Bush in other matters, are concerned about the killing of their members by criminals with handguns and even automatic weapons.

With the aid of John Ashcroft, the former Attorney General, and with help from Alberto Gonzales, the Attorney General who wrote the legal opinion calling the Geneva Convention rules regarding the treatment of prisoners "outmoded," civil rights suffered a major setback during the Bush administration. The torture of Iraqi prisoners at Abu Graib is a direct offshoot of this lack of respect for human rights. And as a result, our own soldiers may be in danger of torture or death when taken prisoner in this and future wars. An undercurrent of sexual predation underlies much of this sadism. The sodomizing of prisoners by our police, the pedophilia scandals in the churches, and the widespread perverse assaults on prisoners in Afghanistan and Iraq suggest that we have a very repressive culture. The assaults are not committed only by males. In Abu Graib prison in Iraq, young American women soldiers have stripped and taunted prisoners till they got erections, and they have smeared their victim's faces with red ink to mimic menstrual blood. This technique was suggested by an Iraqi interpreter, who was well aware of the strong taboos on menstrual blood among Muslim males.

The salience of torture is evidenced by the headlines it is making in 2009. By Obama's orders, and by a lawsuit under the Freedom of Information Act by the American Civil Liberties Union, the memoranda detailing the U.S. torture of terrorists have been made public. The administration originally took a position against prosecution of the lawyers who wrote the documents condoning torture, and the people who actually did the torturing. In April of 2009, Obama still opposed the prosecution of CIA operatives who actually performed the torture, but said it would be up to his attorney general, Eric H. Holder Jr., to decide whether to prosecute the lawyers who wrote the torture laws. Waterboarding (simulated drowning) of suspects was reported to have been repeated a total of 266 times on two individuals. These recent reports have led many liberal critics of the administration's policy to demand prosecution of the lawyers who wrote the laws permitting torture.

Note that the law and order doctrine has *fear* as its underpinning. Remember the use of the African American Willie Horton, who killed while out of jail on parole, to win an election for Republicans? Blacks and Hispanics are jailed much more frequently for crimes than are whites. Although these minorities commit more crimes, due to their lower position on the social ladder, and their lack of education and jobs, they are also "profiled" more often, resulting in the arrest of innocents. Thousands of Muslims have been profiled and arrested, but only a handful of convictions have resulted. Unfortunately, the 9/11 attacks have opened the floodgates of attacks on the innocent. This happened in World War II, when Roosevelt, who was certainly more conscious of civil rights than Bush Jr., put innocent Japanese Americans in concentration camps and confiscated their homes and businesses. The Patriot Act endangers every one of us. It ignores habeas corpus, the right to trial, the right to counsel, the prohibition of unreasonable searches, and all else that we hold dear about our system of laws.

6. Character Assassination

Anyone who has followed the news for the last dozen years has been exposed to stories of attacks by members of both parties on opposing candidates. That has been part of American politics going way back, even to May, 1856. Senator Charles Sumner, a Massachusetts antislavery Republican (a "Massachusetts liberal" like John Kerry?) was not just verbally but also physically attacked on the floor of the Senate. He had criticized Stephen Douglas and Andrew Butler, both Democrats, for being pro-slavery. He said that Butler took as his mistress "the harlot, Slavery." Butler's kinsman, Representative Preston Brooks of South Carolina, strode into the Senate and beat Sumner into unconsciousness with a metal-topped cane. Brooks was acquitted, but died at age thirty-seven. Sumner recovered.

This near-assassination was not as lasting in its effects as some of the recent GOP verbal attacks on several Democrats. Everyone knows of the smear campaign against Bill Clinton when he was a sitting president. Granted that he should not have dabbled with intern Monica Lewinsky, but the intent of the "right wing conspiracy" was to impeach him. The betrayal of Monica by her older "friend," Linda Tripp, suggests the bitter hatred Tripp must have felt toward Clinton and the Democrats. A group of conservative lawyers in Washington, D.C. were funded by Richard Mellon Scaife to pursue the perjury and obstruction of justice case against Clinton. These charges were brought up during the suit by Paula Jones against Clinton for sexual harassment. Jones' lawyers were given evidence of Clinton's dalliance with Lewinsky, which included the DNA match of semen from the blue dress that Monica gave to Special Counsel Kenneth Starr, on the advice of Linda Tripp. Clinton was finally acquitted by the Senate in February, 1999, but not before his name was dragged through the mud. What would be an extramarital indiscretion in most countries was turned into a puritanical three-ring circus, which certainly qualifies as character assassination.

The retaliation against Joseph Wilson is another instance of a vicious attack, this time on a couple who thwarted part of Bush's plan to claim that Saddam Hussein was rebuilding his nuclear "weapons of mass destruction," known as "WMDs." Joseph Wilson was a retired diplomat who was sent by the CIA in 2002 to investigate claims that Iraq had bought "yellowcake" uranium ore from Niger. When Wilson denied that there had been any sale in a *New York Times* Op-Ed article, the Bushies tried to smear him and his investigation. In revenge, they blew the cover on his wife, Valerie Plame, who was a covert CIA agent specializing in tracking WMDs. Robert Novak, a conservative columnist, outed Plame on the word of two senior administration officials. These informants committed a crime in identifying Plame as a secret agent. They must have had access to secret or top secret information. A special prosecutor, Patrick Fitzgerald, investigated the "leak." Karl Rove, the brains behind George W., and I. Lewis (a.k.a. Scooter) Libby, Vice President Cheney's chief of staff, were both called to testify. Libby, the fall guy, was indicted. (See Addendum at the end of Chapter Four for an update, and the Timeline.)

John Kerry, the Democratic candidate for president in the 2004 election, was a decorated Vietnam War hero. This gave him a leg up on Bush, who served stateside in the Texas Air National Guard, thus avoiding any overseas service. This disparity in war service probably prompted the GOP to start a campaign to impugn Kerry's war record. A group of Vietnam veterans got together and with considerable financial help published a book, *Unfit for Command: Swift Boat Veterans Speak Out Against John Kerry*, which claimed that Kerry lied about his actions in combat. The senior author was John O'Neill, a critic of Kerry since 1971. When Kerry testified to the Senate Foreign Relations Committee that U.S. troops had committed war crimes in Vietnam, O'Neill, a graduate of the United States Naval Academy who took command of PCF 94 after Kerry left, became incensed. When Kerry used his war record to promote his candidacy, some thirty years later, O'Neill, now a Texas lawyer, and his co-author, Jerome R. Corsi, a Harvard Ph.D. and "expert" on the antiwar movement, got support for their publication and recruitment of anti-Kerry veterans. Bob Perry, a Texas millionaire and Bush contributor, gave $200,000 to the Swift Boat Veterans for Truth.

Texas Republicans also launched a smear campaign against Kerry, employing Spaeth Communications, the same outfit that smeared John McCain in 2002. Senator McCain, a Vietnam veteran, strongly criticized the Swift Boat campaign, and publicly asked Bush to denounce its tactics. Bush did not respond. Other vets went to bat for Kerry. In his book, *Shame on Swift Boat Vets for Bush: John Kerry Saved My Life* (Rassman, 2004), Jim Rassman wrote that Kerry pulled him out of the water under fire and saved his life.

It is interesting that in the world of right-wing politics there is often someone with a grudge (Linda Tripp, John O'Neill) and someone with money to turn that grudge into a legal or political smear campaign (Richard Scaife, Bob Perry). These people make a perfect marriage, like Jack Sprat and his wife.

Howard Dean is another victim of smear tactics. Dean seemed a front runner in the Democratic primaries. At his closing rally in Iowa, he was videotaped, yelling along with an audience of yelling supporters. The directional mike used for the video effectively "stripped off" the sound of the yelling crowd, making Dean look like a screaming nut. The GOP public relations team called his speech "I have a scream." The video was shown over and over on television and very likely cost him the primary.

Dan Rather, the former CBS anchorman, made the mistake of criticizing Bush's service in the Texas Air National Guard, without having his staff thoroughly authenticate the source of documents containing much negative information. Rather said that using the documents on his show, *60 Minutes*, was a mistake in judgment and that he was sorry.

The right wing immediately attacked. Bryan Curtis, a staff writer for *Slate*, wrote *The Anchor Is a Madman* (Curtis, 2004). Rather had always been a target. In 2001 David Limbaugh, the brother of the talk radio host, awarded the "Sore Loser's Award" to

Rather at the Media Research Center's annual banquet. (Rather had criticized Katherine Harris' declaration that Bush had won Florida.) Rather also won the "Flakiest Comment Award." In response to Bill O'Reilly's stacked question, "Do you think Bill Clinton is an honest man?" Rather said, "I do. It is possible for a man to be honest and lie about any number of things."

Rather lost his post as anchor due to this error, caused by his dependence on his staff to verify the report of Bush's Air National Guard service problems. Several people who had prepared the *60 Minutes* text were fired. Rather is now suing for millions.

There are many cases of character assassination, smear tactics, and retaliation by the GOP. Neither party is above using these tactics, but the Republicans seem to have been especially harsh and vindictive in trying to defeat, or succeeding in bringing down, their opponents. (Character assassination is one thing, but actual assassination seems to attack centrists and liberals more often than conservatives. Martin Luther King and John and Robert Kennedy are cases in point. The attempted assassination of Ronald Reagan was clearly not a conspiracy. It was done by the mentally disturbed John W. Hinckley Jr., who wanted to show off to his imaginary loved one, the actress Jodie Foster.)

II. PREPARATION FOR DOMINATION

At this point, I don't want to go into too much detail about the apparent preparation for a one-party system by the GOP. I will just review some of the acts (most of which were previously mentioned) that suggest a concerted effort to strip power from the Democratic Party, and to weaken any opposition to the GOP.

Since four Supreme Court justices were old enough to step down, Bush had a chance to pack the Supreme Court (and lower federal courts) during his second term. The Supreme Court has lifetime appointments, so the composition of the court determines the direction of the legal decisions for at least a generation. The court was already about five to four conservative. Democrats and Republicans have historically used the filibuster to block judicial appointments. The GOP wanted to push through the nominations of ten federal nominees (out of 299 Bush nominees in his first term) that were blocked by the Democrats as being ideologically too extreme. In addition, Chief Justice Rehnquist died of cancer in 2005. He was replaced by John G. Roberts, Jr., a conservative.

Tom DeLay and Bill Frist, Bush's hatchet-men, were pushing for further control of the Supreme Court. To keep the Democrats from blocking any of these nominees Frist said he would resort to the "nuclear option," which by a vote of the GOP majority would have ended the use of the filibuster to block judicial nominations. V.P. Cheney, as presiding officer of the Senate, could have ruled that the filibuster is unconstitutional. Then a simple majority (fifty-one) would uphold the ruling. It usually takes sixty votes to break a filibuster.

Just in time to avoid the "nuclear option," a bipartisan group of senators hammered out a compromise, allowing some of Bush's minor nominees for federal judgeships to get an "up or down" vote (no delays in committee or in hearings, no procedural maneuvering). While attention was focused only on a replacement for Rehnquist, Judge Sandra Day O'Connor announced her retirement. She was considered a "swing voter," who voted sometimes with liberals, and sometimes with conservatives. Bush picked John G. Roberts Jr., a former federal judge with a consistently conservative record, as her replacement.

When Chief Justice Rehnquist died, Bush picked Roberts for that post. Roberts was confirmed after much wrangling. Someone was still needed to replace O'Connor. Bush nominated Harriet Miers, who had been his right-hand legal adviser and factotum for years. The right wing criticized her credentials as a conservative. She was not radical enough for them! Bush was forced to drop Miers and nominate Samuel J. Alito, whose conservative "credentials," especially on abortion, are clearer than those of Miers. (See Addendum, Chapter Four, for an update on Alito.) The issue, of course, is the overthrow of *Roe v. Wade.*

Roberts was similarly attacked by the left with spot ads on the Fox and CNN cable networks, paid for by Naral Pro-Choice America. Bush managed to pack the Supreme Court with *two* radical conservatives (to replace Rehnquist and O'Connor) thus making a long-term impact on our legal system. This gives the conservatives a five to four majority. The overthrow of *Roe v. Wade*, and the civil rights issues raised by the Patriot Act are only two of many serious cases that the future court may face. The Court has already upheld a "partial birth abortion" ban (2007). Roberts is in his mid-fifties. The Supreme Court appointments are for the life of the candidate. Bush has, in effect, "packed" the Supreme Court, much as Franklin Roosevelt tried to pack the court in the opposite direction.

By saying the Democrats are "against people of faith," Bill Frist used the old technique of divide and conquer. Would you expect this kind of statement from a Harvard graduate and a transplant surgeon? The answer is "Yes." There have always been plenty of well-educated right-wingers. Look at e.e. cummings, T.S. Eliot, and George Bernard Shaw, all three anti-Semites, and cummings a fascist as well. Charles Lindbergh the pilot and his wife Anne Morrow, the author, were highly intelligent, but supported Nazi Germany. Henry Ford was smart enough to build the Model T and an empire, but was an anti-Semite, and far to the right.

By attacking the balance of powers, carefully constructed by the founding fathers to create a system of checks and balances between the Administrative, Legislative, and Judicial branches of the government, the GOP has overstepped the boundaries of proper political behavior. The president rushed from his Texas ranch to Washington, D.C. to sign an administrative order to stop the Florida court's decision to remove a feeding tube from Terri Schiavo. Terri was a Florida housewife who suffered cardiac arrest and massive brain damage. She was in a persistent vegetative state from 1990 to 2005. Her husband had petitioned to have her feeding tube removed. Bush's administrative order was a most unusual interference with the courts at the state level, and it finally did not succeed. It was obviously a sop to the evangelical right-to-lifers.

It might be argued that the swing toward conservatism during the Bush administration was merely part of the normal oscillation between the extremes of right and left. In fact, the oscillation has been getting smaller, especially since the Democrats started playing "me too." If the political pendulum stops swinging, the two-party system may just collapse. The legal system in Germany, for example, failed as a check against fascism, because Hitler packed the courts with Nazi judges.

Bush continued to break down the wall between Church and State. Money was fed to churches for social intervention with little or no supervision.

Issues like prayer in the schools and the teaching of evolution are still hot-button items for the GOP. The promotion of the teaching of "intelligent design" theory by the government (including Bill Frist) and by many school boards is a direct assault on science and the Darwinian theory of evolution.

The Patriot Act, whose creation was possible only under the blanket of fear created by the 9/11 attack, and its exploitation of that fear by the administration, has stealthily and savagely curtailed our civil liberties. Records of books and documents borrowed from libraries can now be examined without a warrant. Searches of personal documents and computer records are now easier to make. U.S. citizens who are suspected of potential terrorism can be held incommunicado, without formal arraignment, and without access to counsel. Other suspects were subjected to "extraordinary rendition." They were flown to countries friendly to the United States, where torture is tolerated (Egypt, Syria) with the ostensible goal of obtaining intelligence. Obstetrical records have been seized with the spurious goal of curbing sexual abuse of teen girls. The real purpose was to bring pressure to bear on abortion clinics, in line with the religious right's drive against abortion, contraception, and stem-cell research.

The furor over Supreme Court replacements is due to the stated goal of the GOP to overthrow *Roe v. Wade* and make abortions illegal once more.

The attempt to privatize Social Security suggests the establishment of a giant kleptocracy, where people with low incomes put their savings into the stock market. Wall Street would profit immensely. Brokers would get richer. Since the skullduggery of Enron and WorldCom, the cooking of the books by Arthur Andersen & Co., and the 2007–09 recession, who can trust the market? Even the Wall Street insiders didn't know which investment instruments were sound, and billions have been lost worldwide due to the complexity of "derivatives."

Later on, I will go into more detail about "preparation for domination."

III.   THE KEY TO THE PUZZLE

The puzzle, stated before, is how so many poor, working class and middle class people voted against their own economic self-interest. Several people have addressed this question. Thomas Frank has suggested that the Republicans have used a program of "carefully cultivated derangement" of economically depressed places such as Kansas to further their conservative goals.

> While earlier forms of conservatism emphasized fiscal sobriety, the backlash mobilizes voters with explosive social issues—summoning public *outrage* over everything from busing to un-Christian art—which it then marries to pro-business economic policies. Cultural *anger* is marshaled to achieve economic ends (Frank, 2004, p. 5, emphasis mine).

Frank then goes on to mention some of these "economic achievements" of the backlash: the international free-market consensus, with its accompanying privatization, deregulation and de-unionization, and globalization. We could add outsourcing of jobs and the curtailment of civil liberties and legal procedures such as class action suits.

My question would be, what is the *source* of this outrage? Whence the anger directed at gays, liberals, elites, intellectuals, atheists, abortion, and not least, justifiable anger at Saddam Hussein and terrorists? That question can be tackled after some more discussion of the puzzle, or "derangement." Paul Krugman (*New York Times*, February 25, 2005) sums up Frank's thesis:

> The message of Mr. Frank's book is that *the right has been able to win elections, despite the fact that its economic policies hurt workers, by portraying itself as the defender*

of mainstream values against a malevolent cultural elite
(emphasis mine).

Krugman describes the smear tactics used against the AARP by the same people who smeared John Kerry with the "Swift Boat" propaganda. The AARP had taken a stand against privatization of Social Security, so they were tarred with being anti-soldier and pro-gay marriage. The Swift Boat smearers published a picture of a soldier crossed out, and a gay couple in tuxedos with a check mark; (i.e., "A vote for Kerry is a vote for gay marriage, and Kerry is not a soldier—he doesn't support our troops.")

John A. Lawrence, Democratic staff director, House Committee on Education and the Workforce, refers to the labeling of a cartoon character, SpongeBob SquarePants, as gay by Dr. James Dobson. Dobson is the founder of Focus on the Family and a right-wing activist. Lawrence sees this seemingly ridiculous smear of a cartoon character as part of the same ongoing political strategy that Frank and Krugman deplore.

> Dr. Dobson and other cultural conservatives exploit such dubious threats as SpongeBob SquarePants to illustrate their allegations of a liberal assault on religion, family, and children. These well-planned campaigns are designed to lead voters to overlook conservative policies and their own economic self-interest and vote for those who position themselves as defenders of cultural normalcy. After all, why should politicians address falling wages, prolonged unemployment, crashing pensions, evaporating unemployment insurance and outsourced jobs when you can get millions of voters to go for the cultural head fake and take out their *anger* on cartoon characters (Lawrence, 2005, emphasis mine).

The key to the puzzle is the source of this widespread anger, which is directed against targets chosen by the Republican right. How can people be so easily misled? How can gay marriage, Spongebob, and the substitution of Happy Holidays by some people for Merry Christmas trump jobs, education, and health-care?

While it is clear that a great deal of anger is being directed at specific targets, that these targets have been carefully selected to fit the Republican "family values" agenda, and that the purpose of these targets is to deflect anger away from the Republicans onto the Democrats, the question of the sources of the anger have not been pinpointed. I think there are two main sources.

The first and most powerful source is the very loss of jobs and health insurance and the failure of public education, along with the host of other losses inflicted on the poor and middle class. The motor power that drives the anger comes from the cutbacks in funding social programs. Either by dumb luck or through Machiavellian genius, the right wing has hit on the exact means of creating anger through fear of loss of status. As Americans see their own financial prospects narrowing, and realize that their children will not "do better" than their parents—the dream of every generation—their anger builds up.

Why don't they direct their anger at the Republicans, who are so clearly behind the cutbacks and the broken promises? My premise is that many Americans have suffered early psychological damage during their childhood and that this damage has created an anger that preceded their current anger over the economy. They couldn't express that early anger because they were beholden to their parents for sustenance and protection. (They learned to "suck it up.") That anger is due to poor and uncaring parenting on a widespread scale. Once they learned to repress their anger at authority figures (their parents) they were primed to repress their anger at George Bush & Co. As kids, they learn to take it out on classmates, in sports (the other school is the enemy) and on dweebs and nerds and any kid who is different, including minorities. As adults, they have the tailor-made targets of gays, Iraqis, or liberals constantly held up to them as evil.

At first it may seem hard to make the connections between current politics and psychological damage in early childhood. To make those connections clear, I have to go back to some research data that I gathered in a 1969–1984 study of 2000 families, to show how much poor parenting there is, even in a "sophisticated" metropolis like New York City. Then I have to assume that parenting doesn't differ that much between the Red states and Manhattan. My guess is that rural areas are more likely to be harsher, if anything, in bringing up their children than are the urbanites in New York City.

IV. PARENTAL PRACTICES CREATE ADULT ANGER

Before examining the behavior of this sample of parents, it is necessary to look at the theory of how parental practices damage children and create anger. Several sources contribute to a theory of early damage and anger. In *The Insanity of Normality*, Arno Gruen, a former professor of psychology at Rutgers University, now practicing psychotherapy in Switzerland, sets forth the process by which anger is created by the parents' behavior, and then deflected away from them onto the self or other objects.

Gruen assumes (and rightly so) that the child is essentially helpless, dependent on the parents for nourishment and protection—in fact, for survival.

> The child adapts to the needs of the parents rather than to his own needs, to assure this protection. In order to be able to share in the power that subjugates them, children substitute obedience and adaptation for responsibility for their own actions. If we lose the connection to our own interior world, then we can relate only to a false self, to an image-oriented self attuned to behavior and feelings pleasing to our surrounding world. The need and perhaps also the compulsion to preserve this image-orientation take precedence over all one's own personal perceptions, feelings and empathy. The resulting inability to be rooted in oneself is what engenders destructive and evil behavior (Gruen, 1992, p. vii).

The kind of parental "love" that engenders self hatred and its consequent anger is often called "narcissistic." The parents punish or demand conformity "for your own good." Gruen points out that "A solicitude...whose object is to keep another person dependent and thus under one's control, ought no longer to be seen as a 'loving' solicitude." Narcissistic parental behavior occurs when the parents put their wishes and needs ahead of those of their children. This in turn produces a "narcissistic injury" to the child. Gruen sees this as developing a false-self and self-hatred. The process by which the need for love and protection is turned into self-hatred (or in our language, low self-esteem) is laid out by Gruen:

> To deny their inner needs (*which their parents have ignored*) children must either completely or partially split them off…in order not to be forced to perceive that father and mother are causing them pain, children will search in themselves for the cause of their despair. This tragedy, which leads to children's surrender of the self, consists not only in the dissociation of their inner world but, beyond that, in the fact that—in order to maintain the life-giving bond with mother and father—they must see the lack of parental love as the result of a defect in themselves (Gruen, 1992, p.19, italic insert mine).

The strength of this desire to maintain a good image of one's parents is shown in two well known case histories of multiple personality: Sybil and Miss Beauchamp. The outright rejection of these patients by their mothers was not a deterrent to their pitiful attempts to maintain a picture of the "good mother." "On three occasions, Sybil's mother came close to killing her" (Schreiber, 1973, p. 200). Yet Sybil felt she herself was at fault.

> What was most disturbing to Sybil was her feeling that she had no reason to be unhappy, and that, by being so, she was somehow betraying her parents. To assuage her feelings of guilt she prayed for forgiveness on three counts: for not being more grateful for all she had; for not being happy, as her mother thought she should be; and for what her mother termed 'not being like other youngsters'" (Schreiber, 1973, p. 94).

Again, in Miss Beauchamp, Morton Prince noted the self-blame of the victim of a cold, rejecting mother.

> Ms. B. was a nervous impressionable child…Her mother exhibited a great dislike to her, and for no reason,

apparently, excepting that the child resembled her father in looks...her presence having been ignored by her mother except upon occasions of reprimand. On the other hand, she herself idealized her mother, bestowing upon her an almost morbid affection; and believing that the fault was her own, and that her mother's lack of affection was due to her own imperfections, she gave herself up to introspection, and concluded that if she could only purify herself and make herself worthy, her mother's affection would be given her (Prince, 1906, p. 12).

Although these are two extreme cases (Sybil especially being the victim of her mother's excessive violence), I think the dynamics are similar across the wide range of parental damaging behaviors. Wanting your child to be the ballerina or the baseball star you never were is a much milder form of rejection, but this "living through" your child ignores the child's needs. It gives first priority to the parents' needs. This produces the self-rejection and consequent anger and depression in the child. In the case of the so-called "multiple personality," (currently referred to as "dissociative identity disorder") this rejection, often accompanied by violence or sexual abuse, results in a severe splitting, or dissociation,

How does the behavior of the rejected or abused child toward his or her parents relate to our previous national authority figures—our parent substitutes, Bush and Cheney? If many of our population have traded in their original selves for an obedient "false self" that has not grown independent of their parents, it is not surprising that they may have looked to Bush & Co., or to John McCain, to tell them what to do. They have not become "autonomous" human beings, in Gruen's view.

When we speak of individual rather than political autonomy (the independence of a country or nation), there are many synonyms, depending on the discipline of the user. Some of these are "inner-directed," "self-reliant," "self-sufficient," "self-directed," "non-conforming," and "non-enculturated." Many people have written about self-reliance and autonomy, among them Emerson, Kant, and Carl Rogers. Maslow (1962) thought that an important trait of the "self-actualizing" person was "autonomous functioning," defined as being "relatively independent of their social and physical environment."

The non-autonomous individuals will have that residual anger left over from the loss of their original (childhood) self. The current economic squeeze only adds more anger. What is the result? Low self-esteem (fear of losing status) and a double dose of anger that has to be directed away from the self. Dick Cheney and Karl Rove showed us where to direct that anger: at gays, Iraqis, liberals, elitists, and those of little faith.

Why wasn't the anger directed at the figures who hurt so many citizens—Bush, Cheney, Rove, and Rumsfeld? One major factor may be the preparation during childhood for identification with a damaging or unloving or narcissistic parent. *If you have been trained to give up your true or inner self to maintain your parents' love and support, you are vulnerable to the same kind of maltreatment later in life. You join with the guys with the power— your parents, and then the Bushies.*

Does this seem too simple? There is more evidence for this tendency to join forces with the "strong" guys, even though they may be hurting (or killing) you. Bruno Bettelheim noticed that in a German concentration camp, some of his fellow prisoners— Jews and political prisoners alike—wore abandoned or worn out armbands of their Nazi captors. In so doing, they borrowed power symbolically from the enemy. Bettelheim called this "identification with the aggressor" (Bettelheim, 1943).

Another famous case of similar identification was Patty Hearst, who was kidnapped in 1974 by the Symbionese Liberation Army, a radical gang. People were shocked to see the front-page newspaper pictures of Patty, the daughter of one of the richest men in America, holding an automatic rifle while robbing a bank. She had been kept in a closet and had forced sex with her captors. "Identification with the aggressors" probably saved her life.

The lesson to be learned is that when someone has power greatly superior to yours, you may join forces with him to save your life. There was probably nobody in the world in as powerful a position as George W. Bush. He reinforced this aura of power by posing in an Air Force jacket on an aircraft carrier for a photo-op declaring (prematurely) victory in Iraq. Why not join with this man, who also had his soft side—the joking Joe Six-Pack, "Dubya"? (See later section on the faces of George W. Bush.)

So you have a large portion of the population that has been trained to forgive their parents' aggressions to maintain their love and protection. You also have a natural tendency for people to identify upward with those in power over them, the "aggressors." Many people were primed to forgive the Republicans their aggressions and vote them in—even after two terms of Bush.

All of us are "sinners," since we all have done something (or thought of doing something) in our lives—even pulling the cat's tail—that we were ashamed of. Bush renounced his past drinking, carousing, and other "sins." As a born-again Christian, he has been forgiven by God. Surely we can forgive him if he has been forgiven by God! We can forgive him job loss, health care chaos, and education "left behind." We are sinners too, and we hate those elitists who pretend to be so holy! (The attraction of the denial of carnal and other pleasures by charismatic leaders has always been a main source of their power. The chastity of priests and nuns, the starvation diet of Mahatma Gandhi, and the suffering and passion of Christ come to mind. Maybe George's born-again renunciation helped him win votes.)

What a great scam this Bush/Cheney program was. It was a closed system. Cut back on social supports, spend down on war, and cut taxes for the rich until you can't pay for those supports ("starving the beast"). Then direct the anger *you have created* in the jobless, outsourced, insurance-less, squeezed middle and working class away from these cutbacks and deprivations, and toward your hot-button targets (gays, elitists, liberals, intellectuals, etc.). Sex, religiosity, social control, jealousy, fear of complexity—these are all thrown into the "family values" mix.

V. THE FAMILY RESEARCH PROJECT: PARENTAL PRACTICES AND CHILD BEHAVIOR OUTCOMES

You may ask, "How do we know that parents are behaving selfishly toward their children, and in so doing are creating adults who are still angry, and trained early to give up their autonomy and even their own self-interest to powerful leaders (parent figures)? The Family Research Project, which I directed for sixteen years, looked at the children in approximately one thousand families selected randomly from the borough of Manhattan, New York City and one thousand families on Welfare from the same geographical area. Mothers were interviewed initially for an average of two hours, and re-interviewed five years later with a questionnaire that focused on one of their children between the ages of six and eighteen. While a great deal of information was gathered from community records (mental hospitals, welfare records, schools, and police records), the questionnaire looked primarily at the parental child-rearing practices and parental relationship and at the children's behavior and psychological symptoms. Project psychiatrists visited a subsample of several hundred families to validate the material gathered by the questionnaires.

A factor analysis of parental behaviors, based on the mothers' reports, yielded three major factors: Parental Coldness, Parental Lability, and Punitive Parents. It is interesting that coldness and punishment were fairly independent or separate ("orthogonal") factors. Apparently parents who punished were not necessarily cold. (A factor analysis attempts to maximize the differences between the factors—that is, low intercorrelations between them.) Lability in the parents was tapped by questions dealing with the inability of parents to maintain control over their anger with the children. Losing their temper, and being alternately loving and angry, are good examples of the questions in the "lability" factor, (originally called "Mother-Excitable-Rejecting").

To summarize, when the children's behavior was correlated with various factors, such as the child's physical health, social class, and race of the parents, the relationship between the parents ("Parental") and parental behavior toward the children ("Parent–Child") the Parent–Child factors were by far the strongest predictors of psychological problems in the children. This was in spite of the fact that many of the behaviors, such as hitting the child, or "losing your temper often," were socially undesirable. The mothers were assured of confidentiality, and the reports of mothers' or fathers' violence toward the children were surprisingly frequent.

For those who have statistico-phobia, it might be best to skip the next few pages. However, you will miss the richness of the statistical data which I am using to relate child and adolescent experience to adult political behavior.

Let's take a look at the independent variables, those that we tested for their effect on the dependent variables (child behavior and symptoms). First were the demographic (background) variables: Spanish-speaking, being black, a High Number of Addresses in New York City, Number of Natural Parents (primarily father absent), Large Number of Children in the Household, and Not Always in Natural Mother's Care. These factors had rather weak associations with child behaviors. Being Spanish-speaking accounted for 3.7% of unique variance in the Isolation score (few friends) and 2.9% for the Weak Group Membership score. What does this mean?

Before explaining the meaning of unique variance, it is necessary to discuss the meaning of correlation and correlation coefficients. A simple correlation in statistical parlance describes the relation between two factors, variables, or measurements, such as height and weight. If one gained a pound for every inch of height, that would yield a coefficient of correlation of +1.00. If one lost a pound for every inch of height (a dismal prospect), the coefficient would be −1.00. If there were no relation between height and weight, the correlation coefficient would be zero.

To understand these results, we should start with the simple correlation equation formula $y = mx + b$, which describes a straight line (drawn through the calculated center of a "scatter plot" of values by the "least squares" procedure) with one independent variable (such as High Number of Addresses) represented by x, and one dependent variable y (a child behavior score such as Weak Group Membership), where m is the slope of the line, and b is the y-intercept (the point at which the line crosses the y, or vertical, axis).

In the Family Research Project we used multiple correlation equations, since there were many predictor (or "independent") variables related to child behavior outcomes ("dependent variables"). These predictor variables were the demographic variables, the parental factors (the relationship of the parents, and the mother's physical and emotional health), and the parent–child factors (usually known as "parental practices"). These predictors were put into a series of multiple regression (or multiple correlation) equations of the form $(y = a + b_1x_1 + b_2x_2 + b_3x_3...b_px_p)$ where y is the value of the dependent child variable that we are predicting or explaining, and x_1, x_2, x_3, etc. are the independent factors or "predictors," explaining the variance in y. In addition, b_1, b_2, b_3, etc. are the weights or strengths (slopes, or Beta coefficients) of these factors in their association with the particular child behavior factor (y) in question.

These b values (regression coefficients or Beta coefficients) indicate the independent contribution of each independent variable to the prediction of the y, or dependent, variable. You could say that $x1$ correlates with y after controlling for all the other independent variables ($x2$, $x3$, etc).This is also known as the partial correlation. The term a is called the "constant," the equivalent of b in the simple correlation.

When a great many predictors are put into the equation, the unique or independent contribution of each successive factor entered ("stepwise regression") has been weakened by its overlap with all of its predecessors. The unique contributions, then, while small due to the methods we use, nevertheless point to *relationships* between predictors and child psychopathology. It is the relative strength of the (weakened) unique contributions that tells us what factors are injuring children.

Another cause of diminished partial values is "multicollinearity," when many of the predictor variables are highly intercorrelated. Then some of the predictors are redundant. We attempted to reduce the intercorrelations using factor analysis. Another problem is the assumption of linearity. Some predictors are curvilinear, not linear. These need to be broken down into linear segments, if possible. Some predictors are categorical, such as sex (although in our society this variable is rapidly becoming linear). These variables are entered as "dummy variables," with values of 0 and 1 (for example, with 0 = male, 1= female).

There was one multiple regression equation for each of the eighteen child behavior factors. When examining the relation within the first wave of the study (Time 1) these weights could better be called associations. When looking at Time 1 factors' associations with Time 2 child behaviors, the factors might be called "predictors" of later behavior. At this point, we will look only at associations. We will look at the cross-section sample, which is a representative random sample of households with children in the borough of Manhattan, New York City.

When we look at unique variance (partial R^2, which reads as partial R squared), we are looking at the contribution of a predictor all by itself; not at its interactions with other variables in the predictor set of twenty-five variables. What do we mean by "variance?" A score varies from a low number of symptom items to a high number, and each individual got a score on each variable. For example, the predictor Being Hispanic accounted for 3.7% of the unique variance in the Isolation score, independently of all the other twenty-four independent factors.

How can we judge the strength of the relationships? We can look at the R^2 (correlation squared). In studies of this kind, correlations are never very high. An example of the highest association of all the symptom scores is that between the twenty-five independent factors and Delinquency. The correlation (R) was .78. The R^2 is the proportion of variance in the dependent variable, y, that is explained by all the x variables in the equation taken together. To see the percentage of variance in Delinquency accounted for by all twenty-five factors as a set, we have to square the R (multiply it by itself, or .78 × .78). This yields .60, or "60% of the variance in Delinquency." That is quite a lot of variance explained, but it still leaves 40% unaccounted for. Other environmental factors (pollution?), heredity, and measurement error might account for the shortfall.

As a guideline, correlations (R) and variance accounted for (R^2) are shown in Table 4.

TABLE 4

R	R^2	% of Variance
.50	.25	25%
.25	.06	6%
.20	.04	4%
.10	.01	1%

In our study, we usually considered 1% of the variance (or more) worth looking at when considering *unique* contributions (partial R^2). The unique contribution of a single factor within a set of predictors (using multiple correlation analysis) is given by the partial R, or Beta coefficient. When this is squared ("partial R^2"), it yields the percentage of variance in y contributed by a single predictor, net of all the others in the predictor set. (When looking at the overall power of a *set* of factors, we look at the multiple R, not the partial R's. We expect and obtain much higher correlations, and a greater percentage of variance accounted for.)

The demographic variables are often called "social background" variables. Being black contributed 1.8% (a partial R^2 value, contributed uniquely, or by itself, without overlap with other factors) to Mentation Problems (e.g., concentration and memory difficulties) and Demandingness (1.1%). "Moving to many different addresses" accounted for unique variance in Delinquency (1.4%), and Fighting (1.2%).

Overall, except for the association of being Spanish-speaking with Isolation and Weak Group Membership (another aspect of social isolation), the power of the demographic variables is not very great.

The Parental Factors were based on numerous questions about the parents and the marital relationship (if any), and a number of psychophysiological "screening items" that distinguished patients from non-patients in previous studies (Langner, 1962). The screening items (such as "can't get going," "frequent headaches") were asked of the mother about herself. The Parental Factors were:

Mother's Physical and Emotional Illness
Traditional Marriage
Mother's Economic Dissatisfaction
Unhappy Marriage
Unleisurely Parents
Parents' Quarrels

The only strong parental factor was Mother's Physical and Emotional Illness. Typical items in this score were "mother's health is poor," "she has periods when she can't get going," "feels weak all over," and " is often bothered by nervousness." The partial R^2 values linked to it were:

Regressive Anxiety (2.1%)
Fighting (1.1%)

TABLE 5

Traditional Marriage was linked to:	
Compulsivitiy	3.5%
High Group Participation	2.3%
(Less) Fighting	1.1%

Table 5 suggests that a traditional marriage fostered good peer relations and controlled fighting, but paid a slight price in terms of compulsivity (hand-washing, etc.). It was not a predictor of serious psychopathology.

A very different story is told by the Parent–Child Factors. I will list them, giving a few examples of items that "loaded" onto each factor, the item correlations with the factor score (or loadings), and then the partial R^2 for various child symptom scores. The Parent–Child factors averaged 10 questions each.

The strength of these parental practices in their association (and prediction) of child behavior problems and psychopathology is part of my evidence for widespread damage to children in the United States. That early damage, in turn, is one factor that I think led so many adults to vote for George Bush and against their own best economic interests.

TABLE 6
MOTHER EXCITABLE-
REJECTING

	Correlation with Factor Score (R)
Mother Excitable-Rejecting ("Labile")	.
Mother often screams at child	.39
Is very changeable in handling him (her)	.37
Has problems which keep her from getting pleasure from him (her)	.29
	Partial R^2 (%) Unique Contribution
Conflict with Parents	8.9%
Regressive Anxiety	4.0%
Fighting	3.8%
Sex Curiosity	3.2%
Isolation	2.0%
Self-Destructive Tendencies	1.9%
Conflict with Siblings	1.9%
Mentation Problems	1.5%
Competition	1.2%

The fact that this lability in the mother is making independent (unique) contributions to so many children's symptoms is startling. We tend to think of this maternal behavior as less damaging to children than outright physical punishment. Yet the intermittent

72

periods of warmth (due to her "changeability") will tend to bond the child, and thus may create as much or even more of a conflict than outright violence. The prevalence of this type of maternal behavior is clearly greater than outright physical violence. For that reason, we might suspect that it damages political judgment in even more adults so exposed than does parental punitiveness. *It again sets voting adults up for bonding to oppressive figures who do not have their individual needs at heart.*

The second most powerful Parent–Child factor is "Parents Cold." This deals with both father and mother. Typical items are:

TABLE 7
PARENTS COLD

Parents Cold	Correlation with Factor Score (R)
Parents rarely hug and kiss the child	.43
Parents do not show affection easily to child	.40
	Partial R^2 (% of unique contribution)
Conflict with parents	7.8%
Fighting	2.1%
Conflict with siblings	1.5%
Undemanding	1.0%
Delinquency	1.0%

Parental Coldness was not quite as strong a factor as lability in mothers. However, the first three behaviors (Conflict with Parents, Fighting and Conflict with Siblings) are common to both Parental Coldness and mother's lability. Interestingly, Undemandingness and Delinquency scores were related only to Parental Coldness. The Undemanding children were more prone to early independence, were older, and were probably not bonded to parents as much as to their peers. Delinquents have been shown to exhibit peer reference (older male siblings and gangs) rather than parental reference in many studies. (See Albert Cohen, *Delinquent Boys*, 1955.)

TABLE 8   PARENTS PUNITIVE

Parents Punitive	Correlation with factor score (R)
Parents spank child with strap or stick	.63
Parents often use deprivation of privileges	.60
	Partial R^2 (% of unique contribution)
Fighting	2.6%
Conflict with parents	1.9%
Regressive Anxiety	1.0%

Punishment, physical and nonphysical, reflects the first three child behaviors associated with labile mothers. However, it lacks two of the more serious associations with lability: Self-destructive Tendencies and Mentation Problems. (In later analyses, boys who received physical punishment by their fathers after age nine had the highest scores on Delinquency, and reported school problems and arrests based on school and police records. Early punishment (ages six to nine) was linked to *non*-delinquent symptomatology.)

The same factors that showed strong associations with children's symptoms during the first waves of interviews (Time 1) also predicted children's symptoms at Time 2, five years later. This supports the predictive validity of the mothers' reports. Further validation was gained from community records (school, police, Welfare).

A final piece of evidence about how common poor parenting is in our culture is the simple prevalence of what is nowadays considered to be child abuse. Seven percent of the mothers in the cross-sectional (representative) sample said they beat the child with a strap or stick as punishment, while 21% of the Welfare mothers said so. While only twenty-five child-abusers (2.5%) were *officially* reported in the cross-section sample, seventy-two mothers (7% as mentioned above) reported beating their children with an object. *The real rates of this form of abuse could very well be three times as high as the reported rates nationally.* This didn't include punishment by fathers, or verbal, emotional, and other forms of abuse. Given the social undesirability of hitting children, we could expect that many more parents, particularly in the middle class, did not report hitting with an object. While the borough of Manhattan, New York City, is not representative of the country as a whole, the data presented suggest widespread abuse of children nationally. Rural areas, the Midwest, and some Southern states are likely to have even higher rates of abuse and poor parenting, due to authoritarian family structures.

Figures for reported child abuse and neglect for the nation as a whole are available in a summary published in 2005, *Child Maltreatment 2003: Summary of Key Findings*, National Clearinghouse on Child Abuse and Neglect Information (Childabuse, 2005):

> An estimated 906,000 children were determined to be victims of child abuse or neglect in 2003...60% of child victims experienced neglect, almost 19% were physically abused, 10% were sexually abused, and 5 % were emotionally maltreated. In addition, 17% were associated with 'other' types of maltreatment, based on specific State laws and policies...In 2003, an estimated 2.9 million referrals concerning the welfare of approximately 5.5 million children were made to CPS (child protective services) agencies throughout the United States. Of these ...an estimated 1.9 million were accepted for investigation or assessment...57% of all reports that alleged child abuse or neglect were made by...professionals ...*Approximately 80% of perpetrators were parents.* (Italics are my emphasis.)

If we apply the ratio of unreported abuse to reported abuse found in the study of Manhattan children to the national figure of 906,000, we come up with a figure of about three million abused nationally. If we were to add to this figure the children who suffered not only physical abuse ("punitive parents") but also parental coldness and lability, the figure for the incidence of general poor parenting could be in the neighborhood of ten million nationally. Since incidence is a count of new cases per year, the prevalence figure (the number of cases existing at any one time) would be much higher. It would contain the accumulated cases of child abuse and poor parenting over time.

Descriptions of the Family Research Project and some of the statistical data discussed above can be found in various publications (Langner, 1962; Langner et al., 1974, 1976; Gersten et al., 1974, 1976; Eisenberg, et al., 1975; McCarthy, et al., 1975). At least ten other publications deal with this research project.

Many studies have found that these factors (or closely related factors) predict child and adolescent psychopathology. I have used data from the Family Research Project to illustrate how epidemiology can complement the findings of clinical practice (Bowlby, Miller, Gruen, and many others.) A recent study confirms the hypothesis that strain increases in linear fashion with increasing stress due to parental behavior, among other factors (*Adverse Childhood Experiences Study: Major Findings*, Centers for Disease Control and Prevention; see Adverse, 2005).

A score was made of abuse, neglect and traumatic stressors labeled "adverse childhood experiences" (Aces). "The ACE score is used to assess the total amount of stress during childhood and has demonstrated that as the number of Aces increases, the risk for… health problems increases in a strong and graded fashion." Some of the health problems mentioned are alcoholism, depression, illicit drug use, and suicide attempts, among many others. A large number of "life events" studies have shown a relation between stressful events and physical and emotional disorder in both adults and children.

VI BAD PARENTING'S EFFECTS ON ADULTS

What is the effect of parental lability, punitiveness, coldness, and mother's physical and emotional illness on children once they become grown-ups? I have previously cited Gruen's description of the child's denial of his inner needs in order to maintain parental love and protection. This results in a "false-self." (The child denies his inner needs for affection, independence or autonomy, and sexuality, and presents a façade to the family and the world of seeming conformity with their demands. This façade gradually becomes a rather stable false self, as the original "true" self is lost and abandoned.) Children then blame themselves, not their parents, for their despair. This produces self-hatred, which is turned onto (projected onto) people or groups outside the family. Adults with a "false self" lack autonomy, and are trained to obedience. They are more likely to vote for someone like Bush, or for any powerful authority figure (like their father or mother) who tells them what to do in simple terms. They are also accustomed to authority figures who do not have their best interests at heart Later on, I will go into more detail about the patterns of parental abuse. I'll discuss the work of Alice Miller. She has focused on the tendency, particularly in Freudian psychoanalytic therapy, to blame the child for aggressive and sexual instincts, rather than the parents for real, not imagined, abuse of their children. Her discussion of the beatings and humiliation that Adolf Hitler suffered as a child, and his subsequent destructive rage, can make us fear for the fertile soil of child abuse in our country and the dictator and followers it might produce.

The question of whether child abuse (sexual, physical, verbal, or other types) is real or a fantasy as reported by adult patients is discussed briefly in my book *Choices for Living: Coping with Fear of Dying* (Langner, 2002, pp. 81-82, under "recovered memories").

VII. WHAT'S IN THE FUTURE FOR AMERICA?

If you have a nation with many conformist self-hating people who fear losing what little status they have, you have a nation ripe for fascism. We're not there yet, and the election of Barack Obama will probably keep us from the brink for at least two terms. But let's look at the conditions, both economic and psychological, that might lead to fascism. Some of these factors were present in Weimar Germany, and led to the German peoples' endorsement of Adolf Hitler.

A. Loss of Identity

I have discussed the loss of identity, or "loss of self," that so many children experience in order to maintain their relationship to their parents. In pre-World War II Germany, a country known for its authoritarian family structure, this loss of early identity, of the "true self," must have been widespread. The *Haustyrann* (house tyrant) of the German family was not interested in the needs of his children, but was busy asserting his authority. Max Weber's father is a good example, for he demanded that his son excel at saber-dueling, while his mother sought to bring out her son's gentler side. Weber became a world-famous sociologist, but he suffered from the conflict between his parents' expectations.

Meanwhile, Germany had lost its national identity. With the Versailles Treaty of 1919, the country lost much of its territory (Alsace and Lorraine, Prussian Poland and part of West Prussia, Danzig, the Saar, and various colonies). Limits were placed on the German armed forces. There was great resentment over the payment of heavy reparations. The stage was set for a widespread paranoid feeling of victimization.

B. Loss of Self-Esteem

When there is loss of identity, there is also loss of self-esteem. If you have given up your true self and traded it in for a false self, you are angry at the loss. That anger is turned against the self, rather than at the parents. Anger directed at oneself over this bad "bargain" results in low self-esteem.

The self-esteem of the German people was very low after World War I and the Versailles Treaty. In particular, historians have noted the loss of status among the *Kleinbeamten*, who comprised the backbone of the Nazi Party. These were the petty officials—bus conductors, school teachers, government workers, many of whom wore uniforms on the job. They were hit hardest by the subsequent economic depression.

C. Loss of Love and Affection

The child of punitive, cold, or labile parents suffers a loss of the love and affection that is needed for proper nurturance and growth. In Germany up to World War II, child-rearing was known to be particularly harsh. The stories in the children's book *Strubblepeter* (also *Struwwelpeter*) are a nightmare of parental punishments and threats. For example, *Daumenlutscher* ("little suck-a-thumb") was warned by his parents not to suck. At night the tailor came, and cut off both his thumbs with a huge scissors. Imagine a child confronted with the full-page illustration of *Daumenlutscher*, blood dripping from his thumbs onto the floor!

Max und Moritz were bad little boys. They particularly annoyed their irascible father. In the end, they were ground up by the miller and fed to the chickens. This book was the inspiration for the American comic strip *The Captain and the Kids*.

My mother once asked a close friend, who was raised in Germany in the early 1900s, if he wasn't terrified by the *Grimm's Fairy Tales* and these other lurid books. He said he never worried, because "I was a good little boy." Here is a good example of social control through childhood literature—through fear.

I don't think the average American parent is as authoritarian as the German parent of the 1900s, but there is growing evidence of opinion in favor of physical punishment over "permissiveness." There has also been a strong push for capital punishment for those younger than eighteen. The *New York Times* ran an article several years ago about a boy who suffocated in pig feces on a correctional farm run by a friend of the former Attorney General, John Ashcroft. There have been other instances of privatization of correctional facilities for juveniles that have resulted in serious injury to the inmates. In addition, the widespread occurrence of prison rape of juveniles has for years been tacitly condoned, and has only recently been subjected to strong criticism. Moreover, the United States still allowed capital punishment for juveniles until Supreme Court decision in 2005.

D. Loss of Social Supports

We have listed the loss of social supports due to the Bush administration. The obvious supports are health, education, and welfare. Jobs are of critical importance, not only for sustenance and support of the family, but also for a sense of belongingness. Many people identify with the organizations for which they work (even if they are exploited by the companies).

In the United States, the workplace as a source of financial and emotional security has declined sharply. In part, this is due to the ebbing of union membership. Job security was a lifetime commitment in large corporations like General Motors until a few years ago, but corporate attitudes have changed markedly in the United States. Corporate retirement programs and pensions are virtually disappearing, except at the CEO level. In 2008 the country was shocked to hear that General Motors, Chrysler, and Ford might go out of business. Republicans have blamed the United Auto Workers for the meltdown, saying that the UAW wages were $73 an hour, while those at Toyota, for example, were $30 per hour. In fact, the difference is due to the benefits agreed to in the past by management. If health and pension benefits are subtracted from the $73 figure, Detroit UAW workers get only $28 per hour. Foreign car makers are not committed to offer these benefits. It has been suggested that if universal health care were passed into law, the auto companies could survive this crisis. Of course, the conservatives have blamed the unions and not the management of these companies.

The church has always been a source of support, both emotional and financial. The decline of church membership has taken away some of this support, even while the evangelical ideology of about one fifth of the nation has invaded the political sphere. Parochial schools and church-run hospitals have been closing.

Jobs and the church were both in decline in Germany after World War I. The people looked to the government for the missing emotional and financial support. When Hitler offered membership for the little guy in the Nazi Party, he quickly recruited the disaffected. Remember that he was a wounded World War I veteran, and a frustrated artist who ended up as a house painter after the war. His story was the story of the struggling and forgotten average guy.

E. Loss of Control over Life Events

None of us has control over when we will die, but we can usually put that final event on a back burner until some catastrophe brings this basic fear back to the front. With the bombing of the twin World Trade Towers, Americans felt their lives threatened.

Sadly, there is increasing evidence that the Bush administration took shameful advantage of this vulnerability. It is now clear that our fears were purposely enhanced by the administration, with a system of colored alerts. Every time there was a political gaffe, it was covered up by a shift from an orange to a red alert. While most of the nation stayed on yellow, New York City was constantly on orange.

In 2009 there was further corroboration of the manipulation of the public by the Bush/Cheney/Rove team. In his book, *The Test of Our Times* (September 1, 2009) Tom Ridge, the former Secretary of Homeland Security, said that Attorney General John Ashcroft and Defense Secretary Donald H. Rumsfeld pressured him to raise the national threat level a few days before the 2004 national election. They justified this action because of a videotape released by Osama bin Laden. Ridge refused, and suspected it was wanted by the administration to help Bush win the election.

Bush & Co. had a windfall with the 9/11 bombing, because from then on they were dealing with a frightened, anxious, and perhaps hypervigilant public. Now was the time to talk of mushroom clouds caused by weapons of mass destruction (which Saddam Hussein didn't have). Now was the time to concoct reports of yellowcake uranium bought by Iraq, which never happened. These were fears concocted and promoted by our leaders.

Not all the fears were tailor-made by Cheney and Rove. There were plenty of events that contributed to feelings of loss of control. The preemptive war in Iraq was bringing home pictures of wounded soldiers and civilians and grieving parents of the dead. Then, a tsunami in the Indian Ocean created more evidence of the helplessness of man in the face of natural disaster. Later on came Hurricane Katrina, which devastated New Orleans and other cities on the Gulf. The delayed and inadequate response to this catastrophe, even though there was a warning of several days, speaks to our impotence in the face of such cataclysms. It also showed how unprepared the Bush administration was to protect us. The inability of the former GOP-dominated government to act promptly and even-handedly in this crisis questions its posture as the sole party providing national security.

If these events triggered anxiety due to loss of control in the United States, similar events were at play in Weimar Germany. The control of Germany's fate was in the hands of the Allied Powers. Jobs were scarce. Territory was lost. A nation with a proud military tradition could not admit that it had been defeated, and it talked of betrayal from inside.

F. Rapid Social Change

In his study of communities in Stirling County, Nova Scotia, Alexander Leighton found that rapid social change had a negative impact on mental health. Rates of mental disorder were highest in communities where there had been rapid change, while stable communities showed low rates. (See Hughes et al., 1960, page 4, for a discussion of "preliminary indicators of [community] disintegration.") These indicators were: "A recent history of disaster, widespread ill health, extensive poverty, cultural confusion, widespread secularization, extensive migration, and *rapid and widespread social change*" (italics mine). Any or all of these factors could have an effect on voting behavior. I have looked at only a few of them in any detail. More than a hundred years ago Emile Durkheim, the famous French sociologist, found that deregulation (the loss of or change in laws and customs governing behavior) was associated with high rates of suicide and other forms of social pathology, such as divorce (Durkheim, 1897). He coined the term *anomie* for this deregulated state of society. While he claimed to eschew psychology, he clearly implied that individuals were upset by this societal state. Durkheim did not use "regulation" in the sense that we use it to describe the [supposed] control of the SEC (Securities and Exchange Commission) and the Federal Reserve Board over the stock market. However, it is not beyond possibility that Alan Greenspan's lack of concern with regulation, and the Republican focus on deregulation, created something like a state of general societal deregulation that Durkheim called anomie. Greenspan admitted to the failure of his free-market philosophy. "Those of us who have looked to the self-interest of lending institutions to protect shareholder's equity (myself especially) are in a state of shocked disbelief....The whole concept of self-regulation through self-interest is now dead" (Greenspan, URL).

In the United States we have had rapid changes in attitudes toward sexuality and in marital relations. The power of women has increased with respect to men. The population has moved from the farms to the cities in three generations. Only 2% of workers are now in agriculture. We have also experienced rapid changes in the workplace, in religious affiliation, and in the centrality of religion. These changes have aroused a great deal of anger among those who feel slighted. White men, the religious right wing, and rural folk are most affected. Minorities—blacks, Hispanics, and Asians—have succeeded in many industries and occupations, often replacing white men.

These changes, to mention a few, have set us up for an angry, dispossessed set of subgroups that are grist for the fascist mill. They are the potential for a massive shift to the right. "Patriotic" fringe groups have already gone over to the fascist model. They are mirrored in dozens of violent movies about militias and rabid cults. But these are not the real danger to our country. That lies in the possibility of a one-party reign that gradually moves to the extreme right, using the anger generated by these rapid changes, as well as losses of identity, self- esteem, affection, supports, and control. The recession that began in 2007, and is still with us in 2009, may well have helped to avoid this radical right trend, by its shock effect (see the "Stubborn mule" hypothesis in the Introduction).

G. The Longing for Authority, Religion, and Community (Gemeinschaft)

Fritz Stern is a survivor of Nazi Germany. He suffered as a boy because he was Jewish. He was taunted and excluded by Aryan boys in school. Fortunately his family was able to flee, and he now lives in New York City. In 1985 he warned, as I said before, that there were three conditions in pre-Nazi Germany that were widespread, and seemed to set the stage for Hitler's hijacking of the government: *a longing for a new authoritarianism, with some kind of religious orientation, and above all a greater communal belongingness"* (Stern, F., 1985). In an acceptance speech upon receiving the Leo Baeck Medal presented by the German Foreign Minister, he said:

> ...the Nazis didn't realize that they were part of an historic process in which resentment against a disenchanted secular world found deliverance in the ecstatic escape of unreason. German elites proved susceptible to this mystical brew of pseudo-religion and disguised interest. The Christian churches most readily fell into line as well, though with some heroic exception (Stern, 2005).

Stern has warned about the parallel he sees between what happened in Germany and the spinning of public opinion, the lying, and the intimidation in our country during Bush's two terms. His insight into *resentment against secularism* is a second cousin to what I have called *Gemeinschaft*-longing in discussing the work of Ferdinand Toennies.

Longing for Authoritarianism

It is not difficult to see the trend toward authoritarianism in America today. I mentioned the backlash against the "permissiveness" of the Dr. Spock era of child-rearing. The harsh treatment of juveniles is a goal of the law-and-order crowd, but it is being fought in the courts, most recently with regard to capital punishment for those younger than eighteen. The United States has been one of only two nations to allow such "cruel and unusual" punishment. The responses to questions about physical punishment support the argument that a high degree of authoritarian upbringing still exists in our country.

A good example of an authoritarian father (although he is rather extreme) is "Bull Meechum" in *The Great Santini* (1979). Robert Duvall plays a Marine officer who longs for a war during peacetime. He treats his family as he treats his recruits. The children have to call him "sir." He is cruel, dictatorial, and egocentric. His son Ben, seventeen, suffers, being torn between his father's authoritarian character and his love and need for him. This is the very conflict we discussed, which often results in loss of identity and poor self-esteem.

A recent dismissal of a graduate student in education from Le Moyne College gives some insight into the influence of early punishment on later attitudes. Scott McConnell (now in his late twenties) was paddled with a foot-long piece of wood for being disruptive in elementary school in Oklahoma. "As a child he moved from Texas to Florida to Oklahoma as his mother pursued marriages to 'bad men.' He is an evangelical Christian. He wrote a term paper stating that 'corporal punishment has a place in the classroom,' and 'I will help the child understand that respect for authority figures is more important than self-esteem.'" In an interview he said that he disliked "anti-American multiculturalism" as a teaching method (Anon., 2005).

> New York is one of 28 states that ban corporal punishment; most of those that allow it are in the South and West. Most states did not ban corporal punishment until the late 1980's, after parents, educators, and other advocates began pressing for the laws. More than 342,000 students received corporal punishment in the 1999–2000 school year, in the most recent figures from the Federal Education Department. (Anon., 2005)

The links in his brief history seem destined to lead to McConnell's adult attitudes: (1) The "bad men" of his early childhood suggest authoritarian stepfathers and physical abuse, or at very least a lack of good male role models. The successive divorces may have left him in a state of deregulation—a lack of consistent discipline as his father-figures changed. (2) His paddling in school set him up for acceptance of this type of treatment for others. (3) His scorn of self-esteem in favor of respect for authority suggests that he made this bargain himself early on. Thus, his self-esteem is probably low, a condition for attraction to right-wing movements and ideology. (4) His views have also been formed by the evangelical church, so that his hatred of multiculturalism (and presumably minorities and the current target, the Iraqis) stems in part from his former (pre-college) environment. (5) He was an Army private, and that discipline (often harsh, but rationalized because of the dangers of combat) may have reinforced his previous experiences with regulation. All in all, he might have been one of Gruen's case histories: giving up the true self, low self-esteem, anger, projection, feelings of victimization, and possibly violent acting out alone or by joining a right-wing political movement.

Erich Fromm, in *Escape from Freedom* (Fromm, 1941), also spoke of the strong need the pre-Hitler Germans felt for structure and authority. They had been raised in strict families. Suddenly they were exposed to the deregulation of the Weimar period. The old rules were off. Fromm's "freedom" is the equivalent of Durkheim's "anomie" (Durkheim, 1897). It is often pointed out that children sometimes so strongly crave direction and restriction by their parents that they create situations in which the parents are forced to crack down.

It is not beyond possibility that some of the rage against Obama that has grown so rapidly since his election is not merely that standard Republican anger at economic regulation, in a fight to avoid economic losses. It also sounds like a fear of, and rage against, deregulation in the sexual, drug, and interracial spheres. Right-wing protesters call the attempted overhaul of medical care "socialism." Even a speech by Obama to school children exhorting them to attend school and study hard is labeled socialism. It may be a mistake to attribute all this anger to GOP propaganda ("pulling the plug on grandma," "death panels"). The right wing is smaller and more radical as centrists move away. The remainder may feel that their world is blowing apart, and it is time to take guns to public rallies.

In experiments with children's craft classes (making masks) Kurt Lewin created normal ("democratic"), authoritarian, and laissez-faire teachers, who were trained to treat the children in more or less those three modes or atmospheres. The children in the laissez-faire group complained that the teacher showed no interest in them, and they felt rejected.

While most people need *some* structure, if they have been raised in a strict manner, they will feel very threatened in a laissez-faire (free or anomic) situation. Fromm's point (similar to Fritz Stern's) was that the Germans longed for authority, and that longing paved the way for their acceptance of Hitler.

As long ago as 1961, President Dwight D. Eisenhower warned of the power of the "military-industrial complex." Hitler succeeded in appealing not only to the common man, but also to the Army and the Junker officer class (he was a veteran), and to Big Business. Today we see the same Siamese-twin relationship of the military and business. The war in Iraq has been privatized, so that Brown and Root, a division of Halliburton (whose former CEO was Dick Cheney), is acting as a major supplier (quartermaster) to the Army. The tanks, Humvees, aircraft—all the equipment—is making large profits for the suppliers, even with "competitive bidding." Blackwater Worldwide, the security company that was originally hired to protect American diplomats in Iraq, developed into a force as large as the Army in Iraq. The cost of a Blackwater armed guard was $1200 per day, compared to that of an Army sergeant of $190, or six times as much (Popular Mechanics, URL, 2008). Ike warned us:

> In the councils of government, we must guard against the acquisition of unwarranted influence, whether sought or unsought, by the military–industrial complex. The potential for the disastrous rise of misplaced power exists and will persist.

> We must never let the weight of this combination endanger our liberties or democratic processes. We should take nothing for granted. Only an alert and knowledgeable citizenry can compel the proper meshing of the huge industrial and military machinery of defense with our peaceful methods and goals, so that security and liberty may prosper together (Eisenhower, 1960).

With the advent of the Patriot Act, former Attorney General John Ashcroft (followed by Alberto Gonzales) and the Bush administration curtailed our civil liberties. They have done away with *habeas corpus* in cases where the prisoner is not a combatant with a national armed force. They have instigated a procedure called "extraordinary rendition," whereby prisoners suspected of ties to Muslim terrorists are kidnapped in the United States and flown to countries like Syria and Egypt, where they are tortured to obtain information. Libraries are asked to give information on the books our citizens have read. The obstetrical records of girls who have had abortions are commandeered, ostensibly to obtain information on sexual abuse—and so on, ad infinitum. We shall see how far the Obama administration can turn back this assault on civil liberties and the Constitution.

Longing for Religion

There is overwhelming evidence of a strong resurgence of religion, though not necessarily in church attendance and membership. Religion has been politicized. The political argot of today is permeated with religious references, biblical quotations, and moralistic terms. The "family values" package revolves around control of women and their reproductive activities; condemnation of abortion, homosexuality, and stem cell research; and promotion of traditional (heterosexual) marriage. Established religion has historically laid down restrictive rules in these areas. Intercourse during menstruation is forbidden in Orthodox Jewish law. Women's hands should not touch the naked body of a dead Muslim male. Female circumcision and clitoridectomy are still practiced in many parts of Africa.

While religion often sets positive rules governing social relations (do unto others as thou would be done by), the vast majority are restrictive rules (thou shalt not). Thus religion forbids, and in so doing creates the regulation and the authoritarianism that so many people seem to need. It reduces their "freedom" to do many things, like steal, covet their neighbor's wife, or kill. If religion is weakened, then the desire for escape from freedom (or escape from an anomic deregulated society) becomes dominant. So, as previously in Germany, and now in America, there is this strong attraction to religion and pseudo-religious authority. The Bush administration played up to this need. George W. was constantly invoking God in his speeches. He implied that God gave him messages, and is a "higher authority" than his own father. Is he a true believer, or did

Karl Rove teach him to use his born-again status to gain political power with the right wing?

Bill Moyers (Moyers, 2005) sounded the alarm on the relation between right-wing Christian fundamentalist ideology and the trend in U.S. politics. He refers to a twelve-volume series called *Left Behind*, by the extremist religious right-winger Timothy LaHaye. "This is an apocalyptic concoction, based on the Book of Revelations. It predicts an Armageddon, in which all non-Christians (Jews and Muslims included) will be killed." A 2002 *Time–CNN* poll found that fifty-nine percent of Americans believe that the prophecies found in the Biblical Book of Revelations are going to come true. The war in Iraq was seen as a warm-up for Armageddon. Moyers finds evidence that the lack of interest in preserving the environment on the part of the evangelicals stems from their strong belief that God will provide until such time as the Armageddon. Therefore there is no use in worrying about the air, water, or global warming. The Earth will be destroyed, which will be followed by the second coming of Christ and the "rapture," but for Christians only. This attitude toward the environment has been changing among some evangelicals.

Before blaming Bush's re-election on the fundamentalist right wing, it is important to remember that many other forces contributed to this victory. Peter Steinfels (Steinfels, 2005) questions the size of the evangelicals' contribution. "...Mr. Moyers offered only the faintest, glancing mention of the chemical and energy industries. Is their clout, for good or ill, really nothing compared with the Book of Revelations?"

Longing for Greater Communal Belongingness

This type of longing is perhaps more important for setting the stage for fascism (or communism) than are the longings for authority and religion. This is because the desire to belong can be the motive for joining an extreme political group, even if the individual disagrees with some of the group's positions. If the need for love and affection and group support is strong enough, the act of joining becomes the main object. The political positions of the group in such cases do not matter. There are many examples of radicals who became conservatives, and vice versa.

Is there a need for community belongingness in America? When I "googled" the words "Community and Longing," I came up with 730,000 "hits!" Many of these were references to the church as a community. Many were descriptions of loneliness by individuals who decried the loss of community in the United States.

That community is a big issue in our country is attested to by such books as *It Takes a Village* (Hillary Clinton, 1996). How does communal belongingness solve the losses and problems we have outlined above? Joining a movement or a political party, or becoming a member, solves many of the problems confronting the individual in our society.

It solves the problem of *loss of identity*. It gives us a new identity.

It solves the problem of *loss of self-esteem*. Belonging to a group, especially one that is powerful or rich, enhances one's self-image. In *Stardust Memories* (1980), Woody Allen portrays his usual *schlemiel* character (bungler, dolt). Riding on a train filled with bums, drug addicts, and homeless people, he looks across at a train going in the opposite direction. It is filled with generals whose chests are studded with medals, beautiful women in Dior gowns quaffing champagne , and smart-looking CEOs with blow-dried hair and the latest imported Italian suits. He asks, plaintively, why isn't he on that other train?

Communal belongingness solves the problem of *deregulation* (anomie or excessive freedom). The new group has a set of rules. If you join, you get guided limitation. It often gives you a set of goals, which are related to rules.

It often solves or gives promise of solving the *loss of love and affection*, and consequent *loneliness*. How many lonely isolated people have joined extreme cults, in exchange for a little warmth and kindness? Youngsters have often been inducted into cults by using young members of the opposite sex to befriend these initiates. The bonds thus made were in some cases so strong that the parents were unable to regain their child's company, except by paying for a type of kidnapping and brainwashing (known as deprogramming). The "deprogrammers" re-brainwash the brainwashed.

It may solve the problem of *loss of social supports*, depending on the type of group one joins. Many offer jobs. Joining a political party can give access to jobs and contracts, albeit often illegally. In the days of ward organizations, the ward boss could give money and jobs to members. Professional organizations help members find jobs, and often lobby for laws favorable to their constituents. The established churches have traditionally offered food and shelter, and sometimes jobs, to the needy. Hitler promised support to all classes, rich and poor, military and civilian (except for the non-Aryans). In the long run, he didn't deliver on those promises.

Communal belongingness may or may not solve the problem of *loss of control* over life events. It may have minimal effect on such events as severe illness, divorce and death. If the goals of the community are truly focused on the individual's welfare, the impact of some of these events can be minimized. If you belong to a community whose aim is the leaders' personal gain, dominance of one class over another, acquisition of territory, or national hegemony, then you will suffer severe loss of control (unless you belong to the dominant class).

Communal belongingness, especially membership in an authoritarian society, most often tends to solve the problem of deregulation. These regimes are very strict. If anything, the individual will be over-regulated and restricted. Very often such regimes have programs that produce rapid social change, especially if the regime is warlike. In war, there is rapid change combined with stricter regulation, particularly in the area of civil rights. The regulation may be sought by those who wish to "escape from freedom," but they will sacrifice eventually due to over-regulation and loss of civil rights. (Sound familiar?)

How did the Bush administration score on these problems, which are often the forerunners of fascism? Bush *cut social supports* in almost every area. Social legislation is anathema to today's Republicans. They have botched Medicare and threatened to cut back Medicaid and to privatize (eventually destroy) Social Security. They have cut veterans' benefits, allowed jobs to be outsourced, cut back on unemployment benefits and education funding, and have severely limited bankruptcy laws with a "means test." Supports were promised during the Bush campaign. These promises were either broken or subject to "rescission." In October of 2005 the White House and Congress were considering massive cuts in social programs to make up for the costs of Hurricane Katrina. At the same time they were planning to extend tax cuts for the wealthiest 1%.

Since 9/11, Americans have had *less and less control over their life events*. Preemptive wars in Afghanistan and Iraq, the spread of terrorism, the nuclear crises in Iran and North Korea, the heated political activism at home, and the financial meltdown of 2007-2009 have strongly affected the way we live and feel.

While the Bush administration had a program of radical deregulation; of air quality, mining, timber cutting, oil exploration— it *tightened the regulation* of drugs (even medical use of marijuana for pain relief), abortion, euthanasia, and pregnancy prevention by pills ("just say no"). It called for "tort reform," making the initiation of personal injury suits extremely difficult. It promised "freedom," but with the emphasis on free enterprise. Freedom to the GOP means freedom from regulation and the "free market." Meanwhile, personal freedoms, such as confidentiality of medical records and of records of books borrowed from public libraries, have been curtailed. Let's see if Obama can roll back these intrusive laws.

Since the advent of "compassionate conservatism," there has been *rapid social change*. Bush & Co. tried to wipe out all the positive social changes and protections that occurred during and since the Franklin Roosevelt administration. There are also radical changes such as curtailing civil liberties, which have been excused by citing the threat of terrorism.

So Bush *promised* social supports, control over our own lives, and escape from rapid social change. Despite these promises, he *knocked out* these supports, took over much control of our lives, and exposed us to rapid social change—some of it by pre-emptive war, some of it by administrative decisions or by backward-looking legislation.

Those who sought a sense of community belongingness by voting for Bush and by backing his policies should be made aware of their loss of supports, of control over events, and of their exposure to rapid social change.

VIII. COMMUNITY VERSUS SOCIETY: "CIVILIZATION/ GESELLSCHAFT AND ITS DISCONTENTS"

Two great minds, Ferdinand Toennies and Sigmund Freud (among many others*), have considered the factors in modern society, as compared with some ideal primitive or village life, that make for strain and discontent in the individual. Why should we examine these ideas when seeking answers to why Bush won two elections? After all, it is common knowledge that life is tough in our society, even though most of us have shelter and enough to eat. (Thirty million don't, and that figure will only increase from 2008 on for several years, until the recession turns around.) The longing for community, the nostalgia for a pastoral past, may be justified, since we are exposed to rampant competition, severe restrictions on our activities by complex laws, and the constant presence of inequality, which may affect our own standing. In addition, there are usually elements of fantasy in this nostalgia. The community of the little village where you know all your neighbors and everyone is loved and trusted can represent the days of early childhood. The bosom of the family (or mother) is the ultimate community.

*(Jean Jacques Rousseau, 1712–78, in *Discourse on the Arts and Sciences*, contrasted man in a "state of nature" (the "noble savage") with man in society, which corrupted him. He foreshadowed Freud's ideas about repression ("chains") in his emphasis on instinct. However, he saw natural man as good, whereas Freud had a Hobbesian view of man. Freud, Toennies, and Rousseau all viewed society/civilization as constricting and defiling. In his *Social Contract* Rousseau famously said "Man is born free, but everywhere he is in chains." These chains are roughly equivalent to Freud's "discontents" and Toennies' cold, individualistic *Gesellschaft*. On the other hand, Durkheim's *anomie* and Fromm's "freedom" were terms for *lack of regulation*. Both excessive chains and extreme lack of chains have severe consequences. If anyone doubted that excessive deregulation could be damaging financially

and psychologically, he or she would only have to look at the 2007 world meltdown for proof.)

Further echoes of the bucolic fantasy (the ideal community) are found in the many movies set in the days of the pioneers. The rural life, especially the family farm, has almost disappeared. The battles of the cowboys and Indians, or the ranchers and the homesteaders, kept Hollywood busy many years ago. These Westerns are still being turned out despite the fact that the West has completely changed. A great deal of the swagger, shoot-from-the-hip decision making, and tough talk of the Bush administration took its cues from the Westerns. John Wayne, a staunch right-winger, represented the tough American gun-fighter and soldier. When movie heroes like Ronald Reagan and Arnold Schwarzenegger became leading politicians, fantasy and reality fused.

Shane (1953), an ideal picture of the old West, has a villain (Jack Palance) but he is eventually overcome by the often reluctant gunfighter (Alan Ladd). The pioneer homesteading family (Van Heflin, Jean Arthur, and Brandon de Wilde) is saved. This is a far cry from Robert Altman's view in *McCabe and Mrs. Miller* (1971), which pictures a turn-of-the-century Western boom town as a hell hole of paid gunslingers, prostitution and drug addiction—probably a more realistic view of the Wild West.

The Bushies talk Community, but walk (act) Society. What do these terms mean and what do they have to do with winning the election? It seems to me that the term "Community," the rural village of our nostalgia, represents all the "family values" rhetoric used by the White House to win the 2004 election. This is the talk they talked, the "small towns" of Sarah Palin and her "pro-America areas." The walk they walked, and are still walking, is "Society," which represents the complex metropolises and the mass culture in which we now live. Its goals are individualistic, and are mainly about amassing wealth and power.

Ferdinand Toennies (1855–1936) wrote his most famous work, *Gemeinschaft und Gesellschaft* (Community and Society) in 1887 (Toennies, 1957, translated and edited). He saw Community and Society as "ideal types" on a continuum of social change. Without going deeply into his theories, I would like to present the contrasting characteristics of these two types as he saw them.

TABLE 9
COMMUNITY VERSUS SOCIETY

GEMEINSCHAFT (COMMUNITY)	GESELLSCHAFT (SOCIETY)
Rural, pastoral	Urban,. metropolitan
Interpersonal bonds of family and kin	Interpersonal relations
Social; control by "natural" consensus, custom, faith, religious beliefs, heritage	Social control by laws and public opinion
Authority is paternalistic, by elders, possibly authoritarian	Authority is relatively laissez-faire and "permissive," vested in the state and "experts"
Individual is subordinate to the community	Individualism reigns
Reverence for tradition	Focus on "progress," innovation, and "the new"
Social relations are "natural" (intrinsic); people are loved for what they are, not for what they can give you (valued as ends, not means to an end)	Social relationships are seen as means to an end, as in "networking." (instrumental)
Central institutions are family, village, and town.	On the group level, central institutions are business and professional organizations. On the societal level, they are the state and the economy of industrial capitalism.
Production is cooperative, community-wide	Free-market forces reign
Warm	Cold
Identity springs from the community	Anonymity of mass society often leads to loss of identity
Homogeneity, unicultural, common language	Heterogeneity, multicultural, Babel of languages

With apologies to Dr. Toennies, I have taken liberties with the details of his ideal types, to make it more relevant to our own times, and to the ongoing culture wars. From this chart you can see where George W. and Karl R. were coming from. They talk community and *Gemeinschaft*, but they walk society and *Gesellschaft*. They are not totally consistent, but the main point is clearly "talk community, walk society."

Given that both Republicans and Democrats live in a Society, Toennies' description of Society is bound to fit our current situation much more closely than his description of the ideal Community. Let's see what Bush and his speechwriters took from the Community side, and compare it to its counterparts on the Society side. Social control is supposed to be by custom, religious beliefs, faith, and heritage. As a born-again Christian, Bush seemed to be sincere in his talk of religion, his own conversion, and his reliance on a "higher authority." The very name of the conservative group, The Heritage Foundation, seems in line with this Republican predilection for referring to our national past. The emphasis on religion is clearly a means of holding on to the evangelical right, now estimated at thirty million strong. This was a political base that Bush could count on for reelection. *Talk religion, faith, and heritage, walk social control by administrative changes and retrogressive laws* (Patriot Act, Clear Skies, restriction of personal and small business bankruptcy laws, and so on).

When it comes to tradition, Bush referred to it when he needed it. The sixty-year-old traditions of Franklin Roosevelt—Social Security, unemployment support, the Works Progress Administration, the Civilian Conservation Corps, minimum wages—these are already dead meat, or were attacked for privatization, which backfired. *Talk tradition, walk radical innovation* (pre-emptive war; privatization of Social Security; government propaganda delivered as news on television and radio in the United States and in foreign countries; limiting science, as in stem cell research, and so on). (Public opinion has turned the privatization of Social Security into a dead duck. Yes, the people sometimes show great wisdom.)

The authoritarian caste of the right-wing is in keeping with Community values. Paternalistic authority fits in with the "family values" package. The father is the Chief. (Even within the White House, Cheney seemed to be more the father and Bush the son.) When it comes to the economy (not the family) the laissez-faire model and the free market are part of the Republican gospel. *Talk strictness (physical punishment as discussed above) for the family, but walk laissez-faire for the economy and business.* Nobody spanks the CEOs unless they are caught with their hands in the cookie jar (Kenneth Lay, Bernie Madoff, and others).

The picture we are given of the GOP leaders is one of "compassion" and "good old boys." This fits in with the Community emphasis on intrinsic interpersonal relationships; people are to be loved for what they are, not for what they can do for you. In the

Society, as Toennies told us, most friendships are instrumental. In our world you know a lobbyist, who in turn knows someone in Congress or the White House. They get things done for you. If you contribute to the campaign, you have "paid to play." While seeming to be on close terms with both blacks and Hispanics, the White House elevated only a few of them to high ranking jobs (Condoleeza Rice, Alberto Gonzales). When former Secretary of State General Colin Powell had some of his own ideas about foreign policy, he was dumped for Bush's second term. Minority figures, parents who lost a son in Iraq, an Iraqi woman who held up her inked thumb to show she had bravely voted for the new regime, were all trotted out on television for the purpose of showing the administration's sympathy or its success in the chaotic Iraqi elections. These people were being blatantly used as means to an end—the promotion of the Bush agenda. *Talk love of people for what they are. Walk the use of people as objects—as means to your ends.*

Perhaps it is unfair to blame all the evils of modern civilization on George W. After all, he didn't invent industrial capitalism, but he expanded its reach into every nook and cranny of our individual lives—war, abortion, privacy of medical and library records, the environment, financial safety-nets—you name it. You might say he created a radical capitalism, not the conservative kind that emphasized fiscal caution. That's how we went from a large surplus under Clinton to a huge deficit under Bush.

I assume that a majority of Americans "long for community." In the United States we are almost all living in an extreme form of "society." *The more extreme the evils of our "society," the more people will vote for the simplistic pseudo-community, family-oriented propaganda put out by Bush or politicians who come after him.* We all suffer from the evils of our complex heterogeneous capitalistic commonwealth, while at the same time many of us enjoy the goods afforded by capitalism: TV, cell phones, fast food, CDs, and a higher standard of living than in many other countries. However, when an administration exacerbates these evils and weakens the goods, we suffer even more.

Let's take a look at these evils once more, this time in light of Toennies's list of Society's characteristics. (Toennies grew up in a rural setting, and he obviously favored and longed for the *Gemeinschaft*/Community. While he traveled all over, he never left his rural roots.)

Impersonal relations make for loneliness. The decline of the family as the central institution again makes for isolation; it gives control to the state and the experts who are not family members. Individualism combined with laissez-faire economics breeds a state of anomie. This is the "freedom" from which so many wish to escape. In our society, competition trumps cooperation, in stark contrast to some other cultures (especially hunting-gathering cultures, which are becoming extinct). This makes for constant pressure for success, commonly measured by wealth and power. By definition, then, not everyone can be successful. Power implies power *over others*, and wealth tends to accumulate at the top of the power pyramid. Ours is a zero-sum culture. A gain for someone is very often a loss for someone else (as in game theory). Instrumental social relationships predominate. People often complain that they are being used, not wanted for themselves. How often we hear the complaint of a beautiful girl "All he wanted was my body." The wealthy man cries that "She was after my money." This instrumentality of relations pervades our nation. Are the friends you make at the country club just trying to get a business connection? Are your friends just "networking?" These concerns can undermine your self-confidence and self-esteem. The free market may go up, and it may also go down. If you're in stocks, you are entitled to some anxiety. Call it *fear* in 2008. Your dollar fluctuates in value, due to debt, foreign exchange, and recently to loss of confidence and liquidity due to the bundling of subprime mortgages ("collateralized debt," or "securitization"). That's another source of stress.

There's also the anonymity of our mass society. Everybody, except for a few hermits, wants to be known. (The hermits even want to be known for being hermits.) A serial killer, Dennis L. Rader, who called himself BTK for "Bind, Torture, Kill," wrote to the Wichita, Kansas *Eagle*, complaining "How many more people do I have to kill before I get into the news?" He taunted the police with grisly letters, clues, poems, photographs, and phone calls.

The mixture of races, languages, and national backgrounds can be another source of stress. People relate with difficulty to those who have different values and cultures. So the multicultural quality of life, especially in big cities, can be very stressful for some people. We have had race riots in Watts, busing riots in Boston, and years of lynching in the South. In our democracy we try to value all subcultures, and when we fall short of this ideal, stress intensifies. All in all, the qualities of the Society, and especially our advanced state of Society, are stressful, and make for strain, or as Freud put it, "discontents."

However, because of his focus on "instincts," Freud came up with a different short list of stresses than did Toennies. In *Civilization and Its Discontents* (Freud, 1929, 1953, pp. 26–81), he pointed to two main "discontents": suppression (by society) of the sexual and aggressive drives. Without these controls, civilization could not exist. The word *"Trieb,"* which he used, has been translated in many ways, making for some confusion. It can be employed to mean a moving force or impetus, or a drive, impulse, or liking, but the most frequent translation is "instinct."

Toennies came up with a list of the evils of civilization that don't overlap with Freud's short list. Perhaps this is because he was a sociologist, while Freud was a psychiatrist and social psychologist. (A salesman once asked Theodore Abel, one of my professors at Columbia, "What's the difference between a sociologist and a psychologist?" The professor answered "The sociologist deals with groups, and the psychologist with individuals." "Oh, wholesale and retail!" said the salesman. Incidentally, Dr. Abel also wrote on the subject under discussion, in *Why Hitler Came Into Power*.).

In their view of mankind's basic nature, Freud and Toennies were much more in agreement, for they were both strongly influenced by Thomas Hobbes (1588–1679). In *Leviathan* (1651) Hobbes pictured man in a state of nature as being in constant fear of violent death. Freud saw man's fear of death as being due to an instinct of aggression, which pitted man against man. Durkheim saw loss of social control over man's nature leading to a societal state of "anomie," which showed itself in individuals as anxiety, fear, and sometimes suicide.

For Freud, the ideal of "brotherly love," "love thy neighbor," or even more so, "love thine enemy" involved a tremendous sacrifice. Reining in the aggressive drive, in his view, was a major "discontent." He saw man's view of the neighbor as:

> ...a temptation to them to gratify their aggressiveness on him, to exploit his capacity for work without recompense, to use him sexually without his consent, to seize his possessions, to humiliate him, to cause him pain, to torture and to kill him. *Homo homine lupus*; (man is a wolf to man), who has the courage to dispute it in the face of all the evidence in his own life and in history? (Freud, 1929, pp. 50–51)

Freud felt that in order for societies (civilization) to survive, aggressive and sexual instincts had to be controlled by repression and by reaction formation.

> Culture has to call up every possible reinforcement in order to erect barriers against the aggressive instincts of men and hold their manifestations in check by reactionformations in men's minds. Hence its system of methods by which mankind is driven to identifications and aim-inhibited love-relationships; hence the restrictions on sexual life; and hence, too, its ideal command to love one's neighbor as oneself..." (Freud, ibid., p. 51)

Certainly one cannot deny this dark view of humanity in its entirety. The genocides of the Holocaust and obscene experiments in Nazi Germany, in Cambodia's "killing grounds," in Rwanda and Kosovo; the killing and raping in Darfur, the mass raping of German women in Berlin by victorious Russian soldiers; the horrific behavior of young American men and women at Abu Graib prison in Iraq; the mass murder by U.S. troops in Vietnam at My Lai; and the mass rape, genocide, and vivisection of the Chinese by the Japanese all attest to this propensity for violence to and humiliation of others. Freud's and Hobbes's views mirror the Old Testament, where an eye for an eye rules, and God smites your enemies. The New Testament bids us turn the other cheek, to love thy neighbor and help the poor. It forbids us to cast the first stone. These are ideals, and we can't expect to live up to all of them. "The Christian ideal has not been tried and found wanting. It has been found difficult, and left untried" (Chesterton, 1910). Even more depressing; "The last Christian died on the cross" (Friedrich Nietzsche, *Der Antichrist*, 1895).

So, in addition to Toennies's long list of the sacrifices one makes by living in Society rather than Community (such as impersonal relations, rule by law rather than consensus, instrumental use of people to achieve goals, rampant individualism, and the vicissitudes of the free market), Freud added his short list --—the control of sexual and aggressive instincts. That these controls frequently break down is no surprise.

There have been dramatic changes in American sexual behavior over the past century. The Kinsey Reports found that our true sexual behavior varied widely from our ideal sexual behavior. Masturbation, homosexuality, extramarital relations, impotence, and frigidity, among other behaviors and conditions, were found to be widespread. We think that, in the argot of the old cigarette ads, "We've come a long way, baby" toward freedom of sexual expression. But countless frightening incidents remind us that sex and aggression are linked, and are poorly handled by a good portion of our nation.

It startles me to find that the very people who are put in charge of controlling the expressions of sex and aggression seem to have problems in these areas. Perhaps it is not so startling, since we wish to punish those whose behavior threatens our own unconscious but weak controls. The case of Abner Louima in 1997 was horrifying but illustrative. Louima, a thirty-year-old Haitian immigrant, a security officer, married and the father of two, was arrested by police outside a nightclub in Brooklyn. He was taken to a police station, where he was beaten and anally raped with the handle of a toilet plunger. His front teeth were then knocked out when the toilet plunger was jammed into his mouth. He suffered a torn rectum and ruptures in his bladder and intestines. This quickly became national news. The offending white police officer was convicted and is serving time (30 years).

The sexual and racist elements in this case are clear. Racial epithets were used during the rape. Power over the victim is a major motive in such cases, but its expression is through acts simulating intercourse. Similarly, in heterosexual rape, the domination of the victim is expressed sexually. Such extreme violence and cruelty can't help but be suspect. In this case there was probably an element of repressed homosexuality involved on the part of the offending officer.

Another incident was the 1998 torture and murder of a young gay man, Matthew Shephard, in Laramie, Wyoming. The two offenders pistol-whipped him almost to death, then lashed him to a fence, where he died of exposure in freezing weather. Gay-bashing is still widespread, and the perpetrators, to my mind, are always suspect of repressed homosexuality.

A few years ago Arnold Schwarzenegger, the former body-builder, movie actor, and now governor of California, denigrated the "girlie-men" and implied that they were to be found in the Democratic Party.

The Bushies have carried on a campaign against gay marriage. During the 2004 elections, eleven states passed propositions banning same-sex marriage. How Freud would have loved this confirmation of his ideas on cultural control of the sex drive, some seventy-five years later!

> Present-day civilization gives us plainly to understand that sexual relations are permitted only on the basis of a final, indissoluble bond between a man and woman; that sexuality as a source of enjoyment for its own sake is unacceptable to it; and that its intention is to tolerate it only as the hitherto irreplaceable means of multiplying the human race (Freud, 1929, ibid., p. 48).

Freud at first considered his patients' reports of seduction by parents or relatives to be real experiences. Then, under severe criticism by the medical profession, and perhaps because of his own rather strict upbringing, he decided that these reports of parental abuse of his patients were mere fantasies. Now, due to the amassing of data on abuse over the years since Freud did this flip-flop, there has been a very gradual recognition that children are often sexually or physically abused, or maltreated in a number of different ways. (There has also been a cottage industry of lawsuits involving "recovered memories." Several of these lawsuits revealed coaching of plaintiffs by the police and some fringe psychologists. Careful investigation is needed to avoid false accusations of abuse.)

I have already talked about the views of Arno Gruen (1992) concerning the role of parents in creating a "false self" in the young helpless child. The giving up of the true self in order to maintain the love and protection of the parents produces anger, which may be turned against the self or toward others. The creation of individuals who early on gave up their autonomy, their individuality, may lead to attachment to dictatorial leaders.

Alice Miller wrote earlier in this same vein (Miller, 1981, 1983, 1984). She and Gruen agree on the process by which the child is forced to give up his individuality and his own needs. (It should be noted that both Miller and Gruen base their concept of the false self on the pioneering work of Donald Winnicott, 1960.) However, Miller focuses more on the specific types of child-rearing behavior that produce this false self. She also emphasizes her differences with Freudian "drive" theory, showing how orthodox Freudian analytic theory ultimately blamed the patient for having these instincts, rather than the parents for their bad parenting. She blames Freud's flip-flop for this shift of blame; if he had stuck with his original view of patients' reports of abuse by parents as truth rather than fantasy, several generations of patients would not have been betrayed by their therapists (who, in effect, took the side of some abusive parents, and pressed for the patient's reconciliation with them).

Since we are not focusing on the effects of analytic therapy, but on what effects the loss of autonomy can have on political behavior, it seems all right to say that the very small fraction of the population who have had orthodox Freudian analytic therapy (and thus may not have achieved the autonomy Miller hopes for) will not affect the overall proportion of people voting for an authoritarian government or candidate. In contrast, *the general loss of autonomy in our population due to various injurious child-rearing methods could have a huge effect on voting behavior. Early abuse, with its consequent loss of autonomy, could now (and has historically) set people up for submission to an authoritarian leader. The powerless look up to these figures, to "borrow" power.*

I think there is no incompatibility in theory between the Freudian emphasis on suppression of aggression and sexuality (by the parents) and repression (by the child, who must give up some of this behavior) and Miller's emphasis on childhood trauma, while she sees these approaches as totally incompatible. (Miller is rightly concerned that the Freudian therapist's emphasis on drive theory, the child's sexuality and aggression, takes attention away from the actual violence done to the child by the parents.)

> ...it is my belief that these roots (of neurosis) lie in the enforced repression not of the child's so-called instinctual drives but of his or her awareness of having been traumatized and in the prohibition against articulating this.... (Miller, 1984, p. 213)

Let's take an example. A parent who had been punished for masturbation and, early on, given up autonomy, will have unresolved anger over this sacrifice of pleasure and independence. In turn, he or she may take out (abreact) that anger by hitting the child for masturbating. (What I did not dare to do because I was punished for it, you may not do.) The trauma to the child is due *both* to being hit by the parent and to the loss of pleasure and autonomy. The loss of parental love and, simultaneously, of pleasure can be considered a double-whammy. *Parents who were beaten criticize "permissiveness," which is part of the Family Values attack vocabulary.*

Now, what Miller has done, in addition to calling attention to traumatic parenting, is to elaborate on the various ways parents traumatize their children. Some of these parental behaviors can be grouped under the term "narcissistic," because the parent is satisfying only his or her own needs, not the child's.

Parents can satisfy their own needs rather than the child's by interfering with the child's friendships (criticizing friends of different social class, race, or religion); the child's clothing (you can't wear that!); education (you're not smart enough for that school or college); marriage (you can't marry him, he's a____). Miller's point is that these intrusions and controls imposed on the child, if not in accord with the child's needs and individuality, can be very damaging. She does not concentrate on control of sexual expression or aggression or severe toilet training or abrupt weaning, as I was taught to do in anthropological field studies years ago. This was the period when Kardiner, Mead, Bateson and Benedict were dominating "culture and personality" studies. This research made many valuable contributions, but critics dubbed it "pisspot determinism." Miller's sample of parental behavior is much broader and more subtle.

Miller gives a dramatic example of "labile" parental behavior (Miller, 1984, p. 65). A father (her subjects were all German) took out his anger on his young daughter (Miller's patient) by alternately playing with her and then screaming at her and hitting her. After he had humiliated her, he would walk away, and pay attention to other people but not to her. This type of behavior turned out to be a major predictor of later psychological problems in children in the Family Research Project in Manhattan (see Langner, Gersten, McCarthy, and Goff references) It was more predictive of depression and anxiety than of antisocial behavior. This could be expected, because of the bonding of the child during the warm intervals. Children who are beaten consistently (after age nine in our sample) with no warm periods are apt to seek early independence and peer (rather than parental) reference figures. They may end up in gangs and as delinquents. On the other hand, some of them develop a healthy sense of independence. Others develop self-esteem by taking pride in their toughness and ability to endure rejection and punishment. (This is a good example of the "sweet lemon" adaptation.)

It is difficult to describe all the possible combinations of parental behaviors that may affect and even traumatize children. Miller sums it up this way: "We do not need to be told whether to be strict or permissive with our children. What we do need is to have respect for their needs, their feelings, and their individuality, as well as our own" (Miller, 1983, p. xi).

Of course, this respect for your child's needs and individuality must come in part from an understanding of one's own needs and feelings, and this in turn comes from a realistic appraisal of one's own childhood. Only a massive educational program dealing with preparation for parenting and awareness of one's own early traumas can turn around the abuse that is transmitted from generation to generation. Since this would demand an examination of parents' authority, few politicians would be likely to sponsor it.

I do not wish to give the impression that the loss of autonomy is due only to poor or abusive parenting. In fact, conformity and obedience are reinforced throughout the life cycle. Obedience training is continued in school classes and in school sports. After an authoritarian family and poor parenting has robbed a child of his or her autonomy, the schools, especially the public schools, reinforce this loss. This is not the fault of the teachers alone. Since the inner-city schools are badly underfunded, the teacher's main job is often reduced to keeping order in the classroom. (Classic movies depicting these conditions are *Blackboard Jungle* [1955] and *Up the Down Staircase* [1967].)

Many studies have shown the role of schools in promoting and rewarding conformity. In a study of teachers' interruptions of third-grade students, the

> ...active-independent-assertive males and flexible-nonconforming-untidy females were interrupted more frequently than the passive-dependent and rigid conforming students...Since the existence of authoritarian political and social systems depends in large measure on the tacit support of a large group of the population, teacher support of such (conforming) behavior undermines free societies. At the same time it builds the kinds of attitudes that make the establishment of an authoritarian society easier." (Williams and Pellegrino, 1975)

106

Another study gave public elementary school teachers sixteen personality descriptions of students. The teachers reported their feelings of attachment, rejection, and concern toward these descriptions.

> Teachers...felt positive attitudes toward those students inclined to accept authoritarian classroom practices, whereas they rejected those more autonomous students unlikely to accept authoritarianism. To the degree that teachers practice these paternalistic attitudes, they dampen student autonomy and encourage self-effacing conformity. Such classrooms are nurseries not for freedom but for authoritarian political and social environments (Helton and Oakland, 1977).

I don't think it is necessary to give examples of authoritarian atmospheres in training for team sports, nor for training in the armed forces. The brutal Marine or Army drill instructor is a staple of war movies. When I entered basic training, my First Sergeant barked at us "The only rules here come from God and the Army manuals!" The original loss of autonomy due to poor parenting and our educational system is reinforced in adult life in our bureaucracies, where the goal, as Kenneth Burke said, is being "fit in an unfit fitness" (Burke, 1935).

Those who were humiliated or abused in childhood tend to become the humiliators and abusers in adult life. I previously reviewed some evidence of our national problems with sex, such as the sodomizing of Abner Louima. I also mentioned the sexual sadism at the Abu Graib prison in Iraq. The behavior of the guards went way beyond the recommendations for "preparing" the prisoners for interrogation. Given a free rein, several young soldiers performed in a manner that shocked the world and put our nation in a bad light. The leader in these sexual and physical assaults on Iraqi prisoners was Specialist Charles Graner. He had been a former prison guard in the United States. Young women were also involved; Specialists Lynndie England and Sabrina Harmon. Sabrina was photographed showing a smiling "thumbs up" over the body of a detainee just beaten to death. Lynndie was pictured dragging a naked man on the floor by a leash and collar around his neck. (Translation: If you think of people as animals, you can treat them like animals.)

Humiliation was central to these activities. Was this used on the assumption that it would lead to more confessions or better intelligence? Hooding men with women's panties, forcing them to masturbate in front of women, painting them with excrement, and forcing them to eat out of toilets had humiliation as its goal. Alice Miller might say that these soldiers had been humiliated as children, had repressed the feelings of anger this humiliation generated, and were now taking it out on prisoners (as they might on their own children). Testimony at the trials of these abusers confirms that they were not really softening up the prisoners for interrogation (which would be bad enough on its own) but were instead torturing them for their own gratification.

Despite the right wing's complaints about immorality, our nation is still quite puritanical compared to some European and Scandinavian countries. Without repression, you don't have "average" people torturing others sexually. The extent of this prudish attitude is shown in the smearing of political candidates because of extramarital activity. President Clinton's dalliance with Monica Lewinsky (among others) became the spearhead of a vast campaign, funded by Richard Mellon Scaife, to impeach him. Most Frenchmen probably laughed at this fling. Gary Hart had to drop out of a presidential race because of the outing of his affair. Recently Harry Stonecipher, the CEO of the Boeing Corporation, had to step down because he was having an affair with a fifty-eight-year-old woman in "Accounts Receivable"!

Our society is suffused with sexual preoccupation. Whether it is the wiggles of Britney Spears, the trial of O. J. Simpson, or the testimony of the young boys who claimed to have slept in Michael Jackson's bed, we can't get enough of it. It is a joke that the rental of porn movies in our hotels, usually for a period of only a few minutes, is a billion-dollar business. Violence is also a preoccupation, with murders, shootouts, war, and disasters dominating the news. That's what "news" is—bad news, not good news. All of this amounts to yet more evidence of our repressed sexual and aggressive drives.

How does this add up to a potential preamble to some type of dictatorship, or forerunner of fascism? Alice Miller's description of the humiliation of Hitler as a child is gleaned from many sources. In effect, she says that Hitler's father, Alois, was an alcoholic, a domineering but insecure man, who was worried that his biological father might in fact be Jewish. Alois' mother worked as a maid in a Jewish household, and the father of that household reputedly had a child, Alois, by her. When Adolf tried to run away with three friends at age eleven, his father beat him almost to death (Miller, 1983, p. 163). Adolf was beaten almost daily. He was also humiliated; for example, when his father laughed and called him a "toga boy," because he had wrapped a sheet around his naked body after trying another escape.

As a grown-up leader (*Führer*) Hitler took out his repressed rage by killing more than six million Jews, many gypsies, homosexuals, political prisoners, and Catholics, as well as the physically and mentally disabled. More relevant for us is the fact that, with some few notable exceptions, the German people may have wholeheartedly supported him (see Goldhagen, 1996). Both Gruen and Miller point out that most Germans were raised in authoritarian families, presumably had a lot of repressed anger, and were glad to take it out on the Jews and anybody else who was handy.

So, in addition to all the pressures and deprivations of the *Gesellschaft* (the economic depression after World War I, the humiliation of the Versailles Treaty and their defeat by nations less martial), the Germans had been dominated physically, traumatized emotionally, and humiliated by their parents. They were ready to follow a leader who shared their early hurtful experiences.

In Bush we had a leader who probably suffered some early humiliation and perhaps bad experiences as a child. (See "Bush and his Handlers...Early and Later Life, in "Selfishness and Leader Preselection.") He was arrested for driving when intoxicated (DWI). He has had failures in economic ventures, though in a position to get help from his family connections when necessary. He became a born-again Christian, which implies an epiphany of some sort and a renunciation of former ways. He married, had children, and became the leader of the most powerful nation on Earth. His story of struggle and eventual success had an appeal for many. His renaissance is the dream of every American, despite F. Scott Fitzgerald's warning that "in America there are no second acts."

IX. COULD IT HAPPEN HERE?

The 2006 mid-term elections gave the Democrats a majority in the House of Representatives and a tiny majority of one in the Senate. Does this mean that we are no longer in danger of right-wing extremism? The 2008 presidential election brought Barack Obama and the Democrats into power in the Executive and Legislative branches of the government. Lest we be complacent, we should recognize that there was a severe shift to the right during the Bush years. The 5 to 4 conservative majority on the Supreme Court, and the Patriot Act, among many others, herald a continuing loss of civil and individual rights. Many conservative pundits say that the 2006 and 2008 voters voted against Bush and the Iraq war, not *for* the Democrats and their agenda. The reactionary forces are still strong in America.

Are we in a state of proto-fascism? Remember the previously quoted three conditions in pre-Hitler Germany described by Fritz Stern? They were *"a longing for a new authoritarianism, with some kind of religious orientation, and above all a greater communal belongingness."* I think we have those conditions today. Our people are giving up their autonomy. Their privacy is being invaded. Even an arch right winger, William Safire, has campaigned against the violation of our confidential information. Your Social Security number and your mother's maiden name are now available to identity thieves through the "security-industrial complex" (Safire, 2005). Our civil rights are being attacked by the Patriot Act and by campaigns against the courts. The balance of powers was tipped in the direction of the Executive branch during Bush's two terms, and it will be up to Obama to give up some of this power. Religion is still used as a wedge to divide the public into warring camps. The separation of Church and State is being eroded. I have discussed much of this previously.

It has all happened before. People in Germany, Italy, and Spain looked to Hitler, Mussolini, and Franco—dictators all, to whom they gave up their autonomy. This word has synonyms, such as independence, self-reliance, and individualism, and has a cousin named freedom. Isn't it interesting that these are the very words and ideas that Bush kept repeating in his speeches (talked the talk), and that this freedom and independence is what his regime stripped us of (walked the opposite of how he talked). Freedom (democracy) for the Iraqis and for other nations around the world is also a big talking point, but you can't impose democracy from outside and by force. It has to come from the desires of the people, as some Arab intellectuals have recently written.

The people of Europe gave up their autonomy in the 1930s in a Hobbesian bargain or social contract that says "Give the man absolute power, and you won't have to worry about making decisions. He'll protect you from your enemies—keep you from getting killed or dying. He will make rules for living that are clear and simple." (There should be none of that complex analysis and "waffling" that Bush's opponent, John Kerry, was accused of. The leader will make sure that there is no need to fear lack of homogeneity or consensus. In Germany, anyone who challenged *Der Führer* was killed. This was a sure way to get consensus.)

Critics of the Iraq War were labeled "unpatriotic." for "undermining the war effort." Bumper stickers said "Support Our Troops." But many people want to support our troops by bringing them home, and they will come home by 2011. They have seen more than four thousand of our soldiers dead, and thousands wounded. (As of September 1, 2009, official U.S. figures were 4,340 named dead, and 31,483 wounded. Estimates of violent Iraqi deaths due to the war range from 151,000 (Iraqi health ministry, 2006) to 1,033,000 (Opinion Business Research Survey, August 2007). These are probably underestimates, since the surveys are outdated.

How close are we to fascism? In a series of six excellent articles posted on the Internet, David Niewert (2004) used the term "pseudo-fascism," and defined it: "... the conservative movement... is not genuine fascism, even though it bears many of the traits of that movement... it is not openly revolutionary, it is not yet a dictatorship, it does not yet rely on physical violence and campaigns of gross intimidation to obtain power and suppress opposition."

I have already discussed the methods by which the Bush administration grabbed power by using fear after 9/11 and unfulfilled hope for "compassionate conservatism." Niewert mentions Sean Hannity, Ann Coulter, and Rush Limbaugh as Bush administration mouthpieces. Descriptions and critiques of many others can be found in Franken (2003). These right-wing writers and commentators express, often in extreme form, the values and goals of the former administration.

Niewert lists some "mobilizing passions" that may be the foundations of fascism:

> ...a sense of overwhelming crisis...the primacy of the group and subordination of the individual, the belief that one's group is a victim which justifies...action against the group's enemies...dread of the group's decline under the corrosive effect of individualistic liberalism, class conflict, and alien influences...the need for closer integration of a purer community, by consent . . .or violence...the need for authority by natural (male) leaders...the superiority of the leader's instincts over abstract and universal reason...the beauty of violence and the efficacy of will, when they are devoted to the group's success...the right of the chosen people to dominate others. (Niewert, 2004, Part 2, *The Architecture of Fascism*)

The Republican Party has adopted these "mobilizing passions" since the Iraq invasion. Niewert's commentary was written prior to the 2004 election. Since that time, the attack on the balance of powers and civil rights and the force of the Bush attack agenda grew even stronger. The party apparently believed that the narrow margin of victory in the popular vote gave it the mandate to drop the "compassionate" part of their conservatism. The White House delays in rescuing the predominantly black victims of Hurricane Katrina put a crimp in this "mandate," but the administration seemed to believe that a few photo-ops and visits by Bush to New Orleans compensated for the lack of preparedness. The agenda did not seem to change to any degree. The indictment of Representative Tom DeLay, the former House majority leader, for apparent violations of Texas' state election laws, did not slow down the GOP's whirlwind agenda. The Valerie Plame affair and Bill Frist's stock sales put a crimp in Bush's political capital. The Bush push to revamp (destroy?) Social Security died due to strong negative public opinion.

But the tone of several remarks by Republicans still seemed to reflect this perceived Republican mandate and power. Niewert (2004) mentions Vice President Cheney's publicly saying to Senator Patrick Leahy "Go fuck yourself!" He sees it as epitomizing the threat of violence to opponents; a contempt for the weak and the use of power over them; and the abandonment of logic and reason, which are trumped by instinct. We know that Bush often referred to a "higher authority" for his decisions, even though he himself *was* the highest secular authority in the land. By invoking God's power for himself and his decisions, he took on the indisputability of the Biblical prophets.

I referred previously to Governor Schwarzenegger's remark "Don't be economic girlie men" as a put-down to Democrats who were pessimistic about our economy. This labeled the opposition as gay. It may be natural for a former body-builder to make such accusations, but it is unseemly and revealing in the governor of our largest state.

Tom DeLay, under pressure of an investigation into his campaign and other finances, suggested that the judges who refused to have Terri Schiavo's feeding tube removed should be impeached. This attack on the balance of powers and on the judiciary was so extreme that even Bush and Bill Frist, the former Senate majority leader, declined to second the motion, at least publicly.

The Republicans, as evidenced by their radical attack on the balance of powers; their exaggerated sense of "mandate;" their black-and-white (Manichaean) view of the world (whoever doesn't agree with us is the enemy); their support of an apocalyptic view of the future; their war on the separation of church and state; and their assault on liberalism and the Democratic party as weak, effeminate, and elitist persecutors in control of the media (all at the same time!) strongly suggests that they hoped to establish a one-party system in the United States, or at least Republican control for the next century.

Lest I be mistaken for an extreme Cassandra or Chicken Little, let me review what Naomi Wolf (Wolf, 2007, *The End of America*) has called the ten steps of "fascist shift" taking place in our country. She notes that German and Italian fascism was a gradual, or creeping, phenomenon, and she finds "echoes" of these steps in our own society. These are her chapter headings. I have put some Bush era examples in parentheses after each step. (I used Wolf's numbering.)

"2. Invoke an external or internal threat. (Invade Iraq, WMDs)
3. Establish secret prisons. (Abu Graib, rendition)
4. Develop a paramilitary force. (Blackwater)
5. Surveil ordinary citizens. (Patriot Act)
6. Infiltrate citizens' groups. (New York City Republican Convention.).
7. Arbitrarily detain and release citizens. (The "no fly" list contains 45,000 names. Ted Kennedy and Usef Islam were searched, Chaplain James Yee imprisoned)
8. Target key individuals. (Valerie Plame, Prof. Ward L. Churchill, The Dixie Chicks, Bill Maher)
9. Restrict the press. (Dan Rather lost his job.)
10. Cast criticism as "espionage" and dissent as "treason." (Adam Gadahn, 2006)
11. Subvert the rule of law. (Alberto Gonzales, John Yoo)"

Wolf warns against complacency. Despite the Democrats' winning the 2008 election, the Patriot Act and similar laws, rules, and presidential signings are still on the books. It is up to progressives and liberals to make sure that Obama and his cabinet live up to the promises made in the campaign, the "change we can believe in." There is widespread concern that many of the same crew that helped put our country in financial jeopardy (Summers, Gaithner, Greenspan and his disciple Ben Bernanke) could move the Blue party too far to the center/right.

Can a majority of our citizens, because of their social character, be tricked into supporting a fascist government? The fact that a majority of Americans may have been injured by poor parenting does not mean that they are incapable of functioning. Their typical diagnosis would be a character disorder or dysfunctional personality style, and they would be considered "normal," in the sense that their behavior is normative in our culture (a "culturally patterned defect") and that they are also statistically normal. The ability to function means that this large portion of our population can indeed be persuaded, cajoled, and deceived into actively supporting a one-party system—another step toward outright fascism.

There is evidence gathered by two Los *Angeles Times* reporters, Tom Hamburger and Peter Wallsten, that the Republicans were using their "faith-based initiative" to "attract Democratic supporters to the GOP by using the influence of churches and synagogues." They were working on a book called *One Party Country: The Republicans' Plan for Dominance in the 21st Century*. (See *Publisher's Weekly*, April 11, 2005, *GOP's Takeover Plan*, p. 16.) GOP fundraising has usually exceeded Democratic fundraising by a factor of two or three. This initiative failed to cut into or eliminate deep-pocket Democratic contributions in 2008.

Can the GOP eventually succeed in turning us into a "one-party country?" Aside from having most of the deep pockets on their team, they also seem to have an integrated philosophy, which allows them to launch a powerful propaganda attack (family values, patriotism, fear of the enemy). I think that a particular type of childhood experience has prepared a majority of our people to accept that propaganda unquestioningly.

At several points I have posited that the childhood experience of "poor parenting" prepared a large GOP party base and a swing portion of the electorate to vote for George W. Bush, a "poor parent" figure. This is because they have formed a habit, early on, of giving up their autonomy to conform to their parents' needs, rather than their own. The loss of autonomy is synonymous with giving up their independence, and their ability to make rational judgments on issues that affect their self-interest. (Note that those who say they are "independent" voters nevertheless say they "lean" heavily toward either the Red or the Blue. They are swing voters, but they are hardly autonomous. (See Chapter Four on the Pew Center Research.)

I have referred to this "poor parenting" by various names: uncaring parents, child neglect, child abuse, and cold, punitive, labile, or narcissistic parenting. George Lakoff (1995, 2002) has attempted to build a semantic model of two types of parent, each with its own morality: the "strict" and the "nurturant" father. All of the above labels (poor, uncaring, etc.), fall under the "strict" type. He sees these types as metaphors that help to unify the seemingly contradictory political positions (particularly those of the right).

Despite the fact that many aspects of Lakoff's "strict father morality" metaphor can be analyzed from various perspectives (sociological, psychological, and economic, for example) when he combines it with the "nation as family" metaphor, it helps to unify the various and often seemingly incompatible political positions that conservatives have. "It (*strict father morality*) explains why opposition to environmental protection goes with support for military protection, why the right-to-life goes with the right to own machine guns" (*and support of the death penalty*), "why patriotism goes with hatred of government" [italics are my additions] (Lakoff, 1995).

The "nurturant parent" model of the family, according to Lakoff, structures the morality of liberals. This involves caring for others, meeting the individual's desires and needs, living happily, and protecting children from external evils. "The obedience of children comes out of love and respect for parents, not out of fear of punishment. Morality resides in empathy, nurturance, self-nurturance, happiness, and moral growth" (Lakoff, 1995).

The difference between conservatives and liberals is that the former rank moral strength highest, while nurturance is the top ranked value for liberals. Moral self-interest is a middle value for both ideal types. Lakoff is convinced that the reason liberals fall behind is that they haven't organized their values and issues around morality and the family, while the conservatives have unified their values. (They even *call* them "family values.") While this may be true, I think that the lack of cohesion in the various liberal interest groups (minorities, labor, women, gays, intellectuals, academics, social and psychological science practitioners, etc.) is due in part to the basic anti-authoritarian quality of the liberal ethos. If you respect individual differences, then you do not force everyone to march in lock step. One interest group is not the enemy of the other.

O'Donnell (2006) quotes Muirhead's (2006) catch phrases linking two of our presidents to the strict versus nurturant father model. "Think of George 'Bring 'em on' Bush and Bill 'I feel your pain' Clinton." This links the father metaphor and the president/father beautifully.

George and Bill are quite far apart politically. Yet Bill, moving to the center (as it seems he felt he had to in order to get elected and hold onto the middle) drifted far from the nurturant model. George tried to *appear* nurturant ("compassionate") while being a very strict and uncaring father in most of his agenda. When we deal with metaphors or ideal types (Max Weber), we can never find human beings who fit those types exactly. We are all mixtures, and the incongruities of our beliefs and values speak to the internalized value conflicts of our cultures and those struggles in our unconscious minds.

Barack Obama campaigned as a nurturant father. In the foreword of his book, *Change We Can Believe In* (Obama, 2008) he put forth the main thrust of his "vision":

> The people I've met know that the government can't solve all their problems, and they don't expect it to. They believe in personal responsibility, hard work, and self reliance. They don't like seeing their dollars wasted. (*This is the core of the conservative value system; the Protestant Ethic and fiscal conservatism, the strict mode.*) But they also believe in fairness, opportunity, and the responsibilities we have to one another (*the nurturant model*). [italics are my comments].

Notice how he appeals to conservatives and liberals in the same breath. He lists the items on his agenda, and they show his intention to form a safety net for the less fortunate. This net includes growth and job creation, aid for the unemployed or underemployed, tax breaks for the middle class, health care coverage and lower premiums, savings for retirement, investing in early childhood education, and college tuition in exchange for community or national service. This is not very different from the standard Democratic party platform. It is caring, supportive, and humanitarian. Since the Bush years of deregulation and free-market bubbles created what appears to be a severe worldwide economic recession that will take trillions of deficit dollars to turn around, it may be difficult or impossible to fulfill many of Obama's promises.

A good example of the difficulty of classifying a particular parental behavior as either strict or nurturant is the fairly typical mixture of aggressive and loving behavior, which Freud called "affectionate abuse" (Freud, 1900, p. 302). The father of a patient may have threatened, in fun, to "gobble him up." I still remember a rather prognathous friend of my grandmother's playfully saying "You're so cute I could eat you!" At age four I believed she would. Tickling until the child says "uncle" sends another mixed message.

The child reacts to the subliminal message and senses the veiled but (consciously) unintentional threat. Songs and nursery rhymes are loaded with veiled threats and appear to be mindlessly repeated to children, generation after generation. Among these is "Rock-a-bye baby, in the tree top; When the wind blows, the cradle will rock; When the bough breaks the cradle will fall; Down will come baby, cradle and all." There is also "London bridge is falling down …take a key and lock her up." In fairy tales, the child-victim (*Cinderella, Snow White*) usually wins at last, against great odds. However, in many of the *Grimm's Fairy Tales*, and in *Max and Moritz* and in *Struwwelpeter* the children die. Parents have exposed their children to these tales with a mixed message for generations. Today many of us let our children watch all kinds of mayhem on television and in movies. Is this a modern form of affectionate abuse? David Bakan gave an insightful review of the subliminal infanticidal messages in folklore in his *Slaughter of the Innocents* (Bakan, 1971, pp. 57–77).

What Freud, Max Weber, Toennies, Alice Miller, and Arno Gruen and many others have taught us is that the strict and the nurturant father metaphors of Lakoff derive from family structure, parental behavior, major social forces, and historical change (the Industrial Revolution, the rise of Protestantism, and capitalism). The metaphors, the structures of morality, arise from the environment and circumstances of living. In *Social Cynosure and Social Structure*, Weston Labarre (1946) showed how ideal types vary according to cultural conditions. Among the pastoral nomads of biblical times, the young shepherd (David) was the cynosure (a term derived from the North Star in the "dog's tail" of the Little Dipper). In a Mexican village, a strong mature male is needed to plow the hard sun-baked soil. He is the ideal. Without him there is no corn. The warrior, the sage, or the young virgin girl may be the cynosure in other cultures.

The conservative morality (at least in the prudent *fiscally* conservative model) closely mirrors Max Weber's (1904) concept of "secular asceticism." This meant the sacrifice of worldly pleasures, such as fancy food and sex, in order to gain a state of grace. Hard work was evidence of your fitness for salvation. In *The Protestant Ethic and the Spirit of Capitalism* Weber said that in early Protestantism (particularly Calvinism) one's occupation (*Beruf*, or calling, in German) was God-given. God "called" you to your profession. Since salvation was never guaranteed, hard work produced an accumulation of worldly goods as partial proof of grace. Because of this uncertainty, a state of anomie (Durkheim, 1897) was produced. Anomie is a societal state characterized by a lack of limits on behavior (literally, "without law"). This could refer to excessive striving and accumulation of wealth, or to sexual anomie as in widespread debauchery, or any unlimited behavior. Durkheim's "anomie" translates into Fromm's (1941) excessive "freedom," from which the individual tries to escape into authoritarian control. For Fromm, "escape from freedom" was at the root of the rise of the Nazi Party and of fascism in general.

Lakoff describes the conservative mind in terms of a metaphor: "Moral strength imposes a form of asceticism." Hence the right-wing's emphasis on self-denial and self-discipline. (Note that the *leaders* are far from ascetic. They just want the poor and the middle class to be ascetic.) Thus "Welfare and affirmative action are immoral." Failure to "just say no" to drugs or sex, and just being poor, are evidence of moral weakness and deserve punishment. This makes Barbara Bush's previously mentioned comment (reminiscent of Marie Antoinette's "Let them eat cake" remark) on the *benefits* of Hurricane Katrina for its refugees understandable, though still reprehensible.

Another aspect of the "strict father" model is his rigidity. I mentioned before the Manichaean worldview of the right wing. This fits with the strict father model. The "strict father" sees things as black or white. We are good, they are evil.

Bush early on envisioned an "axis of evil" consisting of Iraq, Iran, and North Korea. If you are not for us, you are against us (as in support of the invasion of Iraq). If you don't agree, then you become the enemy. These enemies are seen as traitors, and can be outed, fired, or persecuted. Enmification (Rieber, 1997) and animalization (Langner, 2002) allow you to attack dehumanized others ruthlessly. My favorite of the animal slurs is *Schweinhund*, or "pig-dog." "Son of a bitch" is not far behind. Who said dogs were man's best friend?

Lakoff's "strict father model" clearly mirrors the authoritarian family about which so much has been written. My previous description of the pre-Weimar German family, and of Hitler's father (via Alice Miller) are extreme examples of this model. The mother is subordinate and busies herself with *Kinder, Kirche und Küche* (children, church, and kitchen). The father knows right from wrong, demands obedience, and punishes any disobedience. He holds back on showing affection and emotion. (They are signs of weakness, and possibly of being a "girlie-man.") Grown children are on their own. Lakoff cites "tough love." Here is the root of that oxymoron, "compassionate conservatism."

Lakoff sees the conservative views on feminism, abortion, homosexuality, and gun control as deriving from the strict father model. To me, these views seem multifactorial in origin. Aside from orthodox religious indoctrination, repressed sexuality, and defenses against latent homosexuality, among other explanations, they all seem to be related to asserting and maintaining white-male power. The strict father model is a *means* to power, not an end in itself. It certainly has explanatory power, but the motivation is domination of wives, children, minorities, the poor, the disabled, liberals, and "enemy" nations. (Shortly before the first invasion of Iraq, we were on good terms with Saddam Hussein and saw Iraq as a buffer against Iran. Now we face an Iran with nuclear weapons potential, supported by a Shiite majority in Iraq!)

Let's take an example. Lakoff (1995) says that conservative views on abortion derive from the violation of their model's demand for morality.

> On the whole, there are two classes of women who want abortions: unmarried teenagers whose pregnancies have resulted from lust and carelessness, and women who want to delay conception for the sake of a career but have accidentally conceived...both classes of women violate the morality characterized by the (strict family) model. The first class consists of young women who are immoral by virtue of having shown a lack of sexual self-control. The second class consists of women who want to control their own destinies, and who are therefore immoral for contesting the strict father model itself.

Of course, there is a large *third* class of women Lakoff doesn't mention who also want abortion: poor women with too many children. ("There was an old woman who lived in a shoe, she had so many children she didn't know what to do . She...whipped them all soundly, and sent them to bed." Folk-tales tell us that poor women with too many kids are abusive, or even homicidal, as in *Hansel and Gretel*.) Are these women immoral for being poor, for having sex, and for not using contraception (which is taboo for right-to-lifers) or for all three reasons?

To me, the unifying concept here is control of women, of their sexual behavior and their striving for equality in the work force. In the broadest sense, control of women, children, and minorities is a substitute for control over life's chanciness and over death, which are unpredictable and uncontrollable. Fear of dying underlies much of domineering and aggressive behavior. Becker (1973) showed how killing or dominating others is a means of denying death. In *Choices for Living: Coping with Fear of Dying*, I discuss sixteen different modes of coping with fear of dying (Langner, 2002). Death-fear might very well be stronger in men who have had strict, uncaring, authoritarian, and especially abusive fathers. Remember that Hitler had a doctor in constant attendance to stop the bleeding he imagined would kill him, and he had an extremely abusive father.

There is no doubt that at one level of explanation, Lakoff's strict father model helps us to understand what seem to be diametrically opposed positions. Lakoff's emphasis on the "framing" of values and issues made him of great value to the Democrats in preparing for the 2006 and 2008 campaigns.

I will try to get at a deeper level of understanding of the current political schism than the analysis of semantic models, helpful though they may be in "framing" the issues to appeal to the swing middle voters. If we are to preserve our democracy, we must do nothing less drastic than attempt to slowly change the social character of a good part of the nation. My purpose here has been to show how social character (liberal to conservative, and everything in between) derives in large part from the parenting one receives in childhood. Voting behavior and choice of leaders are based in large part on whether one has experienced an uncaring (selfish) or caring parent. I know of no large-scale data linking adult political behavior and early childhood experience. Survey studies of college students are misleading, because of pre-selection bias. Individual case histories were given by Harold Lasswell (*Psychopathology and Politics*,1930). Alice Miller and Arno Gruen also give case histories with political outcomes.

It is important to state that Lakoff's ideal types grow out of real life experiences and families. In Chapter Six I discuss my study of two thousand families and their children. I found certain types of child character and behavior related to three types of parenting: cold, punitive, and labile. The study didn't follow the children into adulthood, so their voting behavior couldn't be assessed. However, the children of the three uncaring or abusive parent types all had relatively poor behavior outcomes. All three of those parental types were similar to the "strict" model, rather than to the nurturant one. Absence of such poor parenting, and evidence of nurturant parenting, resulted in healthier behavior outcomes on most of the behavioral pathology scores.

Chapter Five describes five "faces" of Bush, one of which is the "uncaring parent" (strict model, abusive, neglectful, etc.).

Chapter Six presents evidence of a high rate of adult psychopathology in the United States These data are both current and from the 1950s. I suggest that high rates of anxiety, depression, drug abuse, and antisocial behavior in the United States have over time created a plethora of uncaring parents. These uncaring ("strict model") parents in turn produced in their children (today's voters) a predilection to choose uncaring leaders modeled on their own strict fathers. This choice is made unconsciously. While some 57% of adults may vote in the same right or left column as their parents (O'Donnell, 2006), the swing voters (the remaining 43%?) in the middle are crucial to winning elections. It is their early experience as children that may determine if they vote for a strict or nurturant leader. If they are truly independents (and have been brought up to be autonomous), they will examine the issues more objectively, and will probably vote according to their economic (and other) self-interest rather than rigid political ideology.

At this time, given the extreme positions of the GOP, I think the autonomous objective voters will always vote for a Democratic leader rather than a Republican. For the Democrats, the question of how to develop more autonomous people and how to appeal now to those who are already autonomous may be a clue to the survival of the party, and perhaps the survival of our democracy.

X. WHAT IS OUR NATIONAL FATE?

Our national fate is inextricably locked into the fate of the world. Here are some of the threats to our nation, and to nations of the past and present, that should be addressed sooner rather than later:

1. War and Military Overextension

There are many examples of nations and empires that have collapsed due to war. The defeat of the United States by invasion is not conceivable in the immediate future, due to the current power of our armed forces. However, the weakening of our country, by military and economic overextension, seems to have already started. Alexander's empire fell apart due to overextension. The Roman Empire lasted for 700 years, partly because conquered non-slaves were given citizenship and protection from other enemies under Pax Romana. We have not given U.S. citizenship to our conquered countries. Napoleon famously lost at Waterloo, partly due to over-reaching. France, England, Spain, and Portugal, once colonial empires, have all lost their colonies. Their great armadas, the armed sailing fleets of the past, have long been sunk.

Kansas Governor Kathleen Sebelius said rescue operations in the tornado-devastated town of Greenburg (May 4, 2007) were severely hampered by a lack of National Guard troops and equipment. Humvees, front-loaders, and trucks were in short supply, due to the war. Fifteen of the nineteen Kansas Blackhawk helicopters are in Iraq. This is a sure sign of the over-extension that may threaten our nation's survival. Similar shortages in New Orleans after Hurricane Katrina helped fuel a much larger disaster.

Nuclear proliferation, most notably in Iran and North Korea, is a worldwide threat. Nuclear materials and manufacturing equipment have been sold by Dr. Abdul Qadeer Khan of Pakistan to rogue nations that are our enemies. Biological weapons are also a threat.

Our lack of preparedness for defense against bio-warfare was highlighted by the anthrax scare in 2001, ending in five deaths. The probable perpetrator was Dr. Bruce Ivins, who worked in a U.S. bio-lab . He committed suicide in 2008, just after being informed that he was to be charged with the crime by the FBI. Two intercepted letters containing anthrax powder were sent to Democratic Senators Tom Daschle of South Dakota and Patrick Leahy of Vermont. Should it have taken seven years to find the culprit, if we were really prepared against bioterrorism?

2. Drought

The civilizations of Chaco Canyon and Mesa Verde in the Southwest collapsed due to lack of water, around 1100 A.D. The entire Southwest in the United States is now in danger of losing its water. Most of southern California is arid. The Sahara Desert moves southward every year, bringing drought to the Sahel region.

3. Natural and Man-made Disasters

These include tsunamis (threats to the rim countries of the Indian Ocean), earthquakes and volcanoes (the Pacific Rim, Pompeii and Herculaneum, and many other cities and areas around the world), and the locust plagues (Egypt, Utah, and the Philippines). The United States has its earthquakes, forest fires, mudslides, tornadoes, and insect infestations (elm beetles, San Jose scale, the Asian long-horned beetle). Our dust storms of the last century were caused by plowing the plains without restoring the prairie grass that held the soil in place. Hurricanes afflict the U.S. Gulf Coast and the southeastern states. Hurricane Katrina recently killed at least a thousand people and devastated New Orleans and one third of the U.S. oil-refining capacity.

4. Diseases

These include The Black Plague, AIDS (in Africa, the United States, Southeast Asia) mad cow disease, Ebola virus, and SARS; in addition, malaria worldwide, Lyme disease, water-borne diseases causing dysentery, and recently avian flu, with the potential to jump to humans. Swine flu (H1N1) has resulted in 5000 deaths worldwide as of October 2009. There is a shortage of the vaccine in the U.S., primarily due to the prolonged incubation period needed to produce it in eggs. This is a pandemic, since more than 199 countries have reported cases.

5. Degradation of the Environment

Global warming has been ignored by the Bush administration. In 1999, more than one hundred and fifty nations signed the Kyoto Protocol, aimed at reducing global warming. Bush would not sign, and said he would substitute the "Clear Skies" initiative instead. This program was been a failure and continued to allow pollution of our air by gases and metals (especially lead and mercury). These pollutants affect the whole world, and hit hardest in our own Northeast (where those "Massachusetts liberals" live), creating acid rain. In the 2005 follow-up meeting in Montreal we again pulled out (though we account for 65% of polluting emissions), saying that the Kyoto Protocol was too expensive and that developing countries such as India and China, though heavy polluters, had not ratified it.

6. Economic Collapse

The United States and world markets lost trillions of dollar value in 2008. There are millions of U.S. unemployed (estimated to rise to 11% or more of the work force). The housing market has tanked. Millions of foreclosures are expected. Commodity prices have been volatile. The price of a barrel (55 gallons) of crude oil went from around $18 in 1945, to $123 in June of 2008, and down again to $33 in December 2008, in inflation adjusted dollars. Self-serve unleaded gasoline went from a high of $4.69 per gallon in June of 2008 to around $2 in January 2009. This volatility in fuel can be devastating. Our economy runs on gasoline. One hurricane can put us at severe economic risk. Unless we curtail our dependence on foreign oil, and turn to alternate sources of energy, we will be vulnerable to economic collapse. Bush talked about alternate energy sources in his State of the Union address, but he drastically cut funding for research in that field. Obama plans to fund alternate energy sources.

We have overspent on the war in Iraq, even borrowing heavily from other nations, such as China. As our dollar diminishes in value, other nations will stop buying our bonds. The euro has already climbed well above the dollar. Other coalitions, in Europe or in Asia, may soon outdistance us in economic power. Outsourcing to India and China has hurt our technological lead. Engineering and science education in these countries have outstripped ours, and their labor is much cheaper. We import much more than we export. Surely this imbalance of payments is a threat to our economy.

7. Overpopulation

China, India, and Africa are all overpopulated. Together they hold more than half the world's population. How will all these people be fed, housed, educated, and given medical care? Before the population explosion, most countries were self-sustaining. An example is Sri Lanka. Early on, when it was called Ceylon, it had enough food growing on trees to sustain its population. That is no longer true.

8. Over-farming and Deforestation

Clear-cutting of forests often leads to erosion of fertile soil. The people of Easter Island cut down their trees and lost their top soil to erosion. Only their huge stone carvings remain. The Mayas of the Yucatan Peninsula deforested their land and suffered soil erosion and drought. Their civilization died out around 900 A.D. (Diamond, 2005). Not surprisingly, Bush wanted to help the lumber companies complete the deforestation of America, including the ancient redwoods of the Northwest.

9. Political and Religious Struggles

There is no end to wars between nations, and "civil" wars within nations: the Trojan War, the Hundred Years' War, the Revolutionary War, World Wars I and II, Vietnam, the Korean War, Afghanistan, Iraq I and II; the list is endless. Civil wars have often cost more in lives than some wars between nations; for example, our own Civil War. In addition to lives lost, the mistreatment of prisoners at Andersonville was on a par with Abu Graib. These struggles always weaken both sides and kill off whole generations of youths, its healthiest and most promising citizens.

The divisiveness of the 2000, 2004, 2006, and 2008 election campaigns, the splitting of the country into the Red and Blue states, and the battles over judicial appointments, abortion, gay marriage, and Social Security can't help but weaken the country. All semblance of bipartisanship has disappeared. It may be inevitable with a two-party system. Obama has promised to heal the rift, but there is pressure on him to prosecute the unlawful actions of the Cheney program of domestic spying, torture, attacks on the press, and so forth.

10. Isolation of Leaders

Jared Diamond (Diamond, 2005) reviews some causes of historical collapse (damage to the environment, climate change, enemies, changes in trading partners, and the response to these factors). Of particular interest is his description of the role of the isolation of the Maya kings in the destruction of their society.

> The Maya kings...could surely see their forests vanishing and their hills becoming eroded. Part of the reason (for their society's collapse) was that the kings were able to insulate themselves from problems afflicting the rest of society. By *extracting wealth from commoners*, they could remain well fed while everyone else was slowly starving...the kings...had to concentrate on fighting one another and keeping up their images through ostentatious displays of wealth. By insulating themselves in the short run from the problems of society, the elite merely bought themselves the privilege of being among the last to starve. (Ibid. Italics are my emphasis.)

This description is chillingly parallel to our own society. The very wealthy live in gated communities, cut off from the bulk of the population. Bush surrounded himself with yes-men and yes-women who told him what he wanted to hear. His audiences were carefully screened, so that he didn't hear dissent. He was isolated from popular opinion. Colin Powell and others (Richard S. Foster, Paul O'Neill, Larry Lindsay, General Anthony Zinni, Jeffrey Kofman, General Eric Shinseki, and Joseph C. Wilson IV) who stood up for their opinions were threatened, reprimanded, fired, outed, or not reappointed for the second term. This is isolation by retaliation.

In 2005, Harriet Miers (former White House counsel) and Karl Rove apparently got together with officials in the Department of Justice, and made up a list of seven U.S. Attorneys who were to be fired for political reasons. They had not toed the party line. In 2007 there were hearings that put Alberto Gonzales on the stand. He and others in the DOJ claimed the seven were fired for incompetence, but it turned out they were exemplary. This is another example of retaliation that isolates those in power, and deprives us of attorneys and other public servants of great integrity

Hasn't "wealth been extracted from the commoners" in our own country? How can Republican tax cuts for the richest 1 percent be justified when there are still so many poor, uneducated, and uninsured in America?

A tsunami struck the countries bordering the Indian Ocean on December 26, 2004. Hundreds of thousands were killed, and more were missing. Only twenty-five days after the greatest natural disaster of the past one hundred years, on January 19, 2005, Bush held his inaugural ball. This might have been toned down in deference to the sorrow that swept the world and the outpouring of money and supplies from governments and individuals. Bush offered a paltry few million dollars in a public announcement. There was an immediate hue and cry, since many smaller nations were giving hundreds of millions. The White House quickly revised its gift upwards, and claimed that the military helicopters and planes it had sent made up for the stingy first installment. Our inaugural balls are always ostentatious, but this was a grave moment in history, and Bush missed his cue. The people at the numerous luxurious inaugural parties and dinners ate well. In Diamond's words, they will be "among the last to starve."

Given the proliferation of nuclear weapons and the advances in explosives, biotechnology, and communications, any U.S. president would have a hard time making decisions about foreign policy. Barack Obama has the added problem of dealing with the destruction caused by the Bush years. Unfortunately, Bush surrounded himself with neo-conservatives and paleo-conservatives. They had a common agenda, which he may or may not have completely comprehended. Their goal seemed to be Armageddon, which fits with the apocalyptic vision of the Evangelist right wing. (Why not clear-cut the forests and mine the national parks, if the second coming will end it all anyhow, and the chosen will go to heaven?)

I have tried to point out some of the techniques used to dupe the American people. The role of "longing for community" and the great need for a sense of belonging and for affection in the American public also seemed to have played a major part in preparing the public to vote for Bush. I have also suggested some of the underlying character structure, formed by widespread poor parenting, that helped Bush win in 2004, and that will make it easier for a dictatorship to arise in our country. Early experience with authoritarianism in the family (as evidenced by physical, emotional, and verbal abuse) may set up whole generations for an authoritarian government. To stop this trend will be difficult. Changes in parenting are very slow and sometimes take generations. Teaching teen-agers (who will soon become parents) about child-rearing could be made a required subject. (We teach them everything else but this crucial course of study.) Who would teach parenting? Only the non-authoritarians— people who are selected to be attuned to the *individual* needs of children and adolescents.

Equally crucial for avoiding the march to a dictatorship is the alleviation of poverty, the improvement of health care, the cessation of unilateral decisions to go to war, and the funding of technological innovation which in itself can lead to more jobs, better health, and a diminution of the rampant anger, jealousy, and greed in our nation.

Two quotations from Abraham Lincoln (who would never be a Republican today!) seem particularly relevant to the previous discussion:

> What constitutes the bulwark of our own liberty and independence? It is not our frowning battlements, our bristling seacoasts, the guns of our war steamers, or the strength of our gallant and disciplined army. These are not our reliance against a resumption of tyranny in our fair land. All of them may be turned against our liberties, without making us stronger or weaker for the struggle. Our reliance is in the love of liberty, which God has planted in our bosoms. Our defense is in the preservation of the spirit which prizes liberty as the heritage of all men, in all lands, everywhere. Destroy this spirit, and you have planted the seeds of despotism around your own doors. Familiarize yourselves with the chains of bondage, and you are preparing your own limbs to wear them. Accustomed to trample on the rights of those around you, you have lost the genius of your own

independence, and become the fit subjects of the first cunning tyrant who rises. (Lincoln, 1858)

If you once forfeit the confidence of your fellow citizens, you can never regain their respect and esteem. It is true that you may fool all of the people some of the time; you can even fool some of the people all the time; but you can't fool all of the people all the time. (To a caller at the White House, from *Lincoln's Yarns and Stories*, McClure, 1904)

Chapter Four
Who Voted Against Their Economic Interests? The Pew Report: Beyond Red and Blue

At this point it may be helpful to summarize some of the conclusions and hypotheses that have been set forth:

I. A SUMMARY OF HYPOTHESES THUS FAR

1. Social character is the key to voting behavior. An authoritarian personality structure favors a vote for a candidate or leader who is represented as strong and inflexible (and even one who is uncaring for his subjects). Social character is formed by continuous experiences within the family, especially by early experiences.
2. Parenting is a prime factor in voting, since it is, along with biological endowment, the primary factor in the formation of social character.
3. Abused and neglected children (injured by parental coldness, lability, and punitiveness) will very likely grow up with a propensity to vote for authoritarian candidates. This simply extends the relationship they have with their parents to the political sphere. There is a continual reinforcement

of obedience and loss of autonomy in our schools, sports, and military training.

4. During periods of rapid social change, people tend to exhibit a longing for the simplicity of the past, a wish to be dependent as in childhood. They long for community (*Gemeinschaft*), but are living in a complex society (*Gesellschaft*). This rapid change (due to war, terrorism, economic upheavals, changing sexual mores, etc.) creates fear and confusion. These emotional states lead people to turn to a "strong man" with a simple message.

5. The war in Iraq, the proliferation of nuclear weapons, the attack on the World Trade Center on 9/11; and the bombings in Spain, England, and Egypt increased fear and uncertainty, creating a shift of the middle voters to the right. Bush used 9/11 and reports of "weapons of mass destruction" to create fear, which gave him a distinct advantage in the 2004 election.

Although I have always believed that self-esteem and social character trump economic considerations when it comes to voting, it is still a mystery how so many people could vote directly against their own economic *best interests*. The questions this section sets out to answer are:

1. How many people voted against their economic best interests in the 2004 presidential election?
2. Who were they?
3. Why did they vote that way?

I considered "those with household incomes of less than $50,000 who voted for Bush" to be "voting against their economic self-interest." I assume that in today's economy, if your household income is less than $50,000 a year, you will have a hard time paying your bills, getting food and shelter, and taking care of your family. In addition, you will have to do without the luxuries of going out to movies, dining out, spectator sports, theater, most museums, and vacations. You will also have to curtail any penchants you have for food delicacies. Many meats and fish are beyond your means. A car, often a necessity, may become a luxury. A second assumption, one that I think is well justified, is that the GOP does not have your best interests at heart, and in fact would do everything in its power to take away or limit your benefits: privacy, medical care, housing, children's education, clean environments, legal representation, job opportunities, and job stability.

The CNN Exit Poll

One of our first questions is "Who voted against their own economic interests by voting for Bush when they were in the lower half of the income distribution/?" Exit polls are conducted as people come out of the voting booths. The CNN exit poll of 2004 (CNN, 2004) gives us an approximate answer to this question. The Table 10 shows that a sizable group of people with incomes below $50,000 voted for Bush.

TABLE 10
PROPORTION WHO VOTED AGAINST THEIR
SELF INTEREST IN 2004

TOTAL	% of Population	BUSH	KERRY
Under $15,000	8%	36%	63%
$15,000-$30,000	15%	42%	57%
$30,000-$50,000	22%	49%	50%
Total of low income group (under $50,000), who voted for Bush	45%	Average 42%	

This figure of 42% is a rough approximation of the proportion of voters who voted against their economic self-interest, according to my definition. However, it has been pointed out that if you look at those of high income who voted for Kerry, they might also be considered to be voting against their own interests. Most of them own stocks and bonds, which the GOP claims to favor. The Republicans have been trying to do away with capital gains taxes, and eventually with inheritance taxes, crying "double taxation."

The GOP tax cuts have been a windfall for the very richest 1%. A look at the same table shows that for those with an income greater than $75,000, an average of 41% voted for Kerry. In a sense they *are* voting for their own interests, if the Democrats develop more jobs, fix the economy, stop the wars, and pay for better schools for their children. They are voting their consciences, but against their pocketbooks.

A few CNN poll questions dealing with economics may throw more light on the low-income Bush voters. Seventeen percent of the sample said they had "lost a job" (though the table did not specify if the job was lost within the last year).

Thirty-five percent of the Bush voters said they had lost a job, vs. 63% of the Kerry voters. Isn't a job-loser who votes for Bush voting against himself?

Seventy percent said they were "very concerned" about the availability and cost of health care. Of these, 41% voted for Bush and 58% for Kerry. If the 41% were very concerned, why did they vote for Bush, when the Democrats have been pushing for universal health coverage for a long time? The Clinton health plan (1993) failed for many reasons, but chief among these was the onslaught of propaganda attacking the plan. Harry and Louise became famous as the couple who virtually destroyed the plan through their television spots, For example, Louise said "If you let the government choose, you lose," a clever, short, rhyming slogan. The insurance companies (Health Association of America, or HIAA), the drug companies (PhRMA), the American Medical Association (AMA) and the hospital lobby stood to lose billions under this plan, and to this day they will fight to protect their bottom line. In 2009, eight months into Obama's presidency, a similar but even more aggressive attack has been launched against the administration's health plan. Senator Grassley has warned that the plan could "pull the plug on grandma" (euthanasia!) and Sarah Palin has cautioned that the government will set up "death panels." It is "socialized medicine." Fear, the favorite tool of the GOP, is being used to prevent Obama from fulfilling his top goal of health care and insurance for all. In the face of this pressure he has even backed down on his campaign promise, the "public option" (a government insurance program that would compete with private insurers). Late on November 7th (a Saturday!) the House narrowly passed a bill overhauling health care. Although it must still be reconciled with a Senate bill, this is an historic step toward health care reform.

Gullibility must open the door for fear and resistance to health reform in this case. The repetition of the negative sound-bites that are so clever (short, easy to remember, and terrifying) can eventually make people believe that they are true. Goebbels repeated the Nazi slogans until they became truths. Edward Bernays, the maven of marketing, said repetition was the key to selling your product. I personally think that these catch phrases can become "truths" only if they fall on the ears of those who lack autonomy. It takes a certain amount of inner-direction, a familiarity with one's own psychological make-up and inner-conflicts, and an ability to make judgments that are independent of the crowd, in order to resist this barrage of lies and fear.

About a third (28%) said their "family's financial situation was worse." Of these, 20% voted for Bush and 79% for Kerry. That 20% should have known that Bush's tax cuts for the very rich were not going to help them with their money woes.

The CNN poll had many questions dealing with the background (demographics) and opinions of those who voted for Bush or for Kerry. One of the most revealing questions was "What was the most important issue?" for the respondent. One of the major questions we are trying to answer is whether Bush and Kerry voters were motivated by different issues, and to what extent. First let's look at how important these "most important" issues were in the general population, regardless of how they voted. First came Moral Values (22%), then The Economy and Jobs (20%), Terrorism (19%), Iraq (15%), Health Care (8%), Taxes (5%), and Education (4%). The low ranking of Health and Education would seem to support our idea that bread and butter issues are trumped by fear and family values. However, The Economy and Jobs ranked second, so the differential importance of economics and social issues is not clear.

When it comes to voting for Bush versus Kerry, the differences by party on issues couldn't be clearer. The Democrats were more motivated by economic issues, the Republicans more by fear (terrorism) and moral values. Of those concerned most with Taxes, 55% voted for Bush versus 43% for Kerry. The figures for Terrorism were 86% versus 14%, and for Moral Values, 80% versus 18%. No real emphasis on bread and butter here. (We have our food. Let them eat cake!)

The reverse is true for the economic issues. Of those who thought The Economy and Jobs the most important issue, 18% voted for Bush versus 80% for Kerry. The same held for Health Care (23% vs. 77%), and Education (26% vs. 73%). Those who ranked bread and butter issues (The Economy and Jobs, Health Care, and Education) high in importance voted heavily for Kerry. Those who ranked Taxes, Terrorism, and Moral Values high in importance voted for Bush (57%, 86%, and 80%). In all fairness, Taxes could be considered an economic issue, especially for the rich.

But our concern is really with those who seemed to vote *against* their self- interest; who they were, and how many of them there were.

Twenty-six percent of those who thought education the most important issue voted for Bush. Likewise, 18% for whom the economy was most important voted for Bush, as well as 23% of those who were most concerned about health care. How could they miss the fact that Bush was not fully supporting health care or education or improving the economy?

The Bush drug program (Plan D) is a giveaway to the drug companies, and it threatens to weaken Medicare and Medicaid. The Bush administration was fighting the states that were trying to make Canadian prescription drugs available to their citizens. The Medicare Part D drug program forbids purchase of foreign made drugs.

The "No Child Left Behind" program has been underfunded and problematic. Many states complain that its new requirements for testing are not covered by the current level of government funding. I think the program should be called "No Child's Behind Left." Under Obama, stimulus money may expand the NCLB program, but many of its flaws, including incentives to teach to the test, are sore thumbs with liberals. Despite the infusion of $100 billion from the stimulus program, massive teacher layoffs have increased class sizes to nearly fifty, compared with the norm of thirty. Many states are in financial crises, and are forced to cut back such essential services as education.

Job creation under Bush II fell far behind its usual pace. Then the recession hit toward the end of his second term, and in August 2009 we are faced with almost fifteen million unemployed (14.9), as well as those underemployed, or simply dropping out of the job market due to failure to find any work at all. Unemployment has reached its highest level in 26 years. This is the legacy Dubya left to his successor. In November 2009 unemployment topped 10%.

The high proportion of Bush voters (86% and 80%) among those who thought Terrorism or Moral Values most important demonstrates how expertly Karl Rove and his spinners (related to Arachnids?) tricked a good portion of the public into voting for Bush.

The Pew Research Report

A source of much more detailed information comes from another poll, but not an exit poll. In May of 2005, the Pew Research Center released the results of two surveys: one of two thousand interviews done on December 1–16, 2004, and a re-interview of 1,090 respondents from March 17 to 27 of 2005. This report, consisting of fifty-eight pages of text plus tables and questionnaires, is a very thorough scientific study of the beliefs and values of recent voters and non-voters. The study was conducted under the leadership of Andrew Kohut, the director of the Pew Center. This report can be viewed online at The Pew Research Center, *The Pew Report: Beyond Red and Blue* (see Kohut, 2005, for URL).

The general findings of the study are that "The GOP had extensive appeal among a disparate group of voters in the middle of the electorate, drew extraordinary loyalty from its own varied constituencies, and made some inroads among conservative Democrats." Divisions within the GOP on economic and domestic issues, and within the Democratic Party on social and personal values "may loom larger in the future." "Foreign affairs assertiveness" now clearly distinguishes Democrats from Republicans. (Republicans approve of the war in Iraq.)

The survey data were used to create a typology of attitudes and values based on nine value orientations, which were formed by answers to two or more questions in the questionnaire: Foreign Policy Assertiveness, Religion and Morality, Environmentalism and Regulation, Social Welfare, Immigration, Business Sentiment, Financial Security, Anti-Government Sentiment, and Individualism (success is/is not within the individual's power).The politically unengaged, or "Bystanders," were taken out of the sample. They constitute 10% of the population, so as non-voters they really should be added to the group that acts (not just votes) against its own economic interests. They were the third poorest group, with 77% having family income of less than $50,000.

A cluster analysis was used to sort the remaining 90% of the relatively engaged portion of the sample into fairly homogeneous groups, based on the nine value orientations, party identification, and self-reported ideology. (A cluster analysis takes a profile of one respondent over various scales and scores, and searches for a best match to that set of peaks and valleys. After finding a good match, the first two respondent's profiles go looking for another match, until certain limits are met. Then a new cluster is formed, and so on, until the sample is completely classified.)

II.   THE PROFILES OF THE TYPOLOGY GROUPS

These are sketches based on descriptions of each type. Only the highlights of each group are mentioned here. For instance, only those groups that are above or below the average age of the sample are described as such. *The typology groups are a good guide to the different categories of people who voted in both the 2004 and the 2008 elections.*

Enterprisers: 81% identify themselves as Republican, 18% Independent, and 98% "lean Republican." They believe in free enterprise, are conservative in values, and are strong on assertive foreign policy (supporting the Iraq war and the Patriot Act). They are anti-regulation, show little support for government help to the poor, and are against gay marriage. But they are no more religious than the United States as a whole. They are predominantly white (91%) and male (76%). (See Table 11 for proportion of each group with income of less than $50,000, the percentage that voted for Bush in 2004, and the percentage of each group that clearly voted against their economic self-interest [a conservative estimate].)

Social Conservatives: 82% Republican, 18% Independent, more religious than Enterprisers, have a cynical view of business, show some support for environmental regulation, and have strong anti-immigrant opinions. They are strong on individualism. Most feel financially secure, though they are not better off than the country as a whole. They are mostly white (91%) and female (58%), older, and Southern. The majority attend church weekly, and 43% are white evangelical Protestants (vs. 21% nationally).

Pro-Government Conservatives: 58% Republican, 40% Independent: strongly religious, financially insecure, favor government support programs, show moderate support for Iraq war. More female (62%), younger, high percentage of minority GOP "leaners" (12% Hispanic, 10% black), poorer, about half with children living at home, and 42% from the South.

Upbeats: 56% Independent, 39% Republican, but 73% are "Republican or lean Republican." Satisfied with government, the economy, and their finances; pro-immigrant, religious, moderate on morality. Young, wealthy, well educated, white, suburban, married, no gender imbalance, Protestant and Catholic (28% and 30%), high stock ownership.

Disaffecteds: 68% Independent, 30% Republican (60% Republican/lean Republican), cynical, alienated, 23% didn't vote in 2004. They like government support, but not environmental and other regulation if it loses U.S. jobs. Less educated, male (57%). Majority (60%) lean Republican. They believe immigrants take away jobs, housing, and healthcare.

Conservative Democrats: Party I.D. 89% Democrat, 11% Independent, 0% Republican, 98% Democrat/lean Democrat. Religious and conservative values make this group differ from other Democratic groups. They are moderates on foreign policy and the environment and want government support for the needy. They are against gay marriage and homosexuality, but average (similar to the sample as a whole) on abortion and stem-cell research. The greatest number oppose the Iraq war. Older women

(27%) and blacks (30%) are heavily represented in this type. People in this group are less educated and poorer than average. Almost half attend church once a week, and a similar proportion attend Bible study or prayer group.

Disadvantaged Democrats: 84% Democrat, 16% Independent, 0% Republican (99% lean Democrat). They are the poorest of all the groups, are against big business, and strongly believe the government should aid the needy. Much more than conservative Democrats, they disapprove of Bush's job performance (91%). Their 82% vote for Kerry was similar to the 81% of liberals who voted for Kerry. They are favorable toward labor unions (71%). Their incomes are low (32% below $20,000 household income), 77% "can't make ends meet," and 60% are women. Minorities are heavily represented (32% black). 14% Hispanic). Most have only a high-school education or less (65%).

Liberals: 59% Democrat, 40% Independent, 1% Republican (92% lean Democratic). Now the largest group of Democrats, they are opposed to the war in Iraq and elsewhere, are heavily secular, and favor environmentalism. They are liberal on social issues such as homosexuality, abortion, and censorship. In contrast to other Democrats, they are pro-immigration (their higher level jobs are not threatened by immigrants) and strongly pro-environment (again probably related to the fact that their jobs are not in construction, lumber, or mining which are strongly anti-environment). They are mostly white (83%), highly educated (94% have college degrees), and are much younger than average. They are not religious, 36% are "never married," they are mostly urban (42%) and from the west (34%). They are the wealthiest Democrats (41% earn $75,000+). Kerry got 81% and Bush got 2% of their vote in 2004.

How can we answer the questions: "How many people voted against their economic self-interest, who were they, and why did they vote that way?"

The data from the Pew survey can help us get some answers, but these will, of course, only be a rough approximation. What income group could be considered to be sorely tried, and discriminated against, by the Bush administration's policies? Again I took a conservative figure, a cutting point of $50,000 household annual income. Note that if these households include children, then they are greatly disadvantaged. Good public schools, particularly in the inner cities and rural areas where most people who make less than $50,000 per year live, are rare. People (and families) who are in this income bracket have trouble getting good medical care. They are unemployed or underemployed at low-paying jobs, and they often lack the education and skills to get better jobs without further training. They are the very people who have already suffered from outsourcing. If they are elderly, their medical needs are barely met by Medicaid. If they are black or Hispanic, their life expectancy is five to seven years shorter than the average white's. Table 11 shows what proportion of each of the typology groups has less than $50,000 income. This constitutes the bottom three fifths of the U.S. income distribution.

Note that 38% of the Enterprisers, 53% of the Social Conservatives, 79% of the Pro-Government Conservatives, 41% of the Upbeats, and 71% of the Disaffecteds were in the "below $50,000" category. Of these, 92%, 86%, 61%, 63%, and 42% respectively voted for Bush in 2004. I focus on these five types because of their heavy GOP vote. (We would need the frequencies from the exact cross-tabulations of voting for Bush by income and typology group to get the correct percentages.)

TABLE 11
PROPORTION OF PEW TYPOLOGY GROUPS WITH INCOMES
UNDER $50,000 VOTING FOR BUSH IN 2004
(*Below $50,000 is lowest three fifths of U.S. income.)

	ENTER PRISERS	SOCIAL CON SERV ATIVES	PRO- GOV'T CON SERV ATIVES	UP BEATS	DISS AFF ECT EDS	CON SER VA TIVE DEMS	DIS AD VAN TAG ED DEMS	LIB ER ALS
<$50,000 FAMILY INCOME % *	38	53	78	41	71	71	78	44
% VOTED FOR BUSH IN 2004	92	86	81	63	42	14	2	2
A: % <$50,000 INCOME X % VOTED FOR BUSH =% WHO VOTED AGAINST ECONOMIC SELF- I8NTEREST	35	46	48	26	30	10	2	1
B: % OF ADULT POPULATION IN EACH GROUP	9	11	9	11	9	14	10	17

The third row of figures (row A) is an estimate of the percentage of people who voted against their economic self-interest in that particular cluster type. For example, I calculated that 35% of the Enterprisers voted against their economic interests. Multiplying the percentage of low income (.38) by the percentage who voted for Bush (.92) yields .35, or 35%.

The percentages of the first five groups who voted against their economic self-interest (for Bush) were respectively 35%, 46%, 48%, 26%, and 30%. This averages 37%, which compares favorably with the 44% we got from the CNN table. (Negligible proportions of the last three groups, conservative and disadvantaged Democrats and Liberals, voted for Bush, and thus did not significantly vote against their economic self-interest.)

(As I pointed out before, rich liberals actually voted against their economic self interest, since Bush's tax policies favored them. Perhaps they were voting their conscience, and right-wing Evangelicals might also be considered to be voting their conscience. But bread-and-butter issues are [or should be] more important for the poor than they are for the relatively wealthy liberals.)

If we take a figure lying between the CNN result (44%) and the PEW result (37%) by averaging, we come up with 40% voting against their economic self-interest.

So about two fifths (40%) of the population probably voted against their economic self-interest! If only a small portion of this group of AESIs (those who voted Against Economic Self Interest) had voted on bread-and-butter issues rather than through fear or because of "family values," Kerry would have won.

The fourth row of figures (B) shows the percentage of the adult population in each of the typology groups. Since these percentages range between 9% and 11% for the five Bush-voting groups we are focusing on, it did not seem necessary to make any corrections to our rough estimate of 40% AESIs among the 2004 voters.

Since about a third of the general population did not vote, we could say that they are also "voting against their best interests" by *not* voting. I assume that most of them are too dispirited, alienated, or poor to vote, or that they were turned away because of criminal records. Even those who were guilty only of misdemeanors were struck from voting lists! Others did not vote due to lack of transportation, or lack of easily accessible voting machines. These disparities in availability of voting facilities, particularly in black neighborhoods, became a big issue in the 2004 elections. The GOP in 2008 tried to make drivers' licenses a necessary form of I.D. in some states. If you don't have a driver's license, or $20 for a voter identification card, you can't vote. This requirement would be the equivalent of a poll tax. Most of those who couldn't escape Hurricane Katrina were blacks, who didn't have cars, and presumably no driver's licenses. Blacks, 88% of whose voters picked Kerry, are still relatively faithful Democrats (along with Jews, 74%). It makes sense for the GOP to attempt to disenfranchise blacks.

Only 41% of whites voted for Kerry. (This figure is based on CNN exit poll percentages.)

III. WHICH GROUPS WERE MORE LIKELY TO VOTE AGAINST THEIR ECONOMIC INTERESTS?

Let's look at the groups that contributed most of this "misplaced" voting. (This, of course, assumes a rational model for man, a wildly irrational creature!) The Pew Report data offer an opportunity to look at some remarkable differences among Bush voters.

The Enterprisers

Table 11 shows that 35% of this group is estimated to have voted against their economic self-interest (AESIs) as defined by having a household income below $50,000 per year and voting for Bush. (Thirty-eight percent had an annual income of less than $50,000, and 92% of the group voted for Bush.) Multiplying $.38 \times .92 = .35$, or 35%. *This makes the assumption that the proportion voting for Bush is distributed evenly across the income levels.* I have not obtained the actual cross-tabulations, so this is the best estimate I can make.)

Since this group had very strong opinions that supported the Bush administration's policies at home and abroad, these opinions alone might have swayed even those of moderate to low income to vote GOP. While I do not have access to a breakdown of the individual opinion items of the AESIs by income, the attitudes and the sex ratio of the Enterprisers seem to tell the story.

The fact that they are mostly white (91%) and heavily male (76%) suggests that they would be prone to support Bush's aggressive foreign policy. In addition, 59% have a gun in the home. They are weekly church attendees (48%) and 36% attend prayer meetings or Bible study. Their primary news source is Fox News (46%), which has a strong conservative slant. Add to this that 23% are veterans, who generally tend to vote GOP.

Enterprisers agree heavily that "Corporations make a fair and reasonable amount of profit" (88% vs. 39% of the sample as a whole). They agree (74% vs. 31% of the sample) that "Stricter environmental laws and regulations cost too many jobs and hurt the economy." They agree (84% vs. 39% of the sample) that "Using overwhelming military force is the best way to defeat terrorism around the world." They also agree (73% agree vs. 34% of the sample) that "Poor people have it easy because they can get government benefits without doing anything in return." These items were selected by the Pew Research Center as typical of the Enterprisers' responses. I have presented their choice of opinion items to represent other cluster groups, with some additions of my own taken from their more detailed tables.

Since 77% of Enterprisers are married, the portion with incomes below $50,000 must contain a good percentage of financially hard-pressed couples. My guess is that white, male, religious gun owners, 30% of whom are small business owners, form an almost stereotypical picture of the Bush supporter. No wonder Bush bowed to the National Rifle Association's wishes. (Remember the *Bush*-master rifle, the XM-15, which is an assault rifle based on the Army's M-16? The CEO of Bushmaster, Richard E. Dyke, was the finance officer of the Bush campaign in Maine, until July 1999. He resigned when a Los Angeles cop sued the company as the maker of the XM-15 that wounded him in a shootout with bank robbers. The sharp-shooting Beltway terrorists of 2002, John A. Muhammad and Lee B. Malvo, tried to extort ten million dollars. They killed ten people with single shots. After they were captured, a Bushmaster MX-15 used in the killings was found in Muhammad's digs.)

Social Conservatives

More than half of this group (53%) were in the bottom three fifths of the U.S. income distribution (that is, less than $50,000). Since 86% voted for Bush, this means that about half of the Bush voters could be considered AESIs (.53 × .86 = .46). The description of the Social Conservatives' demographics is congruent with this impression of half possibly voting against their economic interests. They are white (91%), female (58%), older (average age fifty-two), half live in the South, 51% go to church weekly, and 42% are white evangelical Protestants (vs. 21% of the national proportion).

Older white and poorer Southern religious (evangelical) women conjure up a very conservative picture. They tend to be anti-abortion and anti-gay ("Homosexuality should be discouraged by society"; 65% agree vs. 44% of the sample). They are anti-immigrant ("Newcomers...threaten American customs and values"; 68% agree vs. 40% of the sample). They also agree that "Poor people have it easy..." (68% vs. 34%). However, they also feel that "Business corporations make too much profit" (66% vs. 54%). This last opinion item suggests that some of these AESIs may be dimly aware of the source of their financial problems. This did not, however, deter them from voting for Bush. Again, "values" (and homosexuality and anti-abortion) trump economics. Anti-immigrant sentiment is not surprisingly stronger at lower socioeconomic levels, as this is indeed related to their self-interest, since the immigrant competes for their low level jobs.

What is puzzling is that 88% of the Social Conservatives suggest they are financially secure ("Paying the bills is generally not a problem"), which is comparable to the 88% of the Enterprisers who make the same claim! The Enterprisers are indeed financially secure, while the Social Conservatives have considerably lower incomes.

The large percentage of evangelical white Protestants among Social Conservatives argues for the hypothesis that their opinions are heavily influenced by the sermons they hear in church. The evangelical churches focus on "family values," which often boil down to anti-gay marriage and anti-abortion.

Pro-Government Conservatives

The pro-Government conservatives (PCGs) are the poorest of the Republican-voting groups. About half of their members (49%) have household incomes below $30,000. This group is quite realistic about its financial position. Only 29% say that "Paying bills is not generally a problem," and 68% agree that "I often can't make ends meet." Yet 61% of them voted for Bush!

The PCGs have the largest proportion of AESIs (48% of any of the eight voting profile groups. This was estimated as follows: 61% voted for Bush in 2004, and 79% of the whole group had household income below $50,000. Assuming an equal distribution of voters across income groups, 48% are AESIs (.79 × .61). Ideally, we should like to have the exact cross-tabulation of Democrat and GOP votes by income level, but this was not available.

The Pew researchers named this cluster group's predecessor "Populist Republicans." This captures their social conservatism and their contrasting support for "big government," which is the whipping boy of the GOP. The PCGs want government regulation of industry and morality and government assistance to the poor (a "social safety net"). They back the Iraq war, but not to the extent of the Enterprisers or Social Conservatives. ("We should be willing to fight for our country, whether it is right or wrong"; 67% of PCGs agree, vs. 46% of the sample.)

The PCGs are heavily female (62%) religious, and younger, with more minority members (22% black + Hispanic) than other pro-GOP groups, 6%, 11%, 14%, and 15%). Remember that 79% of PCGs have annual incomes of less than $50,000, the poorest of all eight voting groups.

The PCGs had the second largest percentage of white Protestant evangelicals (37%) after the Social Conservatives (43%) and similar to the Enterprisers (34%). This shows how strong a base Bush had among evangelicals. These three types represent 29% of the adult (voting) population.

Further evidence of the poor financial condition of the PCGs is that 39% reported that someone in their household was unemployed during the previous year. This may have influenced their relatively high agreement (24% vs. 4%, 19% and 12% of the other heavily pro-GOP groups) with the statement "Hard work is no guarantee of success."

My first impression of strong evidence of anti-economic self interest (AESI) in the pro-Bush voting of this group would be their 22% minority membership. Despite Bush's employing and/ or praising minority members (Colin Powell, Condoleeza Rice, Alberto Gonzales, and Clarence Thomas), his policies consistently favored wealthy whites and penalized minorities. My second impression would be that the PCG's poor education vis-à-vis the other three GOP-voting groups interfered with their voting in their self-interest. It might make them less critical of the Republican propaganda. Third, their evangelical membership may very well have served to instill in them a set of "family values" which the GOP successfully used to distract voters from their economic self-interest (jobs, schools, health).

The Pro-Government Conservatives are the strongest evidence that poverty (economic self interest) is trumped by social character and the attitudes that go with it. My best guess is that PCGs are predominantly authoritarian, and that this helped Bush win the 2004 election.

Upbeats

The fourth GOP-voting group, the Upbeats, had about the same proportion of under $50,000 incomes (41%) as the Enterprisers (38%), making them wealthier than the Social Conservatives (53%) or the Pro-Government Conservatives (79%).

The Upbeats have the third largest proportion of Bush voters (63%; only the first five groups listed, from left to right in Table 11, voted significantly for Bush). Again, assuming an even distribution of voters by income, we get 26% of this group potentially voting against their economic self-interest.

"Upbeats express positive views about the economy, government and society. Satisfied with their own financial situation and the direction the nation is heading, these voters support George W. Bush's leadership in economic matters more than on moral or foreign policy issues" (Kohut, 2005). Not surprisingly, they agree (64% vs. 32% of the sample) that "Most elected officials care what people like me think." Since, as stated above, they are a wealthy group (59% have incomes of over $50,000, and 39% have incomes of over $75,000), most officials probably *do* care what they think. They are pro-business. ("Most corporations make a fair and reasonable profit"; 78% agree vs. 39% of the sample.) They are white (87%), suburban, married, and have equal proportions of men and women. They are not heavily female like their two GOP neighbors (Social Conservatives 58% and Pro-Government Conservatives, 62%). They are better educated (37% are college graduates) than the Social Conservatives and Pro-Government Conservatives (28% and

15% of whom are college graduates), but somewhat less so than the Enterprisers (46% of whom are college graduates).

David Brooks, in his column in the *New York Times* shortly after the Pew Report came out on the Internet in May, 2005, pointed to the Upbeats as proof that America's voters were moving to the right and that they were satisfied with the current state of affairs. The Upbeats are "upbeat," in my opinion, because they have more money than most people, are better educated, and in fact have more to gain as a group by voting for Bush. They own stocks (42% of them) and stand to gain, presumably, by the administration's protection of business interests.

However, the 41% of Upbeats who voted for Bush and had incomes below $50,000 per year, or the 18% who had incomes under $30,000 per year and voted for Bush, are a puzzlement. Again, looking at the sunny side seems to be surprisingly unrelated to economic situations. Almost a third (28%) of Upbeats reported someone unemployed in their household during the past year. Were they among the 37% of Upbeats who voted for Kerry? More detailed cross-tabulations could tell us if this was true.

The Upbeats seem to share some values with the liberals. For example, 72% of them agree that "immigrants strengthen our country," versus 45% of the sample. Of course, immigrants pose a threat to the jobs of minorities and the poor, while they provide nannies and manual labor for the suburban Upbeats. In further opinions the Upbeats seem to be more liberal. About one fourth (24%) agreed that "Using military force in Iraq was the wrong decision," versus 5%, 8% and 18% of the other strong GOP groups. Another 27% thought that the "Patriot Act goes too far," versus 12% and 13% of the first two GOP groups shown in Table 11. More Upbeats oppose teaching creationism (59% vs. 49%, 35%, and 34% of the other GOP groups). Again, 26% say "Torture is never justified against terrorist..." versus 10%, 14%, and 22% of the other GOP groups. They also favor stem-cell research, gay marriage, lowering defense spending to reduce the deficit, and more liberal Supreme Court appointments. Their overall opinion of George W. Bush as unfavorable (vs. favorable) was 28%, vs. 3%, 4%, and 19% of the other GOP groups. (Remember that the surveys were conducted in December 2004 and March 2005, after Bush's first term.)

Despite the fact that 63% of the Upbeats voted for Bush, they appear to have a more unfavorable view of him than those in other GOP groups, by a large margin. Do the 28% with an unfavorable opinion of Bush comprise the 14% who voted for Kerry, plus another 14% who disapproved of Bush but despite this voted *against* Kerry (and thus for Bush)? The picture of Kerry as a waffling indecisive patrician who lied about his war record (the Swift Boat campaign) that was promoted by the Bush spinmeisters may have created a group of Bush disapprovers who saw Bush nevertheless as the better of two bad choices. These are questions that can be raised by opinion surveys, but cannot be answered except by in-depth interviews.

The Upbeats, then, share features of both conservatives and liberals. What I find upsetting is that young, wealthy, well-educated, white, married men and women did not see through the smokescreen of false issues. Those Upbeats whose income was greater than $75,00 a year (39%) certainly voted in their own (short-term) economic interests (though not in their long-term interests due to the huge deficit piled up in eight years by the Bush administration and foreign control of our debt), not to mention the breeding ground for terrorists that same administration has created in Iraq. Yet we tried to look specifically at the under $50,000 income group among Upbeats. They were misled by the campaign, but not necessarily by fundamentalist or evangelical leanings. I estimated that 26% of the Upbeats with incomes below $50,000 voted for Bush. Why are people with low incomes so happy? (We might also think them oblivious to their lot, in denial, or simply clueless.) A discussion of their "sunniness" and acceptance of their low income by some of the Upbeats and other GOP groups is discussed after a review of the Disaffecteds.

The Disaffecteds

The last group that voted for Bush with any frequency (42%) was the Disaffecteds. Almost three fourths (71%) of them had incomes below $50,000. That is on a par with the Pro-Government

Conservatives (79%). (Note that the Disaffecteds are more like two Democrat-voting groups [71% and 78% of whom have low incomes], which makes their 42% Bush vote all the more striking.) The previous Pew label for this group was "Embittered," yet 42% of them were not directing their anger at Bush, whose policies favoring the wealthy so clearly hurt their income and their prospects for the future.

The Disaffecteds are less educated than most groups, and are heavily male (57%). They are anti-immigrant. Eighty percent of them, versus 44% of the sample, agree that "Immigrants take our jobs, housing and health care." They show signs of what has alternately been called alienation, anomie, or depression, depending on the discipline of the commentator. This is seen in their responses to several opinion items. "Government is always wasteful and inefficient"; 70% agree versus 47% of the sample. "Most elected officials don't care what people like me think"; 84% agree vs. 63% of the sample. "Hard work and determination are no guarantee of success for most people"; 48% agree versus 28% of the sample.

I must admit to agreeing with all of the last three statements, which seem to make me a Disaffected Democrat. I would have agreed even during a Democratic administration.

Disaffecteds tend to be out of the loop, and this is reflected in their voting behavior. While 42% voted for Bush and 21% for Kerry, 23% said they didn't vote in 2004! Here is a potential target audience for Democrats. They may not be easy to reach, since they don't follow the news. Again, since 72% of them had a favorable opinion of Bush, they may not be easy to convince that the Democrats have their best interests at heart. During December 2003–December 2004 they had the highest rate of unemployment in the household (42%) of any of the five pro-Bush groups. They are the least educated of the five pro-Bush groups. Only 11% were college graduates, versus 46%, 28%, 15%, and 37% of the other pro-Bush groups.

The Upbeats and the Disaffecteds (called "center groups" by the Pew researchers) both shifted heavily from Democratic party identification (I.D.) in 1994 (48% and 51%) to Republican party I.D. in 2005 (73% and 60%). This seemed ominous for the Democrats, but

Bush over-reached militarily and Iraq collapsed in a civil war. The 2006 mid-term elections showed a swing back to the Democrats. The skilled campaigning and fundraising of the Democrats in 2008, combined with the impact of the recession (depression?) in the last quarter just before the election, helped to push Obama to victory. The anti-Bush sentiment no doubt also helped, since McCain and Bush were seen by many as joined at the hip.

IV. SUNNINESS, DEPRESSION, OR DENIAL?

If I am correct that widespread poor parenting (coldness, punitiveness, and lability, as well as more severe forms of abuse, all of which can cause emotional trauma), can create a social character in children that makes them more likely as adults to seek leadership from candidates whose character and behavior toward them is similar to the character and behavior of their abusive parents, then how do we explain the "sunniness" of the lower income Upbeats and others who voted for Bush? What happens to the anger generated by the "loss of self" demonstrated in the case histories cited by Alice Miller and Arno Gruen? How do we explain the "sunny" or "upbeat" vote of the poor, the minorities, and the elderly in the Bush camp?

First of all, the anger of the abused children, it should be remembered, was typically not directed against their parents, but against the self, and later against out-groups (minorities, the "enemy," etc.). They tried to hold onto an image of the "good parent" despite frequent physical violence and destructive verbal disparagement. The very young abused child, in particular, has nowhere else to turn but to the parents. The victim tends to identify with the aggressor, as in the Nazi death camps previously discussed (Bettelheim, 1943). A pitiful picture is presented of a child or adult craving affection so badly that he or she must preserve the false image of a nurturing and protecting parent. Bush posed as a decisive protector of Americans against Osama bin Laden, then against Saddam Hussain and "weapons of mass destruction," later against a "global war on terror" and, after that, with the help of the Republican wordsmiths, by a "global struggle against violent extremism." (That Defense Secretary Donald H. Rumsfeld, General

Richard B. Myers, and possibly Karen Hughes were behind this very temporary change in wording suggests that some in the administration wanted to stop the war rhetoric, withdraw troops from Iraq, and declare "victory" just in time for the mid-term elections. Hence the pressure for an Iraqi constitution, regardless of unresolved issues.) [See Schmitt, 2005.]

The anger of individuals in the case histories of the abused and neglected, including the anger of Adolf Hitler, was directed away from parents and against the self or against minorities and out-groups. This hatred was channeled by the Bush administration against abortion, gays, and Muslims. (Bush foolishly used the words "*crusade* against terror" in one of his speeches, but quickly dropped this phrase after an international hue and cry, because of its racist and historical connotations, namely Christians versus Muslims. Numerous references are now made to a mysterious Muslim goal of "re-establishing the Caliphate." This suggests that the Muslims have their own "crusade.")

The "family values" are code concepts for the underlying race and religious prejudice, which slips out when the more extreme right misspeaks. (Examples are Lee Atwater suggesting the substitution of code words like "states rights" and "forced busing" and even "cutting taxes" for the former non-code word "nigger." More recently, former education secretary Bill Bennett said that if you wanted to reduce the crime rate, "you could abort every black baby in this country.")

Authority figures are not blamed (just as the parents of the abused are not blamed for their abuses). Authoritarian leaders and politicians, big business and its CEOs, are all deemed innocent. This is despite the indictment of the CEOs of Enron, WorldCom, and others.

The propensity for a sunny outlook despite adversity is often made the butt of jokes. Two of many come to mind. Alfred Kinsey is giving a lecture on sex and the American male. At the conclusion, he asks his audience how many have intercourse several times a day. A few raise their hands. Then he asks how many have intercourse once a day, once a week, once a month, and once a year. Each time a few hands go up. Then he asks if there is anyone in the audience who has sex less than once a year. A little old man in the back row raises his hand. "And how often do you have sex?" asks Kinsey. "Once every twenty-five years," says the man. "Then why are you smiling?" asks Kinsey. "Because tonight's the night!"

A second joke involves troubled parents who have twin boys. One child is an incurable pessimist, and the other a confirmed optimist. The parents decide to challenge their children's attitudes. At Christmas, they lock the little pessimist in a room with a magnificent set of electric trains. After an hour they open the door. The child is crying. "I'm worried that there will be a short circuit, and the house will burn down with all of us in it." They turn to the other boy, who has been locked in a room for an hour with a pile of horse manure. Surely he can't be happy about that present. Somehow the little pessimist has found a shovel and shoveled almost all the manure from one side of the room to the other side. "Why are you so happy?" asks the father. He replies "Daddy, with all this manure around, there must be a rocking horse somewhere!"

Why are so many poor and middle-income people smiling? Why are so many Americans sure there is a rocking-horse underneath the manure? So many pundits have asked, Where is the anger?" Psychologists and psychiatrists have used the term "smiling depression" to describe the type of patient who maintains a cheerful façade but is really hiding a depressive state. Part of our national character prescribes a stiff upper lip, or even a smile, when under stress. An article by Revkin (2005) found that objective measures of well-being (gross domestic product, income) do not always correlate with subjective measures of "happiness." Revkin mentions a Harvard study that asked subjects to choose between earning $50,000 a year in a society where salaries averaged $25,000, or earning $100,000 where the average was $200,000. About half the subjects chose to be "half as prosperous but richer than their neighbors." The level of satisfaction is proportional to "relative deprivation," a term used by Stouffer (1949). Soldiers in World War II had levels of satisfaction or dissatisfaction relative to their position vis-à-vis others in their platoon, company, or battalion. For example, a married man overseas, being away from his wife, felt more deprived than single soldiers in the same outfit, who could seek female companionship with impunity (without guilt?) during leaves or breaks in action overseas. Similarly, if your neighbor has a bigger house or better car, you may feel *relatively* deprived.

Revkin discusses two findings relevant to our question about "sunniness." While the U.S. median income has risen between 1974 and 2003, from below $40,000 to above that figure (about $50,000), there has been no concomitant increase in reported happiness over those years, according to National Opinion Research Center surveys. In this study, people in the United States didn't report more happiness with increased income. (Since these 2003 figures may not have been adjusted for inflation, the lack of increased cheerfulness is understandable.)

In a second study (Inglehart, 1999, and data from 2000 and 2005 surveys) wealth (GNP, or Gross National Product, per capita) was plotted against an eight point scale (−2, −1, 0, 1, 2, 3, 4, 5) of reported happiness, by countries worldwide. (GNP per capita tells us what part of the GNP each person would get if the GNP were divided equally.) At the $15,000 to $30,000 level, most countries fell between 2 and 4, the happier end of the scale. These were typically the Scandinavian countries, the British isles and former possessions, the United States (at 3.5) and European countries (Austria, Germany, Belgium, France, Spain, Italy) and Israel and Japan. Since people in these countries are fairly well-to-do compared with those in other nations, one could expect that they would be happier. Here money makes the mare smile

In contrast, in the $0 to $15,000 GNP per capita range, there are two distinct groups of countries. At the unhappy end, which is our expected result—lack of money equals unhappiness—are African countries (Uganda, Tanzania, Egypt, and Zimbabwe), Eastern European and Balkan countries (Hungary, Estonia, Belarus, Lithuania, Bulgaria, Romania, Albania, Georgia, Moldova) and down at the unhappiest level, Indonesia, Russia, and Ukraine. (Later on, we'll see that Ukraine is second only to the United States in high rates of mental disorder!)

In the poor but happy group there was a predominance of Latin American or Spanish speaking countries (Puerto Rico, Mexico, El Salvador, Colombia, Venezuela, Argentina, Chile, Brazil, Uruguay,

Dominican Republic, and Peru). Others were Nigeria, Saudi Arabia, Vietnam, Taiwan, China, Iran, and Turkey. Are we looking at differences in social character here? Are Latins really happier, and is their childhood experience more positive than those in the poor-unhappy quadrant? Or are we being deceived by differences in expression of pain and sorrow? Are there more smiling depressions in the poor-but-sunny group? If cultural differences play a large part in expressions of strain (depression, anxiety, anger) then we would expect the old-line Protestants to be less apt to admit to unhappiness. We can't tell from these data, but the British-U.S. wealthy and happy nations might possibly contain more of the smiling depressions and denials.

If Hispanics living in their Latin-American countries are prone to sunniness, despite low income, what happens to them when they emigrate to the United States? Do they maintain that sunniness in the face of adversity? Do they fare so much better economically after migration that they have reason to maintain their sunniness? Or do they suffer from the "relative deprivation" of being little fish in a big pond after migrating? *If they remain happy, they will be more likely to vote for the GOP. If they feel deprived by comparison with non-Hispanics, they are likely to vote Democratic.* In fact, in 2008, there was a big shift of Hispanic votes to the Democrats. This was felt by some experts to be due to the GOP anti-immigrant campaign. Of great interest would be an examination of the happiness of Hispanic immigrants of the first and second generation, to see if they are preselected for happiness or depression. The first generation can migrate because they are troubled, deprived, or persecuted, or, on the contrary, because they have been more successful and organized than their neighbors in the home country. The Puritans, European Jews, Armenians, and some Argentineans and other Latins have migrated due to persecution. Since the Hispanic population has already outpaced the black population, its vote is crucial to the resurgence of the Democrats. The Pew Research Center probably has the ethnic, generational, and "happiness" data, as well as the 2004 vote, to look at cross-tabulations for answers to these questions.

Social character is part nature (biological endowment and temperament) and part nurture (the physical and social environment, especially parental behavior). So not all Democrats are born with a genetic tendency to depression, and not all Republicans are happy and upbeat (except when they are controlling all three branches of the government). Nor are all Democrats raised by supportive (the opposition would say "permissive") parents, and not all Republicans have had authoritarian parents. There is, however, enough prevalence of abuse and poor parenting to create and maintain a widespread social character that seeks strong authority in these times of stress and rapid social change, and this will exacerbate the shift to the right. The Democratic victory in 2008 notwithstanding, the laws of the land subverted by Cheney, Gonzales, and Yoo and others will cast a shadow over our country for a long time, abetted by a conservative Supreme Court.

I say "exacerbate," since the shift to the right has been going on since the Johnson administration. The "solid South" changed from Democratic to heavily Republican after Johnson led the Democratic Party in support of civil rights legislation. Another major factor has been increased income.

> Since union rolls began shrinking in the 1950's, the income of the typical household has more than doubled, even after inflation is taken into account. Luxuries once restricted to the rich; cross-country airplane travel, home movies, a bedroom for every child— are working-class staples. (Leonhardt, 2005).

Leonhardt points out that these increases in income were due to factors that are unlikely to repeat (as we have seen in the Bush years.) First, women entered the workforce in huge numbers, so that families with two earners often had nearly double the income. Second, there was a tremendous financial bubble in the nineties, which burst. This makes it unlikely that there will be significant pay increases of the same magnitude in the near future. The financial meltdown of 2007–08 has given the *coup-de-grace* to any broad income increases in the near future.

How has the war in Iraq encouraged the expression of the authoritarian social character? It has, by its failure to forcefully "democratize" a tribal nation (previously held together by genocide and torture) created a breeding ground and model for terrorism. This violence has spread to Spain, England, Egypt, and Bali where trains, subways, buses, and hotels were blown up. Taking advantage of the fear caused by the 9/11 attack, and by using false information about "weapons of mass destruction," the *administration in fact created and aggravated the very fears that they hoped would keep the GOP in power.* It was this fear, in part, that prompted many in 2004 to vote for Bush "the warrior" rather than Kerry, who was smeared as the "waffler."

The authoritarian character seeks an authoritarian leader in times of stress and rapid social change. In this case, the leader acted to increase the stress on the average American through fear, lies, and legislation that favored the few over the many. Globalization and outsourcing are producing rapid changes in the economy and in the job market. Seeking a "strong" leader, one who never changes his mind, never admits a mistake, and seemed to have simple and understandable goals (cut taxes, keep government small, fight terror) was the choice of a fearful and bewildered person who was probably brought up in a cold, punitive, labile, over-demanding, or controlling family.

V. SUGGESTIONS FOR A PROGRESSIVE POLICY

Despite the Obama/Democratic victory in 2008, if we don't want to see a dictatorship eventually develop in this country, we had better address the fears and insecurities of the great mass of people, including the poor, the working class, and the middle class. This means (not necessarily in order of importance):

- Getting out of Iraq.
- No more preemptive wars.
- Stopping all forms of torture and humiliation of prisoners, at home and abroad. This is morally wrong, and stopping it will help to protect our troops from the same abuses by others.

- Avoiding unilateralism, and helping the United Nations create an adequate independent peacekeeping force.
- Starting another "war on poverty" to lift up the bottom third of the nation with a "safety net": a living wage, decent housing, child care for working mothers, and access to first-rate medical care.
- Cutting down on outsourcing by offering tax breaks for businesses that keep jobs at home.
- Massive infusion of funds into public education, to develop a technical base and skills to compete internationally. Scholarship programs should be enlarged at private as well as public colleges and graduate schools.
- De-privatization of medical insurance and care, with the government as the sole insurer. This is the "single payer system," a much more desirable plan than the current system, that would save more money than the "public option." The "public option" calls for government and private insurance to compete, but the insurance and drug companies don't want *any* competition. In effect, Obama's reneging on the "public option," is two steps away from the single payer plan used by most of the advanced industrial countries. (Give us all the same quality of care that our President and members of Congress enjoy.)
- Control of drug costs, so that prices are comparable to overseas prices. Allowing prescription drug importation, with controls.
- Targeted funding for protection against terrorism based on actual risk, rather than pork-barrel distribution.
- Reinstatement of civil rights. Curtailment of most of the Patriot Act, especially the portions that invade our privacy, search our libraries, our medical and Internet records. Reinstatement of *habeas corpus*, the right to trial, for legal representation, and access to the evidence against you.
- Maintenance of Social Security, by developing a surplus instead of a deficit of billions.

- Funding development of new high-school curricula that will teach good parenting, based on thousands of studies of families and children already published.
- Prenatal, perinatal, and pediatric care, as well as maternal drug-treatment programs are also needed to avoid early physical damage to children.
- Making abortion available to avoid a national burden of unwanted children who are most likely to be abused, neglected, or abandoned.
- Making contraception available to avoid one million annual abortions. This includes "morning after" medication.
- Federal funding of stem-cell research, full scale, with the hope of fighting diseases such as Alzheimer's, Parkinson's, various dementias, and the potential repair of various tissues, such as the heart, brain, spinal cord, liver, etc. Our nation is being "left behind" in this area.
- Creation of a permanent Commission to Enforce the Separation of Church and State, with lay and clerical members. This would stop the campaign to teach "intelligent design" which attempts to refute Darwinian theory and could eventually undermine our international standing in science and technology.
- Reversing the Bush administration's policy of ravaging the environment in favor of logging, mining, and drilling for oil. Making sure that "clean air" programs really clean the air, by cutting down on mercury, arsenic, sulfur dioxide, and other pollutants in factory emissions; by seeking alternate fuels reduce carbon dioxide emissions that contribute to global warming. Helping the U.S. auto industry compete with foreign car manufacturers through Federal funding of hybrid models, which are the wave of the future. Funding of alternate energy sources. Strive for energy independence.

This list may seem long, but it consists chiefly of stopping wars, controlling terrorism, alleviating poverty, protecting the environment, making quality education accessible, providing health care, lowering abortions via contraception (emphasis on lowering the abortion rate), providing training for parenting, and restoring civil rights and privacy. It is different in only minor ways from the present Democratic platform espoused by Barack Obama.

Jim Wallis, the author of *God's Politics: Why the Right Gets It Wrong, and the Left Doesn't Get It* (Wallis, 2005), focuses on six areas of policy where he thinks the Democrats can find common ground with Republicans. (Do the Democrats really want to base their policy on finding common ground with the GOP? Are the differences too great to bridge? Did Obama's attempts at bipartisanship persuade any of the House Republicans to vote for his economic stimulus bill?) His point, well taken, is that you have to decide on your message and that the "framing" (language, presentation) of that message, which seemed to preoccupy some Democrats, will take care of itself (or at least grow out of the policy vision).

Wallis covers many minor or subsidiary issues, but his main focus is on poverty, the environment, abortion, supporting parents in their childrearing function, renouncing claims to oil or military bases in Iraq, and establishment of an International Criminal Court and an international military force to intervene, for example, in Darfur. I agree wholeheartedly with these choices, but disagree when he suggests how he would implement some of them. For example, he would "support reasonable restrictions on abortion, like parental notification for minors." In some cases this is not a reasonable restriction, since parents might force their daughter to carry an unwanted child to term. The interest of the parents is then put before the interest of the daughter. There is also more than a hint of censorship in his suggestion that "...the Democrats...need to adopt serious pro-family policies, including some that defend children against Hollywood sleaze and Internet pornography" (ibid.). Who will determine what is sleaze and what is a legitimate film?

Almost every policy has its pros and cons, depending on where you stand. If you protect children too vigorously, you are inhibiting freedom of speech. If you over-react to terrorism, you sacrifice civil liberties. The United States made this sacrifice after 9/11 and the Patriot Act. The British, until now zealous guardians of civil rights, have started to ban meetings in certain mosques with jihadist leanings, and have closed down some inflammatory Muslim newspapers since the bombing of London subways and buses.

On August 8, 2005, the *New York Times* printed eight letters to the editor in reaction to Wallis's Op-Ed piece. Two of them struck me as right to the point. Mark Post wrote, "Democrats can join the battle" (the ideological struggle with the Republicans) "with equal vigor, offering a real, radical alternative, or they can lay down their arms. Republican lite is not going to bring voters to the booths in 2008 any more than it did in 2004 or 2000." Andrew T. Jacobs wrote, "But Mr. Wallis's agenda, whatever its short-term utility, doesn't fit the bill. It is little more than a series of old left-wing religious ideas with a few accommodations to the right thrown in." Letter-writers Post and Jacobs both want a new radical or progressive policy vision for the Democrats, but due to space limitations, they couldn't make any concrete suggestions. It is very difficult not to sound "Republican lite," since the GOP has co-opted most of the Democrat's historical positions, at least rhetorically. Obama avoided this trap to some extent, by focusing on "change we can believe in." This emphasis on change (used historically by the challenger to the incumbent in most campaigns) without being too specific about change *to what policies*, bypasses the problem of satisfying the many conflicting interest groups.

VI. A COMPACT COMPREHENSIVE POLICY FRAMEWORK

The policy suggestions I have made above are piecemeal, and are not welded into an overall framework, such as:

PROTECTION FROM: Poverty, War, Terrorism, State-sponsored Religion, and Prejudice.

PROTECTION OF: Health, Jobs, Education, the Environment, Civil Rights and Religion. (This would echo the distinction made between "freedom from" and "freedom to," which is reminiscent of the Roosevelt era.)

Most items on this list are not centrist. They are not GOP-copycat goals. They are not meant to keep the Democrats as Tweedledum to the GOP's Tweedledee. They are not all easy to "frame" so that they will appeal to the extreme right, or to evangelicals. They appeal, I think, to the left and even to the center, which, according to recent polls, was fed up with the war; exacerbation of people's fears, the precarious economy; runaway gasoline, heating oil, and natural gas prices; and the Bush administration's lack of concern for the common man.

This new platform, which is almost identical to that of Obama, helped to get the Democrats back in the running. Before the election, Bush's attempt to privatize Social Security failed (as he admitted in his 2006 State of the Union address to thunderous Democrat applause) despite his thumping the drums. Nancy Reagan, a Republican stalwart, pleaded for more federal money for new lines of stem cells (once her husband contracted Alzheimer's disease). Bill Frist, who seemed to toe the evangelical-right line on all issues, suddenly came out in support of stem-cell research. Whether it was his physician's conscience or a bid for the middle in the presidential race, he did it.

Bush overreached in his second term. (See the Timeline.) He got bad ratings on Iraq as more of our soldiers died. The apparent leak by Karl Rove (via Scooter Libby to Bob Novak) that resulted in the "outing" of Valerie Plame embarrassed Bush. It is clear that his administration played "dirty tricks" just as the Nixon gang of Watergate "plumbers" did. The unconscionable delay in getting help to the victims of hurricane Katrina and the obvious lack of preparedness of the administration for any major catastrophe pushed Bush's approval ratings way down: from the start of his second term till mid-December 2008, his ratings went from 50% to 24%.

The indictment of Tom DeLay, the former House Majority Leader, on charges of money laundering of campaign funds, with its revelations of corruption and cronyism, also hurt the GOP. Former Senate majority leader Bill Frist's "insider" dumping of his family stock called his honesty into question.

Jack Abramoff, the Washington, D.C. "super-lobbyist," pleaded guilty to conspiracy, fraud, and tax evasion. His plea-bargain with the Justice Department prosecutors got him seventy months in jail (five years and ten months; March 29, 2006). His testimony cast a shadow on at least a half-dozen senators and representatives.

Abramoff has been a Republican operative, so the onus fell heavily on the GOP (see Timeline).

Some of the Republicans who have received campaign funds (or gifts) from Abramoff or his clients, many of whom have already given his questionable contributions back to various charities, are Senators John Thune (S. Dakota), Conrad Burns (Montana), Mitch McConnell (Kentucky), George Allen (Virginia), and Representatives Bill Ney (Ohio), John Doolittle (California), J. Dennis Hastert (Illinois, House Speaker), Jo Ann Davis (Virginia), and Tom DeLay (Texas, former House Speaker). Even President Bush announced (through his mouthpieces) that he donated a $6,000 contribution from Abramoff to charity.

In another GOP debacle, a storm of protest arose over the revelation that soon after 9/11, Bush & Co. secretly decided to bypass judicial review and the issuing of a court order when they felt a wiretap was needed for surveillance of U.S. citizens making foreign phone calls. The White House response to this outcry was to demand an investigation of the "leak," rather than to correct this appalling invasion of privacy. Under the protection of the Patriot Act, not only phone calls, but e-mail, the Internet, and library records can be searched. In 2007, Attorney General Alberto Gonzales, who created the illegal rationale for the Patriot Act, was forced to resign. This was triggered by his involvement in the firing of seven U.S. Attorneys, not on the basis of their competence, but because they were *persona non grata* with the White House. (See Timeline.)

Andrew Kohut and Peter Hoey (Kohut, 2005) said "…Mr. Bush's fall in public esteem reflects discontent in a number of areas: Americans are unhappy about economic conditions, the war in Iraq, Washington's intervention in the case of Terri Schiavo and general partisan bickering." Their accompanying chart shows presidential approval ratings, top public concerns, and economic indicators for comparable time periods of the Nixon, Reagan, Clinton, and G. W. Bush administrations. Dubya's record is well below those of his predecessors in all categories.

Chapter Five
The Five Faces of George W. Bush

The way that politicians get elected is by appealing to their natural base. When that base isn't large enough to get them into power, they must broaden their appeal. Bill Clinton did this by moving to the center. Liberal Democrats supported him, but when he promised that he would "change Welfare as we know it," there was dismay in the liberal camp. Obama "reached across the aisle" to attract dissatisfied Republicans and independents. All politicians do it.

To get into power, dictators have appealed to a very broad spectrum of the population. Hitler had a message for the average man, promising jobs and a rebuilding of Germany into a "thousand-year *Reich*." The Versailles Treaty and its reparations exacerbated the economic depression after World War I. Hitler also appealed to big business (I.G. Farben and Krupp) by building up a war industry. His image was a mixture of the bitter unemployed war veteran, a failed artist turned house-painter, and a strong man of simple radical ideas repeated incessantly. Mussolini started out as a socialist, combined this with a Roman revivalist theme, and ended up as a Fascist dictator.

Offering "something for everyone" is the best way of getting elected. Once in power, the leader can keep promising most of what he or she held out as bait before the elections, but doesn't need to fulfill the promises that don't suit his or her covert agenda. This is what I have reviewed previously—how Bush "talked the talk" on education, clean air, and medical care, but didn't "walk the walk." In other words, he failed to fund, or only partially funded, the programs that he found were secondary to his overall plans. What he funded or supported through legislation were the war in Iraq (and the industries that benefited from it), the "war on terror" (funds for Homeland Security were doled out primarily to "friendly" states, not to those that most needed protection); the oil, mining, and lumber industries, and tax cuts for the wealthy. (However, his attempt to privatize Social Security failed.)

The picture of Bush the politician, then, is a combination of what his personality and ideology really are, how his propagandists, public relations doctors (Karl Rove, Karen Hughes) and various spinmeisters painted him, and the unconscious needs of the public (*especially the people's need to resolve the issue of an uncaring parent/leader*). A brief review of the various faces he presented may help explain how he got elected (especially the second time).

I. THE STRONG MAN

Bush is standing on the flight deck of the U.S.S. *Abraham Lincoln* aircraft carrier on May 2, 2003, dressed in a green Air Force flight jacket. A banner behind Bush declared "Mission Accomplished" in Iraq (a Guinness World's record-breaking premature announcement). Although he never saw combat, and did not serve overseas, Bush was trained as a pilot. His speeches have shown an aggressive "tough guy" stance. Discussing the insurgents in Iraq, he said "Bring 'em on." He also used the words "crusade" to describe our role in Iraq, which was a big mistake since it inflamed Muslim sensibilities.

George W. has been photographed ("photo ops") cutting the brush on his ranch, and wearing the appropriate Western outfit. This is his John Wayne image which has been heavily promoted. He is a farmer, a cowboy, and a rancher, and thus partakes of the glories of the West (as in "Western" movies.)

II. THE FAILURE, BORN AGAIN

One of the American Dreams is the re-creation of the self. Every New Year's Day brings resolutions to lose weight, write the Great American Novel, spend more time with the children, or cut loose from that dead-end job and get a new (more creative) career. Contrary to F. Scott Fitzgerald's dictum, there *are* often "second acts" in America.

The sinner redeemed and the success of the former loser are recurrent themes in religion, fiction, and folk tales. Bush managed (albeit with constant help from his family's circle of powerful friends) to re-create himself. From a partying college student with mediocre grades, to an Army Air Force Reserve pilot who was AWOL (absent without leave) in order to campaign, he managed to squeak by. On the way, he was arrested for driving while intoxicated (DWI). He failed at several business opportunities that were handed to him. Then, at least according to his official biographers, he became a born-again Christian. He gave up drinking (at least in excess) and partying, married, and became governor of Texas, then President of the United States.

In a country where the "star system" predominates, only a few are winners, and most of us non-stars are (by default) to some degree losers. This is the zero-sum game of the American Dream. The losers love to see a former loser become a winner. That gives them hope. They can identify with a guy who was really a "ne'er-do-well" in a family of outstanding successes. ("I'm a loser, but George W. gets my vote. If he can pull it off, maybe I can some day—by winning on the horses, the lottery, or in Las Vegas, or perhaps a big break in the stock market?")

The path from loser to winner gives Bush a connection to the common man. He is Everyman. Like Christ, Buddha, Gandhi, and other leaders, he turned away from the temptations of the flesh and either found God or became God. The path from sin through renunciation to redemption is a source of power. If you renounce worldly pleasures, as clergy in many religions do (no sex, drinking, or even no eating for short periods of time) you gain sympathy and power with the masses. You have sacrificed what they are loath to give up. Gandhi fasted to gain power. Robert K. Merton chronicled the success of Kate Smith, a popular overweight singer, who sang without eating for up to eighteen consecutive hours on radio many times during World War II, and sold six hundred million dollars worth of war bonds.

George W. Bush has often been labeled the "prodigal son," after the parable in Luke 15:11–32. A father has two sons, and divides his fortune between them. One goes off to a foreign land, and wastes his fortune on drink and prostitutes. Broke and hungry, he returns home. His father forgives him and embraces him, since he was considered dead but is "born again." Daddy kills the "fatted calf" to celebrate his son's return. The parallel is surprisingly close. George W., the sinner, repents, becomes a "born again" Christian, and wins his father's approval by becoming Governor of Texas and then president. (The only apparent divergence between the two tales is that Jeb Bush, unlike the brother in the parable, presumably did not complain that despite all the hard work *he* had done, George W. got the big rewards, including the fatted calf of the presidency.)

III   THE MOUTHPIECE OF GOD

Religious leaders speak not for themselves, but for God. They are merely the Charlie McCarthy of God the Ventriloquist (apologies to the late Edgar Bergen). When asked if he had consulted his father before deciding to invade Iraq, George W. said that he had consulted a "higher authority!" His decisions were apparently made by a direct Internet connection to the Heavenly Father. His own father had stopped short of taking Baghdad and capturing Saddam Hussein during "Operation Desert Storm." The son would show Dad who was the more macho man. While we know that he consulted with Karl Rove, Dick Cheney, Karen Hughes, Condoleeza Rice, and others in the inner circle, his appeal to the religious right was bolstered by his (apparent) reliance on faith rather than on consultation when making decisions. Barack Obama has promised to listen to his cabinet when making decisions.

IV. THE GOOD FELLA

Bush is known for his "hail fellow well met" façade. He (like many politicians) is a glad-hander. The extrovert is able to reach out to people, shake their hands, kiss their babies, even cry on occasion. The introverts (Stevenson, Gore, Kerry?) are more cerebral, more private, and perhaps a bit withdrawn. Bush is known for having a nickname for each of his close associates. He liked to tell jokes (which apparently fell flat compared with the scripted jokes told by Laura Bush at a famous press meeting.) His persona (or façade) is a "Joe Six-Pack" who seems as if he could hoist a few beers with the guys in the Budweiser ads. (Of course, he can't, since he's a recovered alcoholic.)

This harmless, affable presentation of self hides the willful strong-man. Just when we thought he was Karl Rove's or Dick Cheney's puppet, he took a firm stand against his advisers. Between July and August 2005, the policy line seemed to be changing. The "war on terror" was shifting to the "global struggle against violent extremism." When Donald Rumsfeld and others used the new terminology, implying that non-military strategies (diplomacy?) could be helpful, they were publicly rebutted by Bush, who used the phrase "war on terror" five times in a speech. Rumsfeld quickly kowtowed to the boss, saying publicly "Make no mistake about it; we are in a war on terror." This shifting from the "good fella" to the "strong man" is part and parcel of Bush's will-o'-the-wisp illusory character. He could be God's mouthpiece one minute, and the next minute be beating the war drums (the "axis of evil," or " bring 'em on").

V. THE UNCARING PARENT

This is not a face that Bush presented intentionally to the public through speeches and photo-ops. Simply by hewing to the radical right-wing Republican agenda, he has shown how little he and his cohorts care about the man in the street, the average American. That he himself is indifferent to the needs of the poor and middle class is clear. His unconscionable delay (four days) in responding personally to the catastrophic damage of Hurricane Katrina supports this conclusion. The initial puny offer of fifteen million dollars for relief of victims of the tsunami in the Indian Ocean is an example of personal and governmental stinginess. The criticism from Jan Engelund, United Nations Undersecretary General for Humanitarian Affairs, of the "stingy" contributions from rich nations prompted a quick raising of U.S. relief funds to thirty-five million, and it later increased geometrically.

We don't have much evidence that Barbara Bush was an uncaring parent, but she has a patrician attitude toward the masses that George W. seems to have internalized.

There is no need to document, ad nauseam, the indifference of Bush and his administration to the needs of the poor and the middle class as well. His didn't practice "benign neglect," as Daniel Patrick Moynihan suggested in a memo to President Nixon. ("The issue of race could benefit from a period of benign neglect.") Bush's "compassionate conservatism" was really a cover for *malign* neglect.

This very consistent bias in favor of the rich over the poor seems to be a truism. The Bible says that this has been a fact throughout history. "Unto every one that hath shall be given, and he shall have abundance: but from him that hath not shall be taken away even that which he hath" (Matthew, 25:29). As a rich, faithful born-again Christian, Bush should have been aware that "It is easier for a camel to go through the eye of a needle, than for a rich man to enter into the kingdom of God (Matthew, 19:24).

A major hypothesis of this book is that uncaring, neglectful, or abusive parents severely damage their children, and that this makes them lose their autonomy and vote for authoritarian leaders when they are adults. These parents are focused on their own needs, and they neither satisfy nor understand the needs of their progeny. This is called narcissistic parenting. As Alice Miller and Arno Gruen have shown, the children of abusive or neglectful parents suffer from a loss of their real self, and adopt a false self in order to hang on to an image of loving parents. This in turn creates anger over the loss, which is eventually directed at out-groups (or against the self). My research, and that of many others, has shown that mental disorder from the very mild to severe can result from such early experience. Miller and Gruen both say that *this uncaring parenting can lead to political conservatism, and even to fascism.*

Bush was the leader of the most powerful country in the world. As such, he was a father figure (though a flawed one). The people he led are, in a deep sense, his "children." This is more than a mere figure of speech. At least half of the country looked to him for protection, stability, and well-being (the other half having given up hope that he would change his ways). Those protective and fostering functions are what we normally expect of a president. Since he did not provide that protection, since our country is riven by conflict, and since jobs, health care, education, food, and shelter are lacking for at least a fifth of the nation, he can be considered a neglectful and uncaring parent. How then could some of those least protected and cared for still vote for him? Those who voted against their own economic interests were described in detail in Chapter Three. *My contention is that they unconsciously tried to preserve that image of a good father or mother (or a good president) which they learned to do despite neglect and abuse at their parents' hands during childhood.*

It is now common knowledge, gained from the clinical practice of psychiatrists, psychologists, and social workers, that adult patients tend to choose as marital or sexual partners people who in some way resemble one or both of their own parents as an attempt to resolve some unresolved issues they had with their parents. To further work on and *resolve* these issues, they choose partners who are more likely to exhibit the uncaring, domineering, or abusive behavior of their parent(s).

This mechanism operates in a broad way, so that the poor or the middle class person who experienced uncaring parents may choose the uncaring candidate without consciously thinking of how that candidate would act upon specific political and economic issues that directly affect him or her. He may actually seek the uncaring figure because it is familiar, and because he has learned to make excuses for his early oppressor(s) to preserve the image of the "loving parent."

Despite the current economic and political issues, the preservation of the caring leader/parent must be preserved. When a person was out of a job, she may have wished to preserve her image of Bush as a kindly provider, even though the Bush administration lost many jobs, and did not give businesses tax breaks to prevent outsourcing. She may have blamed herself for her job loss, or minorities and immigrants for taking her job away.

When a teenager wanted to go to college but couldn't afford it, he didn't blame Bush or the powers that be. Bush, just like his father, let him down. Since he was too dependent and scared to fight against his neglectful or abusive father, whose image he preserved as loving, he voted for Bush. He might blame himself, or out-groups.

When a woman who had uncaring parents already had several children, but was unable to pay for an abortion, she may not have blamed Bush for trying to take away her right to choose. Instead she voted for him, holding him blameless, just as she protected her father's image.

What is missing in these people? It is *autonomy*, the ability to stand on your own two feet, and to assert yourself against an oppressive figure. This loss of the true self, the giving up of one's own needs to maintain the love of one's parents, starts in early childhood. If widespread, the authoritarian non-autonomous population may prepare us for slowly becoming a dictatorship, like Hitler's Germany or Mussolini's Italy. If you're used to defending the image of your parents as loving, despite their uncaring or even abusive behavior, then you'll defend the image of each successive uncaring leader.

That uncaring parent/leader is the *hidden* face of George W. Bush. This is an unconscious image in the back of the mind of the poorly parented voter. Bush didn't provide enough body armor for the troops in Iraq, but most of them still seemed to love him (at least his prescreened military audiences did).

On September 15, 2005, Bush spoke from New Orleans in the wake of Hurricane Katrina. "As all of us saw on television, there is also some deep, persistent poverty in this region as well. We have a duty to confront this poverty with bold action. So let us restore all that we have cherished from yesterday, and let us rise above the legacy of inequality." A *New York Times* editorial (anon., 2005) said:

> The Small Business Administration...has processed only a third of the 276,000 home loan applications it has received. And it has rejected a whopping eighty-

two percent of those . . .on the grounds that applicants didn't have high enough incomes or good enough credit ratings...As a result, well-off neighborhoods have received forty-seven percent of the loan approvals, while poverty-stricken ones have gotten seven percent.

Amazingly, Bush didn't suffer major political damage for these broken promises. He (or Karl Rove) thought a few trips to New Orleans and Houston, with staged photo-ops and more promises would make up for them. There was a brief hue and cry, but the public memory of such deceitfulness is short-lived, especially among his supporters.

Awareness or consciousness of being ignored or harmed by the President and his administration can vary greatly from almost total unconscious repression, through "middle knowledge" (Lifton, 1979), to full conscious awareness. This is similar to awareness of our own mortality. We cannot function very well if we are in constant conscious fear of death. The awareness of a harmful and dangerous presidency must be relegated to the level of repression or middle knowledge for those who have been victims of harm in childhood. For those already hurt by abuse and neglect, by cold, punitive, or labile parents, the leader's uncaring image must be put on a back burner. To acknowledge it would be too painful.

The uncaring parent "face" of Bush and the strict parent metaphor of Lakoff discussed in Chapter Three seem to fit neatly into Toennies' ideal types: *Gemeinschaft* (community) and *Gesellschaft* (society). [Are these not also metaphors?] In "community," the father dominates. The mother and children are subordinate and are considered his property. While Toennies considered community to be "warm" and society to be "cold," he was biased, having grown up in village life. The consensus of community left little room for multiculturalism, or for differing opinions within or outside the family.

The father in "society" is a weaker figure. He may be more nurturant (as in Lakoff's model), but he is also likely to be absent physically and emotionally, busy with work, and to cede his family decisions to "experts," such as pediatricians, psychotherapists, and teachers. This is parallel to his tendency to depend on the police and lawyers to defend his family and self rather than using his fists or a gun (as the "strict" fathers who support the National Rifle Association might recommend). "Society" (at least in the United States) is more youth and child-oriented than "community." In the traditional "community," the adult male and the old sage are the cynosures. The "community" seems to favor a gerontocracy, while "society" favors democracy (and bureaucracy). Then again, the cunning old sages have controlled our country during the Bush administration. Are the likes of Cheney, Rove, Rumsfeld, and various CEOs a good fit in our "society?" I think not.

Rather, these Paleolithic leaders and their conservative followers are like the appendix—a vestigial organ hanging on in the changing body politic. The *paterfamilias*, the *Haustyrran*, the John Wayne dad, are figures from the past "community," living on in the "society" of late monopoly capitalism, which itself has turned into globalism. Surrounded by rapid social change, conservatives strike back at homosexuality, abortion, teen and premarital sex, drugs, Welfare, environmentalism, multiculturalism, unions, tort laws, and gun control. "Permissiveness" is a special thorn in the side of the "strict" father, who is living in our more tolerant and relatively open society. (See Chapter One.)

The arguments for and against "Ferberizing" are an interesting example of the deep divide over the strict/nurturant parent dichotomy. Ferber (1986), in *Solve Your Child's Sleep Problems*, said that a child should be left to cry herself to sleep, to avoid having her creep into her parents' bed. This was another instance of "tough love." Some of the middle class took it up, and many found it heartbreaking. Again, these parents ceded their child-rearing decisions to an expert, an aspect of "society." Now Ferber has softened his position. You are allowed to have Junior in bed with you, if you wish. Doing so stops crying and makes nursing easier on Mom, who is usually half-awake during this recumbent procedure, as opposed to getting up and sitting in the rocking-chair.

The middle and working classes have switched positions on the strict/nurturant continuum over the last century. Working class parents used to be easy-going, nursing their kids for a year or two and toilet training them leisurely, although they tended to favor physical punishment over restrictions or denial of privileges. The middle class was strict in most of these areas. As noted before, nursing has become brief as more low-income mothers work outside the home. Other practices got stricter as well. Weaning and toilet training had to be speeded up. The middle class, following the advice in Dr. Spock's popular book, grew more permissive, and probably had more time to wean and toilet train.

The pitiful attempts of a child to preserve the image of a good parent, despite the most extreme abuse, were seen in the previously mentioned case histories of multiple personality disorder (now called "multiple identity disorder"). A recent case (2006) of child abuse ending in murder again illustrates this protective device. Nixmary Brown, age seven, was sexually abused, tied to a chair without food as punishment, and made to defecate in a box of pet litter. Previous to being beaten to death by her stepfather for eating some yogurt without permission and allegedly breaking a computer printer, she had been examined by a doctor. To explain her injuries, she told him that she had fallen out of bed! This lie probably helped to protect her image of him as a good father. Of course, her stepfather may have threatened her if she told the doctor the truth.

There is a hierarchy of failed fathers. Even those who are usually nurturant can occasionally be unwittingly rejecting or abusive. If your biological father fails you, perhaps your teacher or some other mentor will comfort and support you. If your mentor fails, then maybe your president will be a nurturant father. If, like Bush, your president fails to be compassionate, and is definitely more like the strict-uncaring-tough love type of father, to whom can you turn? Well, as billions have found throughout history, the poor, downtrodden, orphaned, starving, emotionally needy, and sick (without medical insurance coverage) can always turn to God. Now God is generally conceived in our culture as a nurturant father. The Lord's Prayer tells us that The Heavenly Father is forgiving ("forgive us our trespasses"), He is nurturant ("give us this day our daily bread"), and He is protective ("deliver us from evil"). Who takes the bad side of this mirror of our own fathers and leaders?

Why, it is the Devil himself! All the torture, punishment, and restrictions carried out by our own fathers and uncaring leaders are assigned to Satan. The Devil (he has at least fifty other names, attesting to his popularity) is the strict father. He allows us to preserve our image of a benevolent God, despite the fact that we are doomed to die, that we are surrounded by evil deeds: war, murder, torture, corruption, widespread slavery, and unlimited greed.

The gods (being a projection of family structure, as Freud [1957] would have it), are usually split into a good and bad father. The Persian gods of Zoroastrianism were Ahura Mazda, god of light, and Ahriman, god of darkness. (Is Ahriman behind the Iranian/ Persian striving for WMDs?) The Norse gods, among many others, reflect this split. Odin was the god of wisdom and magic, old, and generally a good guy. His blood brother, Loki, was the god of fire, a trickster, and a "forger of evil." Fire, evil, and hell are kissing cousins.

So God is the last resort of the mistreated, the underdog. If father failed you, and President Bush failed you, God may yet be your savior. But if God seems culpable and you don't blame your misfortunes on the Devil, then you may blame God and say, along with Jesus on the cross, "My God, my God, why hast thou forsaken me?" (Matthew 27:46) . For many (not just agnostics and atheists), the Supreme Father has failed to keep them from evil and the ultimate harm, death. Hence the illusion of immortality and heaven. If you can't ever die, and God will look after you in heaven, then God's good father image is still preserved.

Since W. took on the cloak of God and become his mouthpiece, it was hard to blame *him* for a preemptive war, poverty, loss of civil rights, or environmental damage. God had spoken through him, so we should blame God, and leave W. blameless. This is another case of "the dog ate my homework" but on a much larger scale.

VI.   THE TABULA RASA: BUSH AS A PROTECTIVE SCREEN

Bush actually was presented to us as at least five slightly overlapping but essentially independent beings: the strong man, the failure born again, the mouthpiece of God, the good fella, and the uncaring parent. This led to confusion on the part of voters, which made it possible to project onto him any or all of those images. The Bush voter could have voted for him because he would protect us from WMDs and terrorists (the strong man) while Kerry said it was wrong to be in Vietnam and eventually said so about Iraq. The religious person could vote for Bush's evangelical stance (anti-gay, anti-science, anti-abortion) and his claim to have had direct consultation with God. Others might have voted for the understandable "good fella," as opposed to what they were told was a complicated, waffling, "elitist" Kerry. (Both candidates could be labeled "elitist," since they both came from the upper-upper class, went to private schools and colleges, and were protected by the status and income of their families when growing up and on into adult life.)

The opposition, of course, does not agree with these images of Bush. They see him as stubborn, not very bright, relying too heavily on his subordinates, isolated from real events by his inner circle, a unilateral preemptive-war monger, a tool of big business, a captive of the evangelical right wing and big business (especially oil, lumber, and mining), a despoiler of the environment, and a champion of the rich and enemy of the poor and middle class. Obviously, slightly more people saw him as good rather than evil, since he won the popular vote (not in 2000, but in 2004). However, he won by a very small margin, and there was much skullduggery at the polls.

There was evidence of strong dissent within the GOP during his second term. Some evangelicals were pro-environment, seeing it as God's gift to man. The churches were also threatening to boycott industries that do business with Israel because they see the Palestinians as victims (and overlook the victimization of the Israelis). This flew in the face of the neo-con's policy within the administration, which strongly supported Israel. The delay in addressing the crisis of Hurricane Katrina cost George W. some political capital but didn't seem to bother his supporters. The explosion of terrorism, motivated in part by the invasion of Iraq, affected his job approval rating. After 9/11 (September 11, 2001) it was 88%, fell to 36% in October of 2005, hit 32% in March of 2007, and 24% in mid-December 2008, a new low for a second-term president. And the hurricane delay was not the only "delay" affecting Bush's mandate. The indictment of Tom DeLay, the House majority whip, opened a window into more cronyism and money-laundering. The investigation of Bill Frist, the former Senate majority leader, for dumping his shares in the family-owned business just before the share price tanked, clearly suggested the use of insider information, which is illegal. The appointment or selection of cronies at all levels of government and widely varying levels of competence (Condoleeza Rice, Karen Hughes, Michael D. Brown [former Under Secretary, Federal Emergency Management Agency] and especially Harriet Miers, Bush's former Supreme Court candidate) shook the confidence of even his ardent supporters. Laughably, the evangelical right attacked his choice of Harriet Miers not because of her lack of experience before the Supreme Court, but because she had not openly stated that she would vote against the *Roe v. Wade* decision on abortion! Last but not least, the indictment of Scooter Libby and the shadow cast on Karl Rove and Dick Cheney by the investigation of the Valerie Plame affair must have cost the GOP many votes in 2008. It had lost its former lock-step cohesiveness.

There were divisions in the Democratic camp too, which are discussed in the Pew Report. These divisions became more obvious during the 2008 presidential campaign, with some bitter exchanges between Obama and Hillary Clinton. After the 2008 elections, Obama has tried to heal that rift by appointing Hillary as Secretary of State, along with some of her former colleagues

What can we say about the faces of Obama? Certainly he is more of a caring father, except to the right-wing "tough love" crowd who see the safety net of the caring father as "spoiling the child," and as that GOP bug-bear, Big Government. He is loving and attentive to his two girls, Malia and Sasha, and this seems genuine, not just a series of photo ops.

He is definitely not the Bush "good fella" or Joe Six-Pack of the Budweiser ads because of his law professorship and Harvard degree. Yet, like Bush's work at the ranch, he gives off proletarian images, such as shooting hoops and one-and-one basketball.

He is not the prodigal son, for he has no known history of drinking and carousing. He has admitted to smoking pot, but that hardly puts him on a plane with George W. His rise from relatively humble beginnings is in sharp contrast to Dubya.

His relationship to his father is similar in some ways to that of Bill Clinton; early loss and absence. However, as far as we know, there was a good relationship with his grandparents, so there has been no direct combat with a male parent figure, as in so many of the militant leaders.

In contrast to Bush's "strong man" John Wayne pose, Obama, throughout his campaigning, and after assuming office, has played it cool and unflappable. There is no hint of "bring 'em on." His responses are measured, and if anything sometimes too unemotional. His strength is in his restraint. Even when rebuffed by the House and Senate Republicans, he kept his temper, but did express regrets that his efforts at bipartisanship had fallen on deaf GOP ears.

Far from being the "mouthpiece of God," as Bush often presented himself, Obama is quietly and deeply religious. His connection to Reverend Wright, though it cost him politically, has given him a strong religious grounding. He may have been raised in a religious household, though his grandparents, and especially his mother, do not sound like routine churchgoers, but more like people of profound Christian principles of charity and love of their fellow man.

All in all, it is hard to see Obama as an uncaring parent. His background of a Kenyan father, white Protestant grandparents and a white mother with ties to African and Asian husbands and a liberal outlook, makes it hard to identify with him directly. Not many people have such a diverse background. But it is possible to see in him an attractive, intelligent, youthful man, husband and father, an intellectual, an American Success, an African American, and someone who is protective. In those roles, and perhaps in others, he is a tabula rasa for the projections of the electorate.

VII. Summary

George W. Bush presented to the 2004 voters at least five different personalities, or images; the strong man, the failure-born again, the mouthpiece of God, the good fella ("Dubya?"), and the uncaring parent. This was confusing, because the images tend to be contradictory. That confusion allowed the voters to choose one or more of the four *conscious* images of George W. they favored, broadening his appeal to various factions: aggressive war-prone males; the religious right and "people of faith;" those who saw in him a fellow failure who made good; people who wanted a pleasant, simple, and understandable leader; and those who feared WMDs and "the enemy." Of course, those who were fully and consciously aware of Bush as uncaring and not meeting their needs voted for Kerry or Nader.

Chapter Six
Stress and Mental Disorder:
How They Helped Put Bush
Back in Office

Previous chapters have asked the question: "Why did many people vote against their economic self-interest in the 2004 presidential election, and how did the GOP campaign persuade the multitude?" In Chapter Four, the question of who voted for Bush despite their low family income (below $50,000) was discussed, and some of these voters' attitudes, opinions, and demographic characteristics were described. This was based on the Pew Research Center report *Beyond Red and Blue*. Chapter Five gave a brief description of the many faces Bush presented to the public and how these faces appealed to disparate groups of voters.

This chapter attempts to relate the various psychological and sociological concepts previously discussed to measures of stress, how stress is related to mental disorder, and how widespread mental disorder, especially anxiety and depression, could have put Bush back in office.

I. A Review of Factors and Hypotheses

Various factors previously suggested as underlying a shift of the political center of voters to the right in 2004 (and possibly since the 1930s):

1. Low self-esteem resulting in upward identification with powerful figures to avoid identification with lower and working classes and minorities. The shift of the South from Democrat to Republican started with Lyndon Johnson's support of the civil rights movement.

2. Exposure to labile, punitive, or cold parenting during childhood, which can lead the victims of such abuse to give up their original "true self" in favor of a "false self" that submits to all the parents' demands. Consideration of the child's individual needs is overlooked by narcissistic parents. This could prepare them to vote as adults for a president who had, in his first term, ignored their needs in a similar manner.

3. In times of rapid social change, economic retrenchment, and national conflict over values (such as occurred in Weimar Germany) people look to an authoritarian leader who promises to solve all their problems with simple oft-repeated promises. The year 2004 brought us to this state. The year 2008 increased these pressures. If not for the economic recession, especially in the fourth quarter, there might have been a victory for McCain. But many people saw McCain joined to Bush at the hip, with identical programs and values, so the Obama message of change was able to win. In the future, these same factors could bring an extreme right-wing leader and his or her party back into power.

4. There is a "longing for community" when people are living in an ever more complex "society." This longing was evident in Germany just before the rise of Hitler, and is evident in our country now. It seeks common values, strong authority in a leader, religious orientation, and communal belongingness.

II. STRESS AND STRAIN: THE MIDTOWN MANHATTAN STUDY OF MENTAL DISORDER

In previously discussing "What's in the Future for America?" I mentioned several "losses" that were present in Weimar Germany and most of which are evident in our country now. These were loss of identity (the "true self"); loss of self esteem on an individual and national basis; loss of love and affection (poor or uncaring parenting); loss of social supports (health, education, jobs); loss of control over life events (war, terrorism); and rapid social change (the changing family structure, high divorce rates, the struggle for racial and gender equality, value conflicts over shifts to more sexual freedom, gay marriage, etc.).

All of the above losses can be considered to be stresses. We frequently use the words emotional stress, tension, strain, and pressure to describe the feeling states associated with these losses and social conditions. In my book *Life Stress and Mental Health* (Langner and Michael, 1963), I discuss the use of an engineering model to clarify the meaning of the terms *stress* and *strain*. Stress is the force acting upon a structure or material, and includes tension, compression, and both shearing and torsion. Strain is the deformation of the structure or material subjected to the stress. When talking about people rather than materials, stress is the social and physical environment pressing on the individual, and strain is the deformation of the personality (the person's typical way of reacting). Many lay people and social scientists use stress as a synonym for mental disorder, which, to my way of thinking, leads to confusion. Mental disorder is the strain due to stress. It is the *reaction* to a stressor.

The Midtown Manhattan Study was one of the first epidemiological studies of mental disorder to look at a random sample of urban dwellers rather than at subjects preselected for treatment in various facilities. A two-hour long sixty-five page questionnaire was administered to 1,660 respondents ages twenty to fifty-nine in their homes. This was a 1.5% sample of the people living in "Midtown," which covered the East Side of Manhattan, New York City, from 59th street to 96th Street. In addition, a Treatment Census of all respondents looked at public and private treatment by psychiatrists, psychologists, and social workers, covering both in-patient and out-patient services and private therapists. (The 13% of the original sample who were non-respondents did not differ significantly in their rate of treatment from those who were respondents—that is, those who were interviewed.)

The content of the questionnaire can be divided into questions representing stress (childhood, adolescent, and adult environment, and demographics) and those measuring strain (symptomatology and role functioning).

The Stress Factors were based on factor analyses of different domains of early experience. The *pre-adult, or childhood stress factors* were: Parents' Poor Physical Health, Parents' Poor Mental Health, Childhood Economic Deprivation, Childhood Poor Physical Health, Childhood Broken Homes, Parents' Character Negatively Perceived, Parents' Quarrels, and Disagreement with Parents.

The adult stress factors are not clearly antecedent to the assessment of adult mental health. (It is also true that adult mental disorder can distort the reporting of childhood experiences, so that, to a lesser degree, even the adult reports of childhood experience bear a reciprocal relationship to adult mental disorder.) To avoid this circularity, I decided after the Midtown Study of adults to do a survey of mental disorder in children ages six to eighteen. The results of that study pertinent to this discussion were given in Chapter Three, Section V, starting with the Summary. It seems counterintuitive to exclude such adult life events as divorce, job loss, and physical illness from an attempt to establish causal relationships between stress and strain, but these life events and stresses in adults may be the *result* of mental disorder as well as causal factors. They then partake of both stress and strain.)

The *adult stress factors* were: Adult Poor Physical Health, Work Worries, Socioeconomic Status Worries, Poor Interpersonal Relations, Marital Worries, and Parental Worries.

The measures of mental disorder, or strain, were based on the exposure of psychiatrists to the symptoms elicited in each respondent's questionnaire. These were judgments of psychiatric impairment called Mental Health Ratings, rated on a scale of 0 to 7. Mental Health I was rated without knowledge of demographic variables, except for age and sex. Mental Health II exposed the raters to the demographic variables as well. This separation was undertaken to avoid circularity of the correlations between, for example, socioeconomic status, race, or ethnic background and mental disorder.

The relationship between Mental Health I and a stress score composed only of childhood items (Childhood Stress Score) was linear. As the number of stresses increased, the average impairment also increased steadily (Table 14-1, "total" column. This table and the following table and figure are not reproduced here, but appear in *Life Stress and Mental Health* [Langner and Michael, 1963].). The same results were obtained when Mental Health I was examined in relation to a Childhood-Adult Combined Stress Score (Table 14-3). Figure 14-1 shows this relationship in graphic form.

The significance of these results for psychological theory are that "the factors associated with mental disturbance are purely additive in their effects," and that "the concept of a single 'traumatic experience" is called into question." *For our purposes, however, the fact that a random sample of people in an American metropolis experienced a large amount of stress in childhood and in adult life, and that this was directly related to their mental health, or lack of it, is most important.*

The distribution of the Mental Health Rating (see Table 8-3 in Srole, L., Langner, T.S., Michael, S.T., Opler, M.K., and Rennie, T.A.C., *Mental Health in the Metropolis: The Midtown Manhattan Study*, Vol. I. New York, McGraw-Hill, 1962) is shown in Table 12.

TABLE 12
MIDTOWN MANHATTAN
MENTAL HEALTH RATINGS

Well	18.5%	
Mild symptom formation	36.3%	
Moderate symptom formation	21.8%	
Marked symptom formation	13.2%	Impaired
Severe Symptom formation	7.5%	Impaired
Incapacitated	2.7%	Impaired, total 23.4%

When the newspapers got word of the high impairment rate, they wrote headlines such as "One in four New Yorkers mentally ill." Worse yet, they said only 18% were mentally "Well," implying that the rest of Gotham (New York City) was very, very sick. Actually, you could get hay fever in the summer or have a mild reactive depression and still receive a rating of Mild symptom impairment. Gotham was used satirically by Washington Irving as a name for New York City. The name referred to a "town of fools," Gotham, Nottinghamshire, in the sixteenth century. Did the newspapers secretly want to make New York City look like a "town of fools" by distorting the research findings?

III. THE WORLD MENTAL HEALTH SURVEY: THE UNITED STATES HAS THE HIGHEST RATE OF MENTAL DISORDER

Since the 1960s, there have been many epidemiological studies of mental disorder using improved instruments. Lest the reader might think that the 1962 level of impairment in a U.S. city like New York was due to the eccentricity of Manhattanites as opposed to the rest of the country, poor methodology, or to the derangement of the research team, I must quote a recent worldwide study.

The World Mental Health Survey Consortium (Kessler, 2004) did random sample surveys in fourteen countries (six less developed, eight developed). They used a WHO Composite Diagnostic Interview, lay administered. They estimated prevalence, severity, and treatment of DSM-IV mental disorders (the fourth revision of the *Psychiatric Diagnostic and Statistical Manual*).

The combined U.S. (12-month) prevalence of Anxiety Disorders, Mood Disorders (Depression, Bipolar Disorders) Impulse-Control Disorders, and Substance Abuse was 26.4%, the highest of all the 14 countries! The next highest was the Ukraine, with 20.5%, whose population has been subjected to a great amount of stress and rapid change since the breakup of the Soviet Union. China, Japan, and Nigeria had the lowest prevalence rates, ranging from 0.8% to 3.1%. Since the questionnaires and methods were standard across countries, the discrepancy in rates between the United States and other countries cannot be dismissed as pure artifact.

The reason I have presented the 23.4% Impaired in the Midtown Manhattan Study and the U.S. 26.4% in the WHO Study is to argue that *our country has had and still has a high rate of mental disorder, and that this helped to make possible the re-election of Bush against the best interests of the majority of voters.*

IV. SOCIAL DISTRESS

Why, when the United States has such a high standard of living, does it have possibly the worst mental health among nations? This is, I think, because we have a high degree of social disintegration and disorganization. Our institutions (family, government, military, education, economy, legal, medical, etc.) are fragmented, our values are in sharp conflict, and our stresses are numerous. Strain (mental disorder) is the reaction to this state of social disorganization and its various stresses. Mental disorder varies from the very mild to the extremely severe and incapacitating.

Dr. Robert Rieber (1997) uses the term "social distress" to describe this societal or community-wide reaction to stress, as opposed to a reaction on the individual level.

> The evidence of widespread social distress as indicated by community collapse and economic stagnation in places like Palermo, Moscow, and Bogota begs the question:

Will it not be one of history's cruel surprises if Palermo and Moscow represent the future of Washington? (Rieber, 1997, p. 156)

If the United States is worse off in terms of mental disorder than the Ukraine and twelve other countries, then there is evidence for great social distress in our country. Since the WHO surveys were conducted in 2001–2003, the results coincide with the Bush administration's watch. [The rate of mental disorder for a huge metropolis such as Midtown Manhattan (23%) could be expected to be higher than the national rate (26%). The 2001–03 national rate suggests an *increase* in mental disorder over the time period.]

My contention is that the lying, the divisiveness, the war in Iraq, the failing economy, and the lack of concern for the middle and working classes and the poor have all resulted over two Bush terms in a sharp increase in mental disorder. In all four categories of the WHO study, the United States leads in the percentage of prevalence in fourteen countries: Anxiety, 18.2%; Mood Disorders, 9.6%; Impulse Control, 6.8%; and Substance Abuse, 3.8%. (These categories overlap, and thus add to more than 26%.)

As mentioned previously, for those classified in *any* of the four disorders, the U.S. prevalence is 26.4%. The Ukraine is next, with 20.5%. Are we on a par with, or even worse off than, a country such as the Ukraine, which has gone through drastic changes, and where social disintegration could be expected after the dissolution of the U.S.S.R.? Are we even worse off than some "third world" countries? The answer is "Yes." Colombia, Mexico, Lebanon, and Nigeria have lower percentages of mental disorder than we have in the United States.

How did the Bush administration helped to create and exacerbate this increase in mental disorder? A look at the diagnoses that went into the four major categories of disorder may help us understand what has happened.

Anxiety disorders include agoraphobia, generalized anxiety disorder, obsessive-compulsive disorder, panic disorder, post-traumatic stress disorder, social phobia, and specific phobia. Mood disorders include bipolar

189

I and II disorders, dysthymia, and major depressive disorder. Impulse control disorders include bulimia, intermittent explosive disorder, and...three child-adolescent disorders (attention-deficit hyperactivity disorder, conduct disorder, and oppositional-defiant disorder). Substance disorders include alcohol or drug abuse or dependence. (Kessler, 2004)

Is it any wonder that Americans are more anxious, and that they tend to panic? The rate of post-traumatic stress disorder is no doubt due in part to exposure to life-threatening danger in Iraq. Minor and major depressions can be expected with the deaths and injuries of the war. Reactive depressions occur with job loss, death in the family, and illness (especially illness without medical insurance). Loss of impulse control is a typical reaction to stress, and is commonest in children and adolescents. Drug abuse is widespread in the United States, whether by prescription medication or by drugs bought off the street. Our anxiety and depression is medicated across all social-class levels.

The preemptive war in Iraq has been a major source of stress. It has done nothing to fulfill the needs of the average American. Now, more than ever, I think the man in the street realizes that his problems haven't concerned Washington in the past eight years. This alienation threatens to carry over into the Obama administration, and may be a hindrance to the recovery of the country.

Rather than be a source of stress, the war suited the aims of the Bushies: oil, dominance (disguised as "benevolent global hegemony" by the neo-cons), unilateralism, acquisition of power at home and abroad, accumulation of wealth, and the deregulation of any laws that interfered with that accumulation. The war has been used to distract attention from national problems of employment, health, and education. The U.S. Army has been privatized. There were 25,000 armed fighters in Iraq hired by American companies as of 2004, with double the pay of the best paid soldiers. Immense war profits have gone to Halliburton and other companies doing business and construction for our forces in Iraq, without much accountability. Contracts for Humvees, armoring, weapons, planes, trucks—all helped Bush's buddies and campaign contributors, the CEOs of large corporations. The top six postwar contractors in Iraq and Afghanistan, ranked by contract value (January 1, 2002 through July 1, 2004) in *billions*, are shown in Table 13.

TABLE 13
TOP SIX POSTWAR CONTRACTORS
IN IRAQ AND AFGHANISTAN, 2002-2004

Kellogg, Brown & Root (Halliburton)	11.4 Billion $
Parsons Corp.	5.2 "
Fluor Corp.	3.7 "
Washington Group International	3.1 "
Shaw Group	3.0 "
Bechtel Group	2.8 "
(See "Contractors," 2005)	

Vice President Cheney was CEO of Halliburton from 1995 through August of 2000. It isn't hard to see why his former company got the largest contracts. The war created more divisions. Bush refused to meet with Cindy Sheehan, a woman whose soldier-son was killed in Iraq. For weeks she camped outside near his ranch, and then at the White House, waiting for him to afford her a few minutes. Responding partly to this, in 2005 thousands held antiwar protest meetings all over the country. Then in 2006, just before Bush's State of the Union address, Sheehan was arrested for wearing a T-shirt showing the number of American soldiers killed in Iraq. There was also more divisiveness over religion, evolution versus "intelligent design," gun control, privatization of social security (a new source of insecurity, since most Americans didn't want it privatized), abortion, gay marriage, sex, and drugs. The issues of "family values" and stem-cell research are stirred up by the evangelical right, and divide us even more. Additional stress is created.

Bush heightened the general anxiety level produced by the 9/11 attacks by starting a war against Saddam Hussein and the Iraqis, while the men actually behind 9/11 were Osama bin Laden and the Saudi suicide terrorists. (Fourteen of the nineteen jihadis were Saudis.) The WMDs that were called a direct threat to our country proved to be nonexistent. Bringing democracy to the Middle East was the next "goal" of the war. At this point, even in 2009, we are still looking at a potential civil war in Iraq, with Kurds, Shiites, and Sunnis each having their own armies. Recently Sunni suicide bombings of Shiites have escalated. This conflict continues, despite the reduction in the level of killing due to the additional troops of the "surge." Obama has announced that combat troops will be withdrawn by August 31, 2010. At the same time, he said that 50,000 troops will remain until the end of 2011. It seems that Iraq and Afghanistan are open-ended quagmires from which we will not soon extricate ourselves.

Uncaring parenting, an authoritarian family structure, and the resulting authoritarian (non-autonomous) social character prepared many Americans to vote against their self-interest. This is not limited to economic self-interest. The jobs, health, education, and environment of many Americans have been compromised. The future of their children has been blighted by a huge national debt. The widespread authoritarian social character, faced with increasing stress, has succumbed to anxiety, depression, antisocial behavior, and drugs. A campaign that told the public that Bush could solve their problems (many of which he had created in his first term) won the vote of a large segment of the political middle in 2004.

We were told that Kerry was a "waffler," while Bush never changed his mind. Kerry was branded as weak and a liar (even though he fought in Vietnam, while Bush stayed in the States in the Air National Guard). These propaganda techniques would not work in a nation of adults raised to be autonomous and skeptical. They would not work in a nation that was well educated, with an ability to look at slogans and promises with a critical eye. They would not work with people who were raised to be "inner-directed" and autonomous, to have "a mind of their own," and who were not heavily dominated by the opinions and values of others.

V. TRAINING FOR PARENTHOOD: CHANGING SOCIAL CHARACTER

The future of our country will depend to a large degree on changing the social character of at least a fair segment of the population. We will have to teach good parenting that avoids cold, punitive, and labile treatment of the child. Training for parenthood should start in high school. This would be a major undertaking, and a political hot potato, since the values associated with what research has shown to be good parenting are often in direct conflict with the widespread U.S. authoritarian character structure. It would emphasize warmth, emotional support, and a focus on the child's individual needs. A self-examination by the parents-to-be of their own needs and unresolved issues would be required. Hands-on training of adolescents by caring for and mentoring young children would be crucial. Fathering and mothering are both acquired skills.

A major problem with intervention *after* parenting starts is that the families and children who come to professional attention have already begun to have fairly severe problems. This is especially true of police and court referrals, rather than self-referrals. The Centers for Disease Control and Prevention (CDC) has sponsored a maltreatment prevention program (see "Parenting," 2004). Their panel of experts recommended a "universal preventive program...introduced early in the parenting process to prevent child maltreatment." The CDC has sponsored a trial of the Positive Parenting Program ("Triple P") at the University of South Carolina. They note, however, that "Up to 50% of families may still be at risk for child maltreatment when services end."

Although programs such as this are a good first step, the best time to intervene is *before* teens become parents—that is, in high school. There should be lectures on the specific issues of parenting, but they should be supplemented with actual placement and supervision in child-care facilities. This is asking for an expensive but much more effective way to reduce abuse and neglect. It also is a way to vastly improve the mental and physical health of future U.S. citizens. Because of the great expense of later treatment and frequent lifelong incapacitation after the child is physically or emotionally damaged, a high school course in parenting would eventually be cost-effective. The program is a potential bridge between the Red and the Blue, both of whom rank stopping crime and strengthening the work force high among various issues. It would also fit comfortably into Obama's plans for expanding education.

A word of caution is needed here. It is much harder to be a good parent when you are poor, uneducated, jobless, a single mother, in poor health without insurance, and a victim of poverty and possible abuse during your own childhood. Thus, it is not surprising that there is more abuse at lower than at higher socioeconomic levels. (See *Risk and Protection Factors for Child Abuse and Neglect*, National Clearinghouse on Child Abuse and Neglect Information, for a review of risk factors.)

However, abuse and neglect are spread over the whole social class range. A good example of abuse at high income levels is Joan Crawford, whose adopted daughter, Christina, wrote that "mommie" beat her with clothes hangers. (*Mommie Dearest*). Bing Crosby's son Gary wrote (*Going My Own Way*) that his alcoholic father beat him and his brothers with belts and canes. Two of Gary's three younger brothers committed suicide. Henry Fonda was given to rages and was extremely cold and rejecting, according to his daughter Jane. She tried all her life to please him and even bought the rights to a film script, *On Golden Pond*, so *he* could win an Oscar, which he finally did. He never thanked her for this effort, and publicly said that he resented the fact that she had won an Oscar before him. (Are movie stars preselected for abuse of their children, or are the abused children of celebrities more likely to get press attention?)

The most notorious middle-class abusers were Joel Steinberg, a lawyer, and his wife, Hedda Nussbaum, a children's book editor at a major publishing house. Joel, a lawyer and a drug addict, beat their adopted daughter, Lisa, to death from a brain injury. Joel also beat up his wife, who failed to report the beatings of Lisa and herself in time.

Any program of parenting education has to be supplemented, perhaps even preceded, by massive improvement in the health, employment, and housing of the lowest third of the nation. What can we do about the top 5%, the professionals and Hollywood stars who abuse their children? In lieu of psychotherapy, perhaps the government could subsidize their children's tell-all autobiographies.

Parenting 101

I am not in the education field, and creating a curriculum is beyond my capacity. Yet there are some topics and approaches that stem from the discussions in this book that might be the basis for creating a program.

1. There should be a brief review in class of child development, with special emphasis on early bonding. Parents should be familiar with developmental stages, so they are not taken aback by changes in the child's behavior. Discussion of the difficulties of the first years should include such topics as colic and the stress it produces, tiredness after delivery, nursing, etc. Books like *What to Expect If You're Expecting* could be quoted.

2. Some time should be devoted to class discussion of discipline: shame, guilt, punishment, withholding privileges, and "time out" seclusion ("go to your room"). These practices have been shown to damage the child psychologically, though they may be *temporarily* effective. Modeling behavior, substitution, or distraction are effective and not damaging.

3. The works of Alice Miller (1981, 1983, 1984) and Arno Gruen (1992), discussed in detail in this book, give us a wealth of information about the type of parenting that is destructive of the child's "true self," and conversely tells us how to be better parents. Concern for the child's individuality, rather than a "one size fits all" approach is crucial to producing an autonomous individual.

4. Some of the teens in this program would already have been subjected to certain damaging parental practices (coldness, punitiveness, and lability) reviewed in this book. To help the teens become good parents in the future, the program should boost their autonomy. The teacher should help the teen with individual projects, and focus on the individual teen's areas of skill.

5. Anger management is crucial for the future parent. There is a large literature on the control of anger. The fragility of the infant's and child's body should be discussed. Shaking causes brain hemorrhages. Lifting the child by one arm can cause a dislocated shoulder. A pediatrician could offer advice in this area. Many of the assaults on children ending in death are by boyfriends of the mother. These are men who have no investment in some other man's gene pool. Respect for children and protection of their relative helplessness should be a goal of the program.

6. There should be discussion of perceptivity—know thyself! The ability to be aware of anger and jealousy and other feelings will help to avoid angry parenting.

7. There should be brief discussion of the stress of marriage (or among unmarried couples). A mother must focus on the newborn baby, often angering the father. Reduction of sexual contact during pregnancy and after birth can create marital tension. There is also the possibility of postpartum depression.

8. Mentoring: There should be an assignment to take care of a child in the first and the sixth grade, as in "big brother" or "big sister." One assignment could be given to visit a nursery school for a day or half day, to see how little children behave and interact. The sixth grader and first grader assigned to the teen should be of the same sex, and the assignment should be made carefully, so that extremely difficult young children are not assigned.

    The teacher should review the progress of the mentoring relationship, allowing the teen to ask questions, seek guidance, and express pleasure or anger and frustration stemming from the mentoring relationship.

9. Peer pressure is always on teens to use drugs and alcohol. The effects of drugs and alcohol on the fetus, and on parental behavior later on, should be covered. Most assaults are drug or alcohol based. The damage to the central nervous system by drugs and excessive alcohol is permanent, and can severely

affect the child of addicted parents. Drugs, drinking alcohol, and smoking during pregnancy should be labeled taboo.

10. Recent changes in premarital sexual behavior ("hooking up") may have an effect on later bonding between husband and wife. This in turn can damage children. Peer pressure on teens in the sexual area is greater than ever, and here again, autonomy should be encouraged. While this is a politically controversial topic, nobody could disagree that a girl or boy should have the ability to control his or her own activity, and this includes the degree of contact with the opposite sex.

11. As an expansion of suggestion no. 1, there should be discussion of early development. Pacifiers are now considered O.K. The importance of "transitional objects" should be discussed. Fear of abandonment (discussed in detail in my book, *Choices for Living*) should be covered in class, so that new parents don't leave the house and abandon their child except in grave emergencies.

The baby cries because he or she is too hot, too cold, hungry, thirsty, or has a wet diaper. Potential parents must be aware that they have to learn to read these signals, and check the various possibilities. The high-pitched crying of babies has a survival value, in that it forces the parent to act. However, this same piercing sound can trigger off physical attacks, especially in young fathers or boyfriends who are not attached to the baby in question.

12. A major goal of the program should be to foster "emotional intelligence" in the prospective parent (see Goleman, *Emotional Intelligence*. New York: Doubleday Dell, 1995). This includes insight, self-examination, internal locus of control. autonomy, and empathy. (Empathy, as defined by the ability to read the feelings of other people through their facial expressions, body language, and tone of voice, is crucial to being a good parent.) All these topics have been discussed in this book. The joys and rewards of parenting should also be emphasized, since an exclusive emphasis on the stresses of child-rearing could simply produce anxiety, and

eventually interfere with a good parent–child relationship in the future. The teen-student's own relationship to his or her parents will doubtless come up during discussions, and the teacher must be prepared to listen sympathetically, but should also comment constructively on what the student says about his or her family atmosphere.

13. Special attention should be given to types of parenting that are injurious to the child, but on the surface seem acceptable. For example, "living through" the child has been discussed as evidence of narcissism on the part of the parent. Insisting on the *parents'* choice of the child's major interests and later occupation, or micromanaging the choice of friends or marital partner, all ignore the child's individual needs.

Another example is teasing and tickling. These are viewed as fun and games, but are often forms of concealed aggression. Many of these parental behaviors are discussed in this text.

14. Funding for innovative educational programs seems unlikely in the 2009–2010 period, but as the economy turns around, it could be a small part of an Obama overhaul of the educational system. If he succeeds in changing the health care industry, maybe he can tackle the problems of our school curricula that have left us far behind many other countries. Adding a semester course in parenting for high-school seniors might be a good idea. A parenting course would be one small step toward changing the selfish, authoritarian, narcissistic social character of a large part of our population. This would change the parent-to-be students' character, but would make even greater changes in the *children* of these students, who would benefit by receiving more caring parenting.

VI. The Democratic Party Needs to Be a Caring Parent: A Party of and for the People, Not Republican/Center/Lite

Our country, once the shining example of a successful democracy, is now in a state of social distress and disorganization. Our educational system is in tatters. Our technical jobs are being

198

outsourced to foreign countries, partly because India, Japan, and now China have more demanding educational programs in mathematics, engineering, and science (and largely because their labor is cheaper). Teaching "intelligent design" along with Darwinian evolution will not help us develop an international leadership in molecular biology. Yet Bill Frist, the former Senate majority leader and a transplant surgeon, suggested that we teach both approaches! He said, "I think in a pluralistic society that is the fairest way to go about education and training people for the future."

In the U.S.S.R. around the time of World War II Trofim Lysenko managed to replace Darwinism with his version of the Lamarckian theory of the "inheritance of (environmentally) acquired characteristics." The popular example was that giraffes stretched their necks to get at the leaves on trees, and that their offspring (genetically) inherited their parents' long necks (long genes!) due to the stretching. The Darwinian explanation is that in times of grassland famine, animals with longer necks (giraffes, generuks) were able to eat leaves off the trees, and thus were better able to reproduce, "natural selection") while their shorter-necked cousins died out. This was "survival of the fittest." The Russians wanted to promote the idea that social engineering could produce genetic change. Of course there *is* some action of the environment on genes, but political considerations prompted the Russian *emphasis* on acquisition of characteristics through the environment. Now, once again, political considerations were propelling us toward a biology founded on faith rather than science. It is up to the new president to reverse this denial and denigration of science. He has already started this reversal, by appointing Steven Chu, a Nobel Laureate in physics, as Secretary of Energy. He has also doubled the funding for the National Institutes of Health after years of flat funding that took no account of inflation.

The new president was elected by a majority of the popular vote, much of it coming from the young, minorities, liberals, and independents. They did not vote for perpetuating any aspect of the previous administration's platform or policies. The defeat of McCain and Palin was to a great extent a vote *against* Bush, though

McCain tried to present himself as a maverick, independent of the previous administration. Max Weber told us of the "routinization of charisma," which consists of the eventual move to the center after the term of a charismatic and innovative leader (such as Obama). Even before the next leader takes over, there is a sort of entropy, a dumbing down of the hopes and promises of the campaign. Though Obama has inherited one of the worst legacies on record, with war in Afghanistan, terrorism, a worldwide financial collapse, global warming, etc. he must not let the iniquities of the past eight years stand because he wants to "reach across the aisle."

Obama and his cabinet need to craft a strong new program that will correct the wrongs perpetrated by Bush, Cheney, Rumsfeld, et al. They need to "tell it like it is," and stop the current GOP practice of lying to the people. They need to assure the man or woman on Main Street and in the suburbs that they have his and her best interests at heart, and that the word *demos* in their party's name really means what it says: "popular government and democracy" (from "populi" and "demos," meaning "the people.") One way they can convince those *people* who voted them into office of the sincerity of their mantra of "change" is to bring the "perpetrators" of the past administration's illegal activities to trial, or at least to create a commission to review these transgressions before the public eye and repudiate them. Some of those illegal activities tricked the United States into war in Iraq, torture, secret prisons, extreme rendition, illegal wiretapping, obstruction of justice, perjury, and conspiracy.

In early January 2009, Barack Obama was asked if he would favor an investigation of criminal behavior by the Bush administration. He said "I don't believe that anybody is above the law, (but) we need to look forward as opposed to looking backwards."

Again, Paul Krugman has expressed the strong feelings of liberals that former Bush administration officials or advisors (I assume he means Bush, Cheney, and Rumsfeld. I would add Libby, Gonzales, Yoo, Frist, DeLay, Rice, Richard Armitage, Paul Wolfowitz, Richard Perle, Katherine Harris, and Michael Brown for good measure) have set a precedent for further curtailment of civil rights under the Constitution. To not prosecute or even publicly investigate their probable criminal activity would allow future government officials to flout the Constitution and the law.

> And to protect and defend the Constitution, a president must do more than obey the Constitution himself; he must hold those who violate the Constitution accountable. So Mr. Obama should reconsider his apparent decision to let the previous administration get away with crime. Consequences aside, that's not a decision he has the right to make. (Krugman, *New York Times*, January 16, 2009)

VII. GEORGE W. BUSH VERSUS THOMAS JEFFERSON

Let's see how George W. Bush stacks up against Thomas Jefferson.

Thomas Jefferson (1743–1826)

> The care of human life and happiness, and not their destruction, is the first and only legitimate object of good government. (To the Republican citizens of Washington County, Maryland, March 31, 1809)

> I know of no safe depository of the ultimate powers of the society but the people themselves... (Letter to William Charles Jarvis, September 28, 1820)

> Men by their constitutions are naturally divided into two parties: (1) Those who *fear* and distrust the people, and wish to draw all powers from them into the hands of the higher classes. (2) Those who identify themselves with the people, have confidence in them, *cherish* them and consider them as the most honest and safe, although not the most wise depository of the public interests. In every country these two parties exist; and in every one where they are free to think, speak, and write, they will declare themselves. (Letter to Henry Lee, August 10, 1824)

(Note that Jefferson saw a "constitutional" [i.e., psychophysiological] difference between the selfish and the caring.

Paul Krugman more recently suggested a personality difference between conservatives and liberals. Recent studies of fear ("threat") responses and twin studies, discussed previously, support the presence of genetic as well as learned differences in the personality of individuals on the broad political spectrum (italics mine, not Jefferson's).

George W. Bush (1946–)

> Our enemies are innovative and resourceful—and so are we. They never stop thinking about new ways to harm our country and people—and neither do we. (Washington, D.C., August 5, 2004, comments during the signing ceremony for a defense bill when the national deficit was estimated at $412,000,000,000.)

> I know it is hard for you to put food on your family. (Greater Nashua, N.H. Chamber of Commerce, January 27, 2000)

> Well, I think if you say you're going to do something and don't do it, that's trustworthiness. (August 30, 2000)

> If this was a dictatorship, it would be a heck of a lot easier, just so long as I'm the dictator. (December 18, 2002)

> My answer is "bring them on." (On Iraqi militants attacking U.S. forces, Washington D.C., July 3, 2003)

> First let me make it very clear, poor people aren't necessarily killers. Just because you happen to be not rich doesn't mean you're willing to kill. (Washington, D.C., May 19, 2003)

VIII. AN ADDENDUM

This addendum is an update of events that may have started earlier than 2007, but had significant changes or resolutions during that year. *Extensive coverage of events during the eight Bush years and the beginning of Obama's first term appear in the Timeline, with commentary relevant to understanding the hypotheses put forth in this book.*

As of March 2007, the conviction of I. Lewis ("Scooter") Libby, Dick Cheney's chief of staff, changed the political battlefront. Libby was convicted on four counts, including perjury, obstruction of justice, and false statements, by special counsel Patrick Fitzgerald. He was sentenced in June to 30 months in prison, but Bush commuted his sentence. He will be on probation for two years, and has to pay a $250,000 fine. As mentioned before, the "outing" of Valerie Plame, a CIA agent, was in retaliation for the *New York Times* Op-Ed refutation by her husband, Joseph C. Wilson IV, of the administration's claim that Saddam Hussein had tried to purchase yellowcake uranium from Niger. Aside from being another revelation of the character assassination typical of the White House staff, the importance of the "outing" is that it was a direct defense of the "weapons of mass destruction" (WMD) rationale for invading Iraq. To say, as Wilson did, that the intelligence was false (and much later was found to be based on a forgery by an unreliable Italian informant) undermined that rationale. Testimony from the investigation suggests that Cheney got Plame's name from George Tenet, former head of the CIA. He then probably spoke with Bush, and also told Karl Rove and Libby to contact as many as six reporters to denigrate Wilson's report, and to punish him by revealing his wife's secret CIA spy role. That revelation, if ever proved, is a criminal offense. The investigation of Karl Rove (President Bush's "brains") has stopped, and Libby has become the "fall guy" for Rove and Cheney.

The Valerie Plame affair, combined with the slow response to Hurricane Katrina, the rising death toll of our troops in Iraq, and the "pay to play" scandal involving Washington, D.C. lobbyist Jack Abramoff have all cast a shadow over the Bush administration. However, the Republican agenda has not really changed one whit. The Democrats have challenged the congressional delays in investigating the steps that led to the Iraq war. They threatened a filibuster to stop the confirmation of conservative judge Samuel J. Alito Jr. to the Supreme Court, but the Senate voted to cut off debate. Alito's confirmation has paved the way for gradual changes in the abortion laws, such as the requirement of parental or spousal permission and support for the "partial-birth abortion" ban, and this might eventually result in the overturning of *Roe v. Wade*.

The 2006 mid-term elections told us the Republicans could not continue to march toward their goal of a one-party system, or at least a generation of GOP control of the presidency, Congress, and the Supreme Court.

The tide of public opinion turned against the Bush administration. The mid-term elections clearly showed that the war, the economy, and cronyism all damaged the GOP. Bush's approval rating dropped to the low thirties. The war in Iraq changed from a war of "insurgents" to a civil war between Shiite and Sunni militias. Pressure to withdraw troops from Iraq increased, with many prominent Republicans supporting withdrawal. Tom DeLay decided to leave the House and his role as the "Hammer," because he was linked to the Jack Abramoff scandal. Abramoff lobbied for the garment industries that ran sweatshops in Saipan. He bilked his Native American clients, the Coushatta Nation and other tribes, of sixty-six million dollars. Money flowed from Jack's clients to Tom's organizations, in return for legislation they needed. (Tom's house that "Jack" built?) DeLay's former aides, Michael Scanlon and Tony Rudy, in addition to their boss Abramoff, pleaded guilty to corruption charges.

A shooting accident revealed the insular lives of Dick Cheney and his hunting pals. Cheney accidentally shot his hunting companion, Harry Wittington, age seventy-eight, with shotgun pellets while hunting quail on the gigantic Armstrong Ranch. There was a delay of one whole day in reporting the accident publicly to a small local newspaper. The White House was silent. This has further tarnished the image of the former White House leaders and their cronies.

Bush's second term, with all its scandals and failures, turned him into a lame duck. While some of his crew left the sinking ship early, the lobbying, the cronyism, and the kleptocracy lived on.

So the Republicans cannot attain their goal of a one-party system right now. But it is prematurely optimistic to think that there will be a major change in the social character of Americans, even though the Democrats won heavily in the 2008 elections. Some of the younger evangelical leaders are focusing on AIDS in Africa, on refugees in Darfur, and the environment. Yet they have not dropped abortion as their central issue. In reviewing the speeches of Republican presidential candidates for 2008, Krugman found that the same old GOP Bush/Cheney policies were supported. He warned the DEMS that Bush-think is still alive and well in the general populace:

> What we need to realize is that the infamous 'Bush bubble,' the administration's no-reality zone, extends a long way beyond the White House. Millions of Americans believe that the patriotic torturers are keeping us safe, that there's a vast Islamic axis of evil, that victory is just around the corner, that Bush appointees are doing a "heckuva" job — and that news reports contradicting these beliefs reflect liberal media bias. (Krugman, *New York Times*, May 18, 2007).

Is Krugman just describing a massive conservative denial, since about half the nation believes in these fairy tales? No! He is describing a deeply entrenched belief system; torture is O.K., all members of outgroups are basically evil, homogeneity is a primary value, networking (in its extreme form of cronyism) is O.K. because it's instrumental. Everyone uses everyone. That's human nature. Contrary opinions in the media or in individuals are seen as biased or just lies.

Here, I repeat, is America's choice: selfish or caring. Let's go back to Chapter One. There I suggested that in order to achieve a better democracy we have to slowly change the social character of a (not so moral) majority—the "GOPS." The traits and values making up the ideal type called the "GOPS" are authoritarianism, selfishness, bellicosity, lack of empathy, imperceptivity (of their own feelings), anti-intraception, rigidity, closed-mindedness, sincerity (as opposed to authenticity), self-reliance, moralism, particularism, favoring homogeneity (us vs. them), instrumental values, pragmatism, and anti-ambiguity (no waffling). In short, this portrait smacks of narcissism.

This mind-set and value system steeped in the Protestant ethic, and fostered by uncaring and narcissistic parents, repeats from generation to generation, to produce more narcissists. Does this sound too pessimistic? I believe in the perfectibility of mankind, but the rate of change of social character is glacial. We still have to learn to control our hypothalamus, the seat of impulsivity and aggression, and the amygdala, seat of the emotions, with the modulating influence of the cerebral frontal cortex. We hark back to both the warlike chimpanzees and their close relatives, the more kindly bonobos. Ninety-eight percent of our DNA is common to both species (DeWaal, 2006). The bonobos are very active sexually, and this may act as an alternative to the chimps' aggressiveness. ("Make love, not war?") They also show evidence of empathy. (See John Kennedy and Bill Clinton as sexually active and less martial leaders in Chapter Two on Leadership Preselection.)

Perhaps the 2008 election victory of Obama will bring about an incremental change in the direction of caring, and away from selfishness. Lincoln's first inaugural address (March 4, 1861), in its immortal prose, catches this hope for peace and union after the secession of eleven Southern states. "The better angels of our nature" gives us a beautiful metaphor as a substitute for the "cortical modulation" of modern neurology.

> ...We are not enemies, but friends. We must not be enemies. Though passion may have strained, it must not break the bonds of affection. The mystic chords of memory...will yet swell the chorus of the Union, when again touched, as surely they will be, by the *better angels of our nature.*

Alas, about a month later, the devils of our nature temporarily took over. On April 12, 1861, the Civil War started with the South's attack on Fort Sumter.

See the Timeline for Further Updates.

Conclusion and Summary

INTRODUCTION

These are some hypotheses that suggest the possible factors causing the apparent lack of economic and general self-interest in the 40% of people with household incomes of $50,000 or less who voted for George W. Bush, in 2004.

1. Parental practices create anger and the selfish social character.
2. Race.
3. The smokescreen or head-feint effect (GOP propaganda).
4. The stubborn mule hypothesis: getting the working class and middle class to focus attention on their self-interest through economic disaster (shock).
5. Conservative policies and propaganda-created stresses that in turn produced an increase in mental disorder.
6. Rapid social change.
7. The working class was swayed to vote GOP by per capita income increases in pre-election year, with weight on the fourth quarter.
8. Election fraud favored the GOP.
9. The United States has become too middle class to vote democratic.
10. The GOP–DEM split may have some physiological or genetic basis.

11. The growth of minorities, especially Hispanics, will tend to favor the Democrats.
12. The United States is a very conservative nation, and we should not expect any sweeping change in the very close split between the right and left any time soon.

Among these factors, I think the influence of parenting on social character and politics is very powerful. In addition, racial prejudice (much of it covert or unconscious); propaganda, stress leading to mental disorder (depression, anxiety, and political passivity); and shock (financial meltdown or war) seem highly influential.

That voting behavior and conservatism/liberalism may have a genetic and a physiological basis is intriguing, but at the same time frightening. A genetic characteristic (such as hypervigilance) may be relatively immune to social intervention. There is always the hope that epigenetic effects will allow the environment to control the expression of genes that might prove in future research to be inimical to liberalism and democracy. Vigilance is necessary to protect our freedoms, but all too easily slips over into hypervigilance. Remember that the founding fathers did not trust men with power, and used the separation of powers (a term created by Montesquieu) to *institutionalize* vigilance. Most of us are not vigilantes. (In 2005 Bush said, "So I say, what the heck! Let's give vigilantism a go and see how things shake out. Why not?")

CHAPTER ONE

In four years, George Bush and his handlers got us into a protracted war in Iraq on false premises, piled up a huge national debt, curtailed our civil liberties through the Patriot Act, and packed the Supreme Court with conservative judges. How could poor people (with household income below $50,000) vote for him a second time, after such uncompassionate treatment? How did we get such a bellicose president, with such an obvious lack of empathy? George Bush's (and Dick Cheney's, Karl Rove's, John McCain's, and Sarah Palin's) policies were clearly in line with the Republican ethos and policies, and not the policies of a maverick.

A personality typology describing the "ideal types," called the "GOPS and the DEMS," is centered around the dichotomy "selfish versus caring." These are core attributes not only of our two political parties, but of societies and individuals the world over. The GOPS and DEMS split on the following traits and core beliefs that together make up two disparate forms of "social character": authoritarian versus permissive, selfish versus caring, bellicose versus peaceful, averse versus empathic, imperceptive versus perceptive, extroverted versus introverted, anti-intraceptive versus intraceptive (feelings and imagination dominate), external locus of control versus internal locus of control, rigid versus flexible, close-minded versus open-minded, sincere versus authentic, self-reliant versus acceptance of dependency, believe in absolute truths versus relativistic truths, faith versus science, particularism versus universalism, homogeneity versus multiculturalism, cynicism and irony disliked versus cynicism and irony accepted as criticism of the establishment, instrumental values versus intrinsic values, pragmatism versus idealism, and intolerance versus tolerance of ambiguity.

Selfishness and the Current Financial Meltdown

There is a direct line between the most extreme espousal of selfishness and the current economic crisis. Ayn Rand wrote many books, including *The Virtue of Selfishness*. It should not be forgotten that Alan Greenspan, the former head of the Federal Reserve Board, was a co-founder of Rand's Objectivist Movement, and was her disciple. His refusal to rein in the housing bubble was consistent with the "invisible hand of the market" philosophy, and the GOP's general unwillingness to regulate the housing and financial industries. This laissez-faire policy, (adhered to by McCain), led to our current housing and financial meltdown.

Human Nature

The GOP view of human nature tends toward the Hobbesian (man is a beast to man, his instincts are intractable and genetically determined), while the DEMS (especially Barack Obama) lean

211

toward a *hope* for man's perfectibility. If man is beastly and intractable, this leads to the conservative view that there is no use in "throwing money" at social problems. I think there is very strong evidence that early experiences affecting attachment and self-esteem that derive from warm and supportive parental practices and family atmosphere, *create* the view of mankind as similarly supportive and perfectible. The lack of early parental warmth and support leads to a view of mankind as basically flawed.

A list of twenty issues on which the GOPS and the DEMS split is offered. The list of the personality traits making up the "social character" of the GOPS and the DEMS seems to fit the issues list like a glove. For example, being averse to "safety nets" fits in with the GOP and Protestant ethic value of independence and their negative view of Welfare as "dependency." A few other examples are: rigid versus flexible (conservative judges favor a strict interpretation of the Constitution, and the evangelicals tend to a literal interpretation of the Bible); faith versus science (science seen as interfering with profits due to regulation of emissions, pollution and drug side effects, and evolution viewed as diminishing man, versus science seen as in the public interest and evolution as evidence of man's perfectibility by social intervention, not by "intelligent design.")

CHAPTER TWO

A major question is how people could vote once again for a man who started a "preemptive" war based on fudged intelligence, or for John McCain, who said he would "stay in Iraq for one hundred years." Why do leaders seem to be preselected for warlike qualities? A look at famous bellicose and relatively peaceful leaders of the past finds that they both, in most cases, suffered some kind of childhood trauma. This may account for the obsessive drive that enables the political leader to get to the top. Beatings, humiliation (both usually by father), father-son conflict, uncertain paternity, severe economic deprivation or deprivation relative to higher social classes, and a façade of early toughness and "compartmentalization" adopted to preserve self-esteem and functioning seem common to these leaders. The childhood experiences of Alexander the Great,

Genghis Khan, Napoleon Bonaparte, Adolf Hitler, and Joseph Stalin show these traumas.

George Bush shared in some of these forerunners of pugnacity. While not severely beaten, his mother Barbara (in brother Jeb's own words) was a "drill sergeant," and due to the usual absence of father G.H.W. Bush, she administered most of the physical punishment. He was humiliated, and suffered from dyslexia, as did his brother Neil. Giving up his "frat boy" self and activities to become a born-again Christian governor and president may have left him with a good deal of anger. This sacrifice may have heightened his militancy. Perhaps "make love, not war" should guide us in choosing the next president and future leaders. (If making love, or at least sexual activity, was the criterion for a great president, Kennedy and Clinton would outshine Washington and Lincoln.)

John McCain was known as "McNasty" in his youth. He is still combative and has outbursts of temper. His father and grandfather were admirals, and he has inherited the necessarily bellicose military point of view. We almost got a president who would keep us in a state of perpetual war. His impulsive choice of Sarah Palin as a running mate with little vetting was careless, especially in a nuclear age.

CHAPTER THREE

About two fifths (40%) of the population with less than $50,000 annual household income voted for George W. Bush in 2004. They voted against their economic self-interest, since in four years Bush had given tax cuts to the rich and cut social programs drastically. Why would they vote against their own interests? Some of the factors leading them to vote against their interests were (*these factors or hypotheses are listed above in the summary of the Introduction*):

1. Self-esteem: The less powerful working and middle classes may identify upward with powerful figures to avoid identification with lower classes and minorities. Downward mobility is feared in a weakened economy. This is a class and race issue.
2. Exposure to labile (emotionally unstable), punitive, or consistently cold parenting during childhood leads the victims

of such abuse to give up their original "true" self in favor of a "false self" that submits to all the parents' demands. High levels of such parental behavior were found in a study, and perhaps three million U.S. children are abused or neglected each year. An incidence (annual new cases) figure of ten million children with "uncaring parents" is estimated. These three types of poor and uncaring parenting were the best predictors of later child behavior disorders.

Those adults with a "false self" lack autonomy and independence. They are trained to obedience and conformity. They will vote for a George W. Bush or a John McCain or any powerful authority figure (like their father or mother) who tells them what to do in simple terms. They are also used to caving in to authority figures (their parents) who do not always have their best interests at heart.

They also saw Bush as a "good fella" or "good old boy" (and saw John McCain that way) because they unconsciously tried to preserve that image of a good father or mother, which they learned to do despite neglect and abuse at their parents' hands during childhood.

3. In times of rapid social change, economic retrenchment, and national conflict over values (such as occurred in Weimar Germany and now in the United States) people look to an authoritarian leader who promises to solve all their problems with simple oft-repeated promises.

4. There is a "longing for community" when people are living in an ever more complex "society." This longing was evident in Germany just before the rise of Hitler, and is evident in the United States now. It seeks common values, strong authority in a leader, and a religious orientation. A return to the community (*Gemeinschaft*) is supposed to solve all the problems of living in a modern society (*Gesellschaft*).

We lost many of our civil rights under Bush. McCain promised to pack the Supreme Court with conservative judges. Remember that the first move Hitler made to gain power was to pack the German courts with Nazi judges.

Chapter Four

Certain U.S. subgroups were more likely to vote against their economic interests. On an international basis, Latin American countries had a "sunnier" view of their lives, despite great poverty. Was this due to depression, to denial? What does this say about the poor and minorities who voted for George Bush and McCain? Further research is needed to explain why some ethnic groups seem to be cheerful despite poverty and extreme hardship.

Chapter Five

George W. Bush presented five faces; the strong man, the failure-born again, the mouthpiece of God, the good fella, and the uncaring parent. These first four multiple faces helped him appeal to a broad spectrum of voters. McCain also had five faces: the strong man, the good fella, the maverick, the tortured sacrificial lamb or Christ-like prisoner of war, and an uncaring parent. The last image, the uncaring parent (or uncaring leader) is too painful for the past-and-present uncared-for adults, so it is put on a back burner and is at an unconscious level, except for most Democrats, who saw Bush and McCain as uncaring, dangerous, incompetent, arrogant, martial, and prejudiced against the poor and middle class.

Chapter Six

5. A fifth factor leading to voting against self interest is that the administration created a great deal of stress in four years. A random sample of adults in an American metropolis reported a large amount of stress in childhood and in adult life. The more stresses they experienced, the worse their mental health (symptomatology and role functioning).

The lying, the divisiveness, the war in Iraq, the failing economy, and the lack of concern for the middle class, the working class, and the poor has resulted in a sharp increase in mental disorder. A Manhattan survey found 23.4% of a random sample of adults age twenty to fifty-nine to have significant psychiatric impairment. In 2003 a World Health Organization (WHO) survey found that the

United States had the highest prevalence rate of mental disorder (26.4%) of fourteen countries studied. Anxiety disorders and Mood disorders contributed most to this figure, as opposed to Impulse Control disorders (anti-social behavior) and drug abuse. The public, faced with increasing stress fostered by the government, has succumbed primarily to anxiety and depression, and to a lesser extent, antisocial behavior and drugs. A campaign that promised the public that Bush could solve their problems (many of which he had created in his first term!) won the vote of a large segment of the political middle. Those promises were not kept. The anxious and depressed, easily swayed, were tricked by a campaign focusing on family values (abortion, gay marriage, stem-cell research, intelligent design) and playing down bread-and-butter issues. This pit-bull family-values approach was again employed by Sarah Palin. She forced her daughter to become engaged to another teenager and to carry her pregnancy full-term. She appealed to the (angry and "bitter") left behind folks who would like to shoot wolves from an airplane and field-dress a moose as she did, if only they had the jobs and money.

Fear of WMDs (weapons of mass destruction) and terrorists were used to sway those already anxious, and to justify unilateral and preemptive war in Iraq. Fears of terrorists and aggressive nations, more justified in 2009, are focused on North Korea, Afghanistan, and Iran.

Appendix Three

A Timeline and Update reviews the Bush years, the 2008 campaign, and the beginning of the Obama presidency. One can only conclude that the Republican Party, with Dick Cheney as mastermind, set out to destroy our constitutional rights, create a one-party nation, and set up an imperial presidency without a separation of powers.

Parting Thoughts

In the short and long term, the Democratic Party needs to be a caring parent, and Barack Obama holds out promise of that role.

The party needs to stand up to the financial experts who want to bail out the failing financial industry, but are loath to give similar help to the millions of Americans who have lost jobs, have lost the value of their homes, and who cannot pay their mortgage or their medical bills. The issues we face and the threats to our future as a nation are many: financial, environmental, political, geophysical, psychological, epidemiological, and many others.

In the long term, we need to change the social character of at least a fair portion of the population. We will have to teach good parenting that avoids cold, punitive, and labile treatment of the child. Training for parenthood should start in high school, so that the children of these current teenagers are not turned into compliant robots who can be easily misled by demagogues, wordsmiths, and stump orators who do not have their best interests at heart.

After reviewing the events of the eight years of the Bush/Cheney administration, with its radical attack on constitutional rights, and the concentration of wealth and power in the hands of a very small portion of the population, I must conclude that we have had a narrow escape from a one-party, military-industrial dictatorship. To prevent this from ever happening again, the best advice is in the maxim often attributed to Thomas Jefferson; "The price of freedom is eternal vigilance."

Since we have reviewed the Bush years in such detail, I think a review of the Obama months is in order here. Perhaps no new United States president other than Franklin Roosevelt has been faced with as many major problems as Barack Obama. The "legacy" of the eight Bush years was a "recession" that still looks more like the depression of the 1930s.

Deregulation that started with Reagan (and included Bill Clinton) created freedom for the banks to invent all kinds of complex investments. Subprime loans were "bundled" and sold by the banks to private investors. "Credit default swaps" were created. This was known as "securitization." Many new types of securities were invented, but they were far from secure. They failed when the subprime loans were found to be essentially worthless, and the banks here and abroad began to fail. Only massive infusions of money saved our own United States banks. The people who had subprime and even market-rate mortgages soon defaulted by the millions, due to job loss or being "under water." (The value of their houses was less than their mortgages.) Many just walked away from their homes, and in effect became homeless. A financial meltdown ensued.

In the meantime, Obama had to juggle war on two fronts: getting out of Iraq, and controlling the Taliban in Afghanistan. He also faced nuclear threats in North Korea, in Pakistan (whose nuclear force could be used against its enemy, India) and in Iraq, whose president clearly intends to have nuclear weapons, and threatens to destroy Israel and other countries in the Middle East.

While Obama early on promised prosecution of those in the Bush administration who promoted and legitimized torture, he later reneged, saying that "we should be looking forward, not backward." Then in 2009 he partially reversed his reversal, saying that an independent commission should be created to look into these illegitimate activities.

As a liberal, I would view Obama as a centrist. His book, *The Audacity of Hope*, is cautious, controlled, and presages his actions once in office. The right wing sees him as a monster, a socialist, a man without a birth certificate who is trampling on the Constitution. On the left, many progressives see him as too cautious and controlled. He is civil even to his tormentors. He hardly blinked when not a single House Republican voted for his economic stimulus bill (January 29, 2009), a bill that was clearly in their own interest (saving the banks).

Perhaps the liberals and the left in general expected too much of him. The attacks on his race, birth certificate, middle name, citizenship, community-organizer background, association with the Reverend Wright, and so on, have been nasty, but he has probably learned throughout his life, that you bite your lip, and that you "grin and bear it."

I agree 100% with Maureen Down in her column, "Less Spocky, More Rocky" (Dowd, *New York Times*, Op-Ed, September 9, 2009).

President Obama is so wrapped up in his desire to be a different, more conciliatory, beer-summit kind of leader, he ignores some verities…

Civil discourse is fine, but when the other side is fighting dirty, you should get angry. Don't let the bully kick sand in your face. The White House should have impaled death panel malarkey as soon as it came up.

Many progressives are deeply disappointed in Obama's tendency to compromise and renege on promises he made (or seemed to make) during his stirring campaign speeches. Strong evidence for this disaffection is found in a full page ad in the *New York Times*, September 10, 2009, demanding that the president fight to include the "public option" (a government health insurance program to compete with private insurance). This ad, in the form of a petition, was signed by four hundred former Obama campaign staffers, twenty-five thousand Obama volunteers, and forty-thousand Obama donors. The ad's headline says "Please demand a strong public health insurance option. Letting the insurance companies win would not be change we can believe in."

Lance Orchid, a Deputy Field Director for Obama in Georgia during the presidential campaign, wrote that after a near fatal accident he made calls for Obama from his recovery bed. He couldn't afford health insurance. His plea captures the feelings of so many who voted for Obama. "I worked for you because I believed you could bring real change on health care. The public option is that change—please don't disappoint me and the millions of people who believed in you."

There are many factors limiting how far Obama can go to effect "change." First among these is the huge budget deficit Bush left (four-hundred and eighty-two billion dollars). Money had to be "created" by the Federal Reserve to pay for the economic stimulus, and for any future expenditures, such as government health insurance, repairing the infrastructure, green technology, and educational reform, Money is needed for the homeless, for those who lost their homes to foreclosure, and to reduce mortgage payments for millions of families, especially the jobless.

Another strong limiting factor is the GOP refusal to compromise. Their attack on Obama and his agenda has been unrelenting. To get his health bill passed, Obama's inner circle threatens to use "reconciliation," a procedural maneuver that allows the bill to pass with a simple majority. This would bypass the sixty votes needed to avoid a Senate filibuster. Alternately, one or two Republicans might vote with the Democrats.

A third factor limiting Obama's choices is the widespread anger and fear generated by the GOP's campaign propaganda against Obama's health reform. The "death panels" and "pulling the plug on grandma" suggest euthanasia The usual public distrust of "big government" has been exacerbated. More people fear a loss of choice, or a medical bureaucracy that would be unresponsive. Choice and bureaucracy are two more of the scary sound-bites that the GOP is employing. Distrust of Obama and his agenda may spread from the health reform conflict to his other initiatives.

The above factors are external roadblocks to change. Yet Obama himself has internal problems which interfere with his ability to get his legislation priorities passed. He has often delayed to strike back at GOP offensives until the last minute. Kerry delayed too long to fight the Swift Boat smear campaign. Dukakis delayed to quell the Willie Horton smear. Obama waited two months to call the death panels and hints of euthanasia just plain lies. His reticence and supernatural coolness in the face of attack may have deep roots.

Obama is biracial. He grew up as a black (as defined by our society) with an absent black father away in Kenya, a white mother, and was raised primarily by his white grandparents. He fits the role of the "marginal man," who has dual loyalties and is torn between them. In classical sociological literature, the foreman was the common example of the marginal man, torn between loyalty to the corporate bosses and the workers he supervised. In a sense, Obama's loyalties were split between the dominant white community to which his mother and grandparents belonged, and the black community. He worked as a community organizer in the black ghettos of Chicago.

One solution to having to please two masters is to please neither, and become radicalized. Another is to become a centrist.

To "reach across the aisle," to compromise, comes naturally to someone who must please two masters from childhood on. Since the white master is much the stronger, it is necessary to be deferential to him first of all. Obama has been trying to be bipartisan and gentlemanly throughout his campaign and the first eight months of his presidency. He looked tense during Hillary Clinton's jibe, "Lifting whole passages from other people's speeches is not change you can believe in. It is change that you can Xerox," but he did not attack back. (See the February 21, 2008 entry in the Timeline.) Unfortunately, blacks still have to be deferential to succeed in the white world of the United States. When this pattern of deference and good behavior is plunged into the fiery pit of politics, it appears as super-cool and over-controlled.

The fight over health care will mark a critical turning point in Obama's presidential course. In his speech to the combined House and Senate, he came on strongly at times, even calling the GOP slurs on his plan "lies." He promised that it would be against the law to deny coverage because of preexisting conditions. He also said that under his plan insurance could not be canceled if you got sick. These are major protections. Yet he did not clearly state that he would fight for the "public option" at any cost. Remember, the White House has made no mention of the single payer (government only insurance) plan. That was the choice of many progressives and health professionals. They have had to settle for the "public option," a plan that includes private health insurance. Private insurance has failed to deliver the care we need at a reasonable cost, yet it is still part of the Democrats' plan. If the "public option" is compromised, there will be little of the "change" that most of the public believed in.

Another internal roadblock to creating the change that Obama promised is that the only people who have the skills to rescue the nation from financial collapse are apparently the very ones who helped create the crisis. Lawrence Summers and Timothy Geithner are part of the banking and Wall Street culture that created the meltdown. So is Benjamin Bernanke, Chairman of the Federal Reserve, who has been credited by many with turning the financial meltdown around, but criticized by some who feel he didn't print enough money to do the job completely. He is also a disciple of

Alan Greenspan, who publicly confessed that his faith in the free market had been misplaced.

Despite the fact that Obama's "honeymoon" is over (and he never had Republicans with him on his honeymoon) the economy is slowly turning around in 2009. Though unemployment is 9.7% (a twenty-six-year high), the Dow Jones is up from a November 2008 low of 7449 to a high of 9627 on September 10, 2009. (That's still a long way from the 13338 high of January 2008.) Major banks have paid back much of the emergency money they received, and the taxpayers got 15% interest on those loans. The rate of job loss has slowed, but this is hardly something to crow about. Consumer spending is low, yet there is hope for improvement with the Christmas season. Obama has shown a great deal more fire in his September 9, 2009 speech to Congress, and that bodes well for the rest of his term.

Further thoughts on the first months of the Obama presidency are given at the end of Appendix Three: A Timeline and Update.

About the Author

My professional experience is described in the preface. As for my immediate family—we live in New York City—my wife and my daughter by this marriage, who is now sixteen. My wife is a children's book editor and author.

Our extended family includes five children by my first marriage. There are also four grandchildren. We try to visit our far-flung family when school permits.

I built our country home in Connecticut over a ten-year period, starting in 1953. Since then I've been busy repairing it. I use three tractors to do gardening and yard work. We hike and swim. My hobbies, when I'm not writing a book, are reading, writing music, carpentry, vegetable gardening, photography, watching movies and political talk-shows on TV, and travel to remote countries.

The following Appendices are an expansion of some of the factors listed and examined in the Introduction, "List of Possible Factors Influencing U.S. Voters to Vote against Their Self-interest."

Appendix One
Fear and Terror Management

In my book, *Choices for Living: Coping with Fear of Dying*, I asked the question "Is fear of dying innate (instinctive or hard wired) or is it learned?" On reviewing the literature, I came to the conclusion that "fear of dying is due to the inevitable momentary abandonments of the infant by the mother and/or father, and the deep threats to the child's existence that these momentary lapses pose" (Langner, 2002, p. 13). This is based on the work of John Bowlby ("attachment theory") and Sylvia Anthony (see p. 29, ibid.). Given the helplessness of the infant, the mother's departure, even though brief, sets off an alarm. The mother's momentary absence may signal her death. "Object constancy" (the stability of the mother's image in the child's mind, even when she is absent) is gradually established by games such as peek-a-boo, and verbal and physical reassurances. Separation anxiety is slowly reduced. This is a stage in the development of independence and *autonomy*.

It is obvious that fear played a large role in persuading people to vote for Bush rather than Kerry in 2004. Just how large a role, the level of consciousness at which it acted, and whether it acted equally on voters of the left, right, or center, are difficult questions to answer at this time, but some of the experiments show differential response to threat (see Introduction, no. 10. "The GOP-DEM split may have some physiological or genetic basis.") Let's first examine the part of "Terror Management Theory" (TMT) as it applies to the 2004 election.

Al Franken, in his book *The Truth* (Franken 2005, pp. 29–31), cites a few TMT studies that seem to test the hypothesis that the fear (about the dangers of terrorism, the "axis of evil," and weapons of mass destruction) generated by the Bush campaign messages after the 9/11 bombing won him the election. TMT is built upon the work of Ernest Becker. The portion of his writing that gave birth to TMT is contained in *Denial of Death* (Becker, 1973). He said that humans need two kinds of defenses against the knowledge (though usually on a back burner, or "middle knowledge") that we must die: self-esteem and a cultural world view (usually limited to one's own membership group). Since death-anxiety (terror) is held in check by the self-esteem provided by this group membership (and the illusion of immortality it engenders), the world view of *other* groups arouses anxiety, anger, and terror.

Most relevant to our search for an answer to why Bush won in 2004, with a large proportion of people voting against their self-interests, is a series of experiments conducted before the election. In one study, ninety-seven subjects were divided into an experimental group who were reminded of their own mortality ("Describe the emotion that the thought of your own death arouses in you, and jot down...what you think will happen to you as you physically die and once you are physically dead.") and a control group who were not reminded of their mortality. The subjects then read an essay praising President Bush's response to 9/11 and the Iraq war. They proceeded to rate their approval of Bush and his policies. The "mortality salience" group rated Bush more favorably (4.16 on a five-point scale) compared with those in the control group (2.09).

In further experiments, the researchers showed that subliminal 9/11 images stimulated unconscious death-related thoughts, that reminders of 9/11 increased support for Bush, and that reminders of mortality increased support for Bush and decreased support for Kerry. These effects took place, regardless of whether the subjects said they were liberal or conservative (Landau, 2004).The fact that *both* liberals and conservatives showed increased support for Bush runs counter to the results of Oxley, Smith et al. (2008), who found that conservatives reacted to threat (pictures of blood and maggots) with greater physiological response than did liberals.

The mortality-salience experiments confirm what we already knew; that Bush's approval ratings shot up after 9/11. When there is a direct attack, such as Pearl Harbor, most citizens tend to support the sitting president. When a presidential election comes up at a time of crisis, we always hear the phrase "Don't change horses in mid-stream." Bush's presentation of self (tough and self-assured), as discussed in Chapter Five, made him the more desirable choice after 9/11, *if* you believed his façade. Were the Bush voters who favored him for his assumed ability to protect them against attack and death just being rational (not irrational, as terror-management theory implies)? In addition, the samples were small and not representative. Despite these problems, this research illustrates how some people in the political middle might have been swayed by death-fear and 9/11 to vote for Bush rather than Kerry. I would add that those who had experienced uncaring parents would be more likely to be anxious and fearful, to be less autonomous, and thus unable to make a rational choice based on *all* the issues discussed during the election campaigns.

It is my conviction that social character determines who will be overwhelmed with fear when a catastrophe occurs. This character is developed early in life. This authoritarian character is induced in children by uncaring and abusive parents. By ignoring the child's individual needs, they deprive him of autonomy. (There may be a connection with narcissistic injury, since the narcissist is overly concerned with death.) The individual with an authoritarian personality seeks a charismatic leader. He is unable to make autonomous judgments. He gave up his autonomy as a child. He votes for an uncaring, dictatorial, and charismatic leader, someone who is more similar to his uncaring parent than a reasoned, logical leader who appeals to the head, not the heart. In this fashion, a large number of people come to vote against their own self-interests, motivated by their psychological fears and anxieties, not by the qualifications of the candidates and the full range of issues.

The 2008 U.S. election results seem to tell us that despite these deep WMD-related fears, the voting public made a choice that served its self interest. But wait! Another set of fears—of the economic meltdown, job loss, home foreclosure, poverty—took over in the fourth quarter of 2008, just before the election. Given the enormity of that economic threat, it is surprising that Obama didn't win by a larger margin. The "stubborn mule" or "shock" hypothesis seems like one of the best explanations of the Democratic sweep.

If world terrorism spreads, as it has to Spain, London, and Bali, and if Iran and North Korea develop or actually use nuclear bombs, American voters, out of fear, may install another radical right-wing regime that will curtail our liberties even further. A democracy can survive only as long as it has a solid base of people who vote with their heads, who consider all the issues, and who don't let themselves be steamrollered by fear and hoodwinked by lies.

Appendix Two
Do the Majority of People Have Basic Economic Interests to Vote Democratic

There are several hypotheses about why the Democrats didn't win in 2004. These are some of the ones that I don't agree with, or only partially accept, and here are the reasons why I don't agree.

1. *FEAR ALONE WON THE ELECTION: TERROR MANAGEMENT THEORY*

(See Introduction, no. 5. "Conservative policies and propaganda created stresses.")

I have taken the position that while legitimate fear was created by the 9/11 attack, the GOP played on that fear with frequent alerts of various "colors." They exacerbated what was a perfectly legitimate fear, by means of propaganda. When it looked as if Saddam Hussein did not buy yellowcake uranium ore to make Weapons of Mass Destruction, they were furious, and punished Wilson by outing his wife, Valerie Plame. Warning: "don't interfere with our fear!"

In addition, I think that those people with an authoritarian social character were more likely to vote for Bush. (This is despite the fact that a single terror management study of a sample of college students suggested that those on the left and right were equally scared by 9/11 and thoughts of death.) It seems logical to me that people who have been abused or neglected in childhood are *more* likely than those with nurturant parents to fear dying, and thus to vote for the man who *claims* to be the stronger (more protective) of the two candidates.

The Swift Boat attack on Kerry was specifically designed to picture him as weak and waffling, thereby making Bush seem strong and a protector against WMDs, Muslims, and terrorists.

2.   FAMILY VALUES ALONE CLOUDED THE MINDS OF POTENTIAL KERRY VOTERS

(See Introduction, #3. The smokescreen or head-feint effect (GOP propaganda

Frank (2005) in *What's the Matter with Kansas?* puts much of the blame for the GOP victory in 2004 on the use of "family values" as a smoke screen, a way of taking attention away from bread and butter issues. While this is true to some extent, these "head feints" and propaganda tricks would not work if there were not a vulnerable population that was ready to fall for them. This vulnerability derives from a failure to develop autonomy in childhood, and to learn critical and independent thinking. Again, it seems to me that uncaring parents and an authoritarian character prepared them to be fooled.

3.   THE GOP STOLE THE ELECTION BY KEEPING MINORITIES AND THE POOR FROM THE POLLS.

(See Introduction, no. 8. Election fraud favored the GOP.)

In *Fooled Again*, by Mark Crispin Miller (2005), the various tricks and skullduggery of the Republican campaign to steal the election are reviewed in horrific detail. While there is no doubt in my mind that Ohio's electoral votes (and those of other states) were won by programming voting machines, by threatening or misleading minority voters, and by making machines accessible for wealthy districts and inaccessible in poor areas, this does not negate the fact that the popular vote was won by the GOP with only a few million more than the Democrats.

If my figures are anywhere near right, some forty percent of the Bush voters actually voted against their economic interests. They had *four years* to see how Bush gave to the rich, and took from the poor and middle class. In Chapter Four the results of the Pew Center research showed that a good portion of Bush voters had lower or lower-middle class incomes. (I used a cutting point of under $50,000 household income.) Again, I interpret this as due to low self esteem, identification upward, to racism (avoiding identification with racial minorities), and to a search for community in the midst of our socially isolating-every-man-for-himself society.

If my suppositions are right (that it is very hard for a family to live on less than $50,000 a year before taxes, with prices for health care and insurance, food, shelter, clothing, heating fuel and gasoline spiraling out of control, or showing extreme volatility), then bread and butter issues should have trumped family values, and even fear of terrorists. But the logical model of human behavior (rational economic behavior) is trumped by the irrational. That irrationality, in turn, derives from early separation anxiety, emotional deprivation, and uncaring parents.

Were it not for this fearful, angry, competitive, hierarchical mind set, there could have been a plurality of twenty million or forty million votes in favor of Kerry, not just a mere three million in favor of Bush.

4.   *"The Majority of People Do Not Have Basic Economic Interests to Vote Democratic."*

(See Introduction, no. 9. "The U.S. has become too middle class to vote democratic.")

So sayeth Steve Rose, in *Talking About Social Class: Are the Economic Interests of the Majority of Americans with the Democratic Party?* (Rose, 2005). Rose decided to specify the proportion of people who would benefit by the government's "safety net" programs. To do this, he looked at the average annual family incomes for "prime age adults" (26–59) over a fifteen year period. The figures he got were"$66,000 for males and $61,000 for females (1999 dollars).

What is wrong with this picture? First of all, by lopping off those between voting ages eighteen to twenty-five, and those sixty and over, he has distorted the results. Don't young adults and over sixties count? Don't they vote? These two groups constitute about *one third* of the voting public, and are also clearly of lower income. The young have not yet achieved their full earning potential, and most of those over sixty are struggling on Social Security or pensions which pay a fraction of what they formerly earned. Rose has already severely slanted his results.

He then does something else which favors his coming out with the result he seems to want; that Americans are too wealthy to see the Democratic Party as their economic safety net. The preselected group he examines has more income, and thus has less need of a safety net. So, by his argument, that group doesn't need to vote Democrat. Since he takes the average (or the "mean") income as his measure, he exaggerates once more the general income level of the population. In first year statistics courses students are taught that the long "tail" at the high end of the income distribution tends to skew or distort the results of the average income, and that the median (the income at the midpoint point of the income distribution) is the preferred income measure. From census data (DeNovas-Walt et al., 2005) I calculated the *median* household income in 2004 for ages 25 to 64 (as close as I could get to Rose's age breaks) at about $56,785. This is well below Rose's figures of $66,000 and $61,000, or a mid-point for both sexes of $63,500! The United States Census figure for median household incomes in 2004 (*regardless of age*), was $44,389. This is getting closer to the $50,000 cutting point which I used to label Bush voters as "voting against their economic self-interest."

Now if we look at "householders" ages fifteen to twenty-four (median $27,506) and sixty-five and over (median $24,509) it is clear that the average *and* the median income will be much lower when all the population is considered. (People of ages fifteen to seventeen cannot vote, but I did not have access to age breaks which excluded them.)

231

Rose's argument, that values trump economics, seems attractive at first, but on further examination it exaggerates the effect of the rising income of the nation by selecting the highest earning segment of the population, and using the average income as a measure.

My cutting point of $50,000 (to define those in each cluster group who "voted against their economic self-interest") is corroborated by Garance Franke-Ruta (2006), who says "...surveys repeatedly show that $50,000 seems to be the threshold income dividing the economically insecure from their more prosperous countrymen, and the average household income in America is now, despite years of stagnant wages, $56,644." (How this average figure was arrived at is a mystery, since it comes out almost exactly at the median for ages twenty-five to sixty-four in 2004!)

I am indebted to David Brooks for quoting Rose in his column *Dollars and Sense* (Brooks, 2006). I can count on him to "cherry-pick" data to support his "Rosy" view of the economy and the state of the union in general. I must credit "Jill," a blogger, with the use of the term "cherry-pick," for it is right on the mark. She also criticizes the Brooks/Rose emphasis on "social anxiety" as opposed to economic worries.

Brooks says, "Middle-class Americans feel social anxiety more acutely than economic anxiety because they understand that values matter most." (Brooks, 2006).

Jill counters, "Perhaps middle-class Americans feel social anxiety more acutely than economic anxiety because they have a sense that social factors are something they can control, whereas economics are in the hands of multinational corporations and the politicians whose favors they buy" (Jill, 2006).

I should point out that the financial and economic meltdown in 2008 has made Rose's 2005 hunch even less tenable. The pocketbook mindset has overtaken the family values mania and the Iraq WMD fears. The Democratic Party has benefited greatly from the recession, and is now indeed attractive to the middle class, which has suffered great losses in income, jobs, retirement nest-eggs, home values, and foreclosures.

Why can people overlook their often desperate economic situation when voting, as did so many in 2004? In Chapter Three I reviewed several reasons, such as a campaign of fear, bald-faced lies and broken promises, a longing for "community" with a homogeneous population and common values, the desire for simple explanations of very complex problems, and last but not least, the redirection of their anger (arising from the loss of their "true self" and uncaring or abusive parents) at target groups by means of the "family values" crusade. "Jill" makes this last reason crystal clear:

"If Americans can point fingers at those they deem unworthy—pregnant women, television screenwriters, actors, and non-Christians, they don't have to pay attention to the erosion of their own economic lives" (Jill, ibid.). This is the "smoke screen" or "head-feint" argument, which certainly fits the facts, in my opinion. What makes voters psychologically vulnerable to the smokescreen is a big issue for me. I don't think people are just plain stupid, as some commentators believe. I think they are *uninformed* and have been duped by highly skilled manipulators in a concerted, well-organized and heavily funded campaign by the Republicans.

5. SUBSTITUTE "BRIDGE VALUES" FOR PROGRESSIVE POLICIES AND ISSUES.

There has been a movement by some Democrats to bridge the gap in values between progressives and those on the right, (ranging from fiscal conservatives to the fundamentalist evangelicals). Hillary Clinton, during her presidential campaign, deplored abortion as a "sad, even tragic, choice," while still supporting the ability of women to choose it if needed, by vowing (as her husband did) to keep it "safe, legal, and rare." She is reaching out to those who hate abortion, and want to ban it. She is saying, as Bill famously said, "I feel your pain" (or rage?). In "bridging" this hot button issue, she prepared to reach a wider base for the 2008 presidential elections.

This can be viewed in several ways. If it is an abandonment of liberal values in an attempt to win election in 2008, then it could be seen as pandering to the right-wing. Some Republican commentators labeled it as a ruse to disguise Hillary's true "radical-liberal" take on abortion. They would say it was a "smoke screen of the left." (If the GOP can blow smoke, why not the Democrats?) A third view is that there has to be some consensus and common ground in America, and that both parties should try to reach "across the aisle" to save our democracy. This third view has been promulgated by Obama during his campaign, and after he won the election. Perhaps the truth lies in a mixture of all these motives.

Franke-Ruta (2006) refers to the American Environics team that counseled Democratic Party leaders and interest groups in 2005. They conducted in-home consumer surveys. Nordhaus and Shellenberger performed a cluster analysis on 117 "values" items using the Environics data.

"Looking at the data from 1992 to 2004, (they) found a country whose citizens are increasingly authoritarian while at the same time feeling evermore adrift, isolated, and nihilistic. They found a society at once more libertine and more puritanical..." (Franke-Ruta, 2006).

These values were factored into four quadrants. One axis is authority (traditional family, religiosity, emotional control, and obedience) versus individuality (risk taking, anomie-aimlessness, flexible families and personal choice). On the other axis is fulfillment (civic engagement, ecological concern, and empathy) vs. survival (acceptance of violence, and civic apathy, sexism, fatalism, and "every man for himself"). They find that over twelve years the values trend has been away from fulfillment, and toward the survival quadrant, and away from authority toward individuality (rage, consumption, sexual permissiveness and xenophobia).

Interestingly, this shift is in the direction of the macho man, the strict uncaring father, and the bully. When the Vice President told Senator Leahy to "Go fuck yourself," he set an example for the nation.(It's my way or the highway!)

Now hedonism, self-centeredness, and ruthless competition are part of what Toennies deplored *121 years ago* (1887) in his depiction of "society" (*Gesellschaft*). He saw people in society (in contrast to "community") as using others for their own purposes (instrumentally) rather than for their intrinsic value as friends or fellow-citizens. (Isn't "networking" replacing friendship?) Relationships in society were impersonal, individualism reigned, there was great anonymity, and the family was replaced by business and the state. Of course, every positive value has its downside. Individuality may lead to social Darwinism (every man for himself).

Franke-Ruta (2006) tells how the governor of Virginia dealt with a population that overwhelmingly supported the death penalty.

> ...once Kaine started talking about his religious background and explaining that his opposition to the death penalty grew out of his Catholic faith, not only did charges that he was weak on crime fail to stick, but he became inoculated against a host of related charges that typically plague the campaigns of Democratic candidates. 'Once people understood the values system that the position grew out of, *they understood that he's not a liberal,*' says Brodnitz (Kaine's pollster) [Emphasis mine].

So is the solution to the Democrats' dilemma for all candidates to convert to Catholicism or other mainstream religions, and to proclaim their membership loudly? (Obama's religiosity certainly did not hurt his candidacy, although Reverend Wright was an albatross.) Clearly the DEMS should drop the "liberal" label pro tem, and they seem to have morphed into "progressives" anyway. If the GOP can use euphemisms, why can't the Democrats? If the Patriot Act (a cover for spying on U.S. citizens and condoning torture and loss of habeas corpus) and Clean Air (an excuse for continued polluting) and No Child Left Behind (an underfunded program that promotes school vouchers that aim to destroy the public school system) and the Medicare Plan D Drug Program (a giveaway to the insurance and pharmaceutical companies) can help the Elephants bamboozle the populace, then why shouldn't the Donkeys use the same tactics? Get the wordsmiths to work!

Here's a new religious pitch. All Democrats are "people of faith." (Who cares that a lot of us have a different slant on faith, or are secularists, agnostics, or even atheists?) We are against sin, especially venality (the cardinal sin of CEOs). We hold charity in high esteem. We give to the poor and needy out of our compassion, which is based on the religion of our forefathers. Didn't Lincoln say "With malice toward none, with *charity* for all..."? Anybody who is a skilled liar can play the values game.

Sure there are underlying value differences in America. But they are being used, twisted, subverted, and purposely exaggerated by demagogues. Even some evangelicals are beginning to see the value of saving the environment, stopping global warming, and fighting child prostitution. They are contributing to campaigns against poverty and sexual slavery all over the world. There is a possible bridge. The danger in "bridging" is that liberals will go past the center of the "bridge" to actually support anti-abortion and anti-gay positions, censorship, the war in Iraq, school vouchers, privatization, intelligent design, invasion of privacy, and all the other Bush/Cheney positions that still threaten our democracy.

Just as in war, we usually become too much like the enemy, so in politics we must beware of being so centrist that there are no longer two parties in America. This slide toward the middle is of great concern to the left that voted Obama in.

The direction of values in America *seems* to be toward the reactionary and illiberal. However, if we look at Ruy Teixeira's (2006) critique of the grim picture painted by Nordhaus and Shellenberger as reported by Franke-Ruta (2006), we find some telling criticisms. Their data were based on a consumer market-research survey over time, but that study was not specifically designed to test values. Several studies show a growing support for women's roles, in contrast to their findings. There are positive (more progressive) trends in other values. Texeira finds the best bit of advice in Franke-Ruta's article toward the end:

> American voters have taken shelter under the various wings of conservative traditionalism because there has been no one on the Democratic side in recent years to defend the traditional, sensible middle-class values against the onslaught of the new nihilistic, macho, libertarian lawlessness unleashed by an economy that pits every man against his fellows. Yet in private

conversations, progressives recognize that there is a need to do something about broad social changes that they, too, find objectionable (Franke-Ruta, ibid.).

Obama did defend traditional values when he emphasized the middle class, not the working class, in his speeches, and sent a message of faith, hope, and charity, as well as "change." (The three holy virgin martyrs' Greek names were *Pistis*, *Elpis*, and *Agape*.) How closely his messages hew to the themes of Lincoln, an obvious role model for Obama. Even his inaugural train from Philadelphia to Washington is modeled on Lincoln's, as well as his optimistic message of hope.

So here is some common ground: the broad social changes that both sides find objectionable. Many of these changes are not new, although they may have been accelerated since the end of World War II. The majority of Republicans *and* Democrats are acutely aware of the "discontents of our civilization" (Freud) and the ills of Toennies' "society." But where they differ fundamentally is *how to go about correcting or alleviating those ills and discontents.*

To look on the bright side, the radical and reckless agenda of the Bushies forced the Democrats to fight back, to formulate their approach, and organize and sharpen their positions and policies. Obama used values to get the necessary votes. The core progressive values are right out of the Bible (B), the Talmud (T), the Koran (K), and all the major religions of the world. B: ("Do unto others ...") "Thou shalt not kill, steal, commit adultery, covet thy neighbor's wife, nor bear false witness against a neighbor." T: "The more flesh, the more worms. The more possessions, the more worry." K: "Wealth and children are the adornment of this present life: but good works, which are lasting, are better in the sight of thy Lord, as to recompense, and better as to hope." We needn't be ashamed of these universal values.

Appendix Three
A Timeline and Update

December 12, 2000. The November 12 presidential election race between George W. Bush and Albert A. Gore is contested. The main dispute is over the "hanging, dimpled" or "pregnant" chads. Chads were the parts that were supposed to be completely punched out of IBM cards used by voters in Florida. If they were hanging or otherwise not completely punched out, they could be counted as a vote or not, depending on the political persuasion of the human vote counters and officials.

In addition to chad interpretation favoring Bush, Florida Secretary of State Katherine Harris and Jeb Bush, Florida's Governor, help brother G.W. by a "computer purge" of fifty-seven thousand blacks and Hispanics from the voter lists, on the grounds that they have criminal records. In August 2003, 38% of Americans polled view the election as stolen.

June 7, 2001. Bush tax cuts for the wealthy, of $1.35 trillion, start.

March 28, 2001. Bush refuses to sign the Kyoto Treaty on global warming.

October 26, 2001. The Patriot Act is created in response to the 9/11 attack. This gives Bush & Co. an opportunity to make draconian methods of social control into law. Among other incursions on civil rights:

Loss of protection against unreasonable searches.

Loss of right to trial and counsel.

No protection for suspects against "extraordinary rendition," which involves flying suspects to countries where they can be tortured.

Suspension of habeas corpus in cases of suspected terrorism. (A writ of habeas corpus demands that a prisoner be brought before the court to determine if the court has the authority to hold him or her in prison.)

Allows "roving wiretaps" (taps on multiple devices simultaneously).

Allows secret warrants for books and records of hospitals, businesses, and libraries. (Hospital records were searched to find the names of girls who had abortions.)

Allows search of Internet and telephone records for calls to and from foreign countries. There is litigation (2008) over whether phone companies are to be held harmless from suits over their divulging personal information.

Creates a permanent police force, the United States Secret Service Uniformed Division, under the control of the Department of Homeland Security. This force is empowered to make arrests without warrants for any suspected felony.

March 10, 2006. The Patriot Act is reauthorized after nine months of debate in Congress. Some of the above provisos have been modified.

February 12, 2008. The Senate votes to broaden the government's spy powers, and gives immunity against lawsuits over invasion of privacy to phone companies that cooperated in Bush's surveillance program. It extends new eavesdropping powers for six years from 2007. The government can eavesdrop on foreign-based communications without getting court approval, as long as Americans are not the targets. The House approved a prior surveillance bill but left out phone company immunity. The two houses must now hammer out a final bill. Obviously, many

Democrat politicians feared losing votes in the 2008 elections if they appeared soft on terrorism.

September 11, 2001. Nineteen terrorists (fifteen of them Saudis) hijack four commercial airliners. They fly them into the twin towers of the World Trade Center in Manhattan, New York City, and into the Pentagon in Arlington, Virginia. The twin towers are destroyed, as is part of the Pentagon. The passengers of the fourth plane overpower the terrorists, and the plane crashes in Shanksville, PA. All together, 2,973 people die. Many rescue workers, including firemen and policemen, die. Surviving rescuers and construction workers are sickened by the pollutants from the attack. The government denies any ill effects at first. Americans are made aware of their vulnerability for the first time since Pearl Harbor. There is an outpouring of support for the victims, and a sense of national bonding.

Bush's reaction to being told by Andrew Card that the second tower has been attacked seems to be paralysis or incomprehension. He continues to listen to a class of children in the Booker Elementary School read about a pet goat.

September 13, 2001. Despite the total restriction of all aircraft from the skies after 9/11, 160 members of the Saudi bin Laden family are flown out of the United States and back home on 787s.

November 18, 2001. No Child Left Behind bill passes Congress.

October 7, 2001. The United States invades Afghanistan.

December 2, 2001. The Enron Corporation goes bankrupt.

January 8, 2002. The No Child Left Behind" act (NCLB) is signed by Bush. This act was sold as "standards-based educational reform." While it had lofty goals, there were major problems. It requires that the name, address, and phone number of every student be given to military recruiters. States set the standards, but these vary widely Critics say that NCLB encourages "teaching to the test," and discourages educational innovation.

NCLB has never been fully funded, leaving the states to pay the bills for creation of standards, curricula, tests, test administration, scoring and reporting, etc.

Students at "failing" schools can transfer to private or parochial (religious) schools at government expense. This defies the rule of separation of church and state. This push for privatization of education is also reflected in the School Voucher program.

March 26, 2007. Senator Ted Kennedy, a lead author of NCLB in 2001, in an Op-Ed in the *Washington Post*, suggested ways to improve it before its reauthorization, which has been greatly delayed. These included, among others, modernization of curriculum, greater funding to provide qualified teachers at all socioeconomic levels, and greater financial support for "inadequate" schools. "Assessment and accountability without the funding needed to implement change is a recipe for failure" (Kennedy, ibid.).

January 2007. Bush is expected to veto any bill containing the Kennedy revisions. Members of both parties are also loath to get behind a bill favored by an unpopular president. NCLB is being *left behind*.

January 10, 2002. A congressional investigation of energy trading by Kenneth Lay, president of the Enron Corporation, results in the eventual conviction of Lay and Jeffrey Skilling, who, along with others, were given prison terms. Many small investors lost their life savings. Confidence in the stock market was shaken. GOP avoidance of its regulating functions is partly responsible. Where was the SEC (Securities and Exchange Commission)?

The Enron collapse was an early warning of the 2006 bursting of the housing bubble due to lack of regulation of bundled subprime mortgages and other exotic investments. The "dot.com" bubble climaxed in 2002, and again many lost their money in Internet investments.

January 29, 2002. Bush calls Iraq, Iran, and North Korea an "axis of evil." He accuses them of sponsoring terrorism and having or developing weapons of mass destruction. During his watch, North Korea has apparently tested at least one nuclear weapon. Iran has been buying and developing centrifuges, ostensibly for nuclear power plants. Unless inspections are permitted, Iran may be stockpiling nuclear fuel to use in weapons. Iraq, which abandoned its nuclear weapons program, was said by Bush to have "weapons of mass destruction." This proved to be wrong. If "WMDs" were the prime reason for invading Iraq, Bush-Cheney-Rumsfeld picked the wrong country. The nations that had WMDs or were on their way to making them are still in the same position. Moreover, this was not an axis, since these three nations were either unconnected, or actually enemies (Iraq and Iran).

February 14, 2002. "Clear Skies" initiative is announced by the White House. This program, voluntary for polluting industries, reverses Clinton's much stricter clean air rules.

May 23, 2002. Attorney General Ashcroft removes restrictions on domestic spying.

June 1, 2002. In a speech, Bush declares the "Bush Doctrine," of preemptive war. This is the doctrine that stumps Sarah Palin during an interview.

June 5, 2002. Ashcroft says Jose Padilla, a U.S. citizen, will be held as an "enemy combatant."

May 30, 2002. Monitoring of political and religious groups is O.K. by new guidelines.

August 26, 2002. V.P. Cheney says Saddam Hussein has "weapons of mass destruction" (WMDs).

October 2, 2002. After Saddam Hussein refuses U.N. inspectors access to his presumed nuclear facilities, Congress authorizes the use of military force against Iraq. Hillary Clinton, John Kerry, and many other politicians later regret their authorization of the Iraq war. In fact, they were presented with falsified intelligence by the administration, even in a speech by the trusted ex-general and then Secretary of State Colin Powell. Barack Obama votes against authorization.

March 7, 2003. Exposure of the "yellowcake uranium" false documents, which reveals the Bush/Cheney twisting of intelligence to justify the war in Iraq.

March 18, 2003. U.S. forces plus a "coalition of the willing" invade Iraq. Saddam Hussein is captured, jailed, tried, and finally hanged on December 30, 2006.

May 1, 2003. Bush declares "victory in Iraq," in front a large banner saying "Mission Accomplished." He appears on the flight deck of the aircraft carrier *Abraham Lincoln* in a flight suit and helmet.

June 2003. Karl Rove, I. "Scooter" Libby, and Richard Armitage tell several newspaper reporters that Valerie Plame (aka Valerie Wilson) was a covert CIA officer (i e., a spy) working on nuclear proliferation.

July 6, 2003. Her husband, Joseph C. Wilson IV, a former ambassador, writes an Op-Ed piece in the *New York Times*, "What I Didn't Find in Africa." He found no evidence of attempts by Iraq to purchase uranium.

July 14, 2003. Robert Novak "outs" Valerie Plame in his article "Mission to Niger." This disclosure exposed the importance to the administration of protecting their claims to "weapons of mass destruction" and to the alleged seeking of "yellowcake" uranium by Saddam Hussein from Niger. Wilson's Op-Ed refuted those claims, and eventually led to the revelation of the longstanding plans of the White House and the neoconservatives (Perle, Wolfowitz, Kristol et al.) to invade Iraq.

March 6, 2007. Libby (the fall guy for his boss, Cheney) is convicted of perjury, false statements, and obstruction of justice. He is sentenced to thirty months in jail and fined $250,000.

July 2, 2007. Bush commutes Libby's jail sentence. (At the end of his second term, Bush refuses Cheney's request that he pardon Libby.)

September 1, 2003. The United States has lost 2.7 million jobs in three years of Bush's first term.

October 21, 2003. Congress votes a ban on late-term abortions. This is part of the right wing's piecemeal attack on *Roe v. Wade*, which includes mandatory "parental notification" of a teen pregnancy by doctors.

November 24, 2003. Medicare Plan D passes. While this seems to be a boon to seniors, it is also a giveaway to the drug companies, since the government is prohibited from bargaining with the companies for lower prices. The "doughnut hole" in 2003 was a gap between $2,250 and $5,100 in annual drug costs during which the enrollees must pay 100% of their drug costs out of pocket, while at the same time paying monthly premiums. Worse yet, the size of the "hole" will increase each year. In 2003, more than half of the Part D enrollees fell into the "hole" trap, and there was a sharp increase in mortality. Insurance companies have increased the deductibles, the co-pay rates, and the premiums each year through 2009.

January 5, 2004. V.P. Cheney and Supreme Court Justice Scalia go duck hunting. Is this a reward for the upcoming court's eventual decision to deny public access to the records of Cheney's Energy Task Force meetings? Where is the regard for the separation of powers of the branches (Executive and Judicial) of the government?

January 13, 2004. U.S. Army Specialist Joe Darby hands over 279 photographs and nineteen videos of torture in Baghdad's Abu Ghraib prison to the Army's CID (Criminal investigation Division). He received them from Charles Graner, a fellow soldier. Detainees were abused, tortured, sexually humiliated, and murdered. Some of the pictures were shown on television (*60 Minutes*). Seymour Hersh wrote a *New Yorker* article, also showing photographs taken by members of the 320th M.P. Battalion who were the abusers. Seven soldiers were courts-martialed, imprisoned, and dishonorably discharged. Sentences of ten years (for Charles Graner, the ringleader) and three years (for Lynndie England, his former girlfriend) were given in trials in 2005.

Techniques used were stripping prisoners of all clothing. prolonged isolation, stress positions (hanging by arms handcuffed behind the back), sleep and light deprivation, painting with simulated menstrual blood (a fearsome taboo for Muslims) threats by savage dogs, and water-boarding (simulated drowning, among others).

March 11, 2004. Madrid train bombings An *al-Qaeda* sympathizer group, or the Basque separatist group ETA, are suspected. 190 die, and 1,755 are wounded.

July 27, 2004. Barack Obama's "Audacity of Hope" speech. The keynote address of the Democratic National Convention.

November 2, 2004. Bush is re-elected, defeating John Kerry by about three million popular votes. Widespread manipulation at the polls by the GOP in Florida and Ohio and other states is suspected. The "Swift-boating" of John Kerry, a decorated war hero, succeeds in smearing his reputation. The campaign against Kerry is financed by Richard Mellon Scaife, who backed the lawyers who smeared Bill Clinton, leading up to the Monica Lewinsky scandal and attempted impeachment.

My response to Bush's winning the popular vote (although by a small margin) was "How could so many poor and middle-class people vote against their economic interests after four years of Bush obviously favoring the very rich.?" It took until 2006 for some of them to wake up, and till 2008 for the tide to turn fully against him. This was a very late "tipping point." It could also be considered a delayed "stubborn mule" response.

November 4, 2004. Bush says he will make privatization of Social Security his major goal in his second term. He announces his intention to create "private investment accounts." Under his plan, workers could divert one third of their Social Security taxes into stocks and bonds. This plan had several goals. First, it would be a huge windfall for Wall Street. Second, it would make little Republicans of the poorer classes, get them to identify with the capitalists, and eventually vote for the GOP. Then, if the Democrats wanted to regulate fuel economy or carbon monoxide emissions, the GOP could say that this regulation would hurt poor old Granny, who held a few shares of General Motors stock

Public opinion was overwhelmingly against Bush's plan, despite a fifty-million dollar campaign to convince people that Social Security was bankrupt. Previously, a counter-campaign was first started after Bill Clinton became interested in establishing private accounts. Then the CAF (Campaign for America's Future) fought Bush's plan, and was joined by the AFL-CIO, MoveOn.org, USAction, and AARP.

The manipulation of language reached new depths during Bush's two terms. The term "private accounts" was changed by the GOP spinmeisters to "personal accounts" when it was found that the elderly (members of a focus group) objected to the word "private." Of course, due to their short-term outlook, the elders were scared of losing their shirts in a market crash. The youngsters, with many years ahead of them, were more favorable to the private accounts. They probably had visions of making hay in the stock market over the long run. The impact of the 2008 financial meltdown would have been even more catastrophic if money from workers' paychecks had been put into the stock market. The failure of his Social Security privatization initiative was a great defeat for Bush, and marked the start of his sharp slide in approval ratings to around 30%.

July 7, 2005. London subway and buses bombed; fifty-six die and about seven hundred are wounded.

August 30, 2005. Hurricane Katrina wipes out many cities on the Gulf Coast. Thousands of poor and predominantly black residents of New Orleans are unable to flee, and are trapped by flooding when levees break. As of 2006, the death toll is put at around 1,300, and still counting. Lack of transportation for the poor despite several days' warning of the storm, underfunding of levee repair by the U.S. Corps of Engineers, and a poor response by FEMA (Federal Emergency Management Agency) are blamed.

Bush cronyism is seen in placing incompetents in crucial managerial positions. The head of FEMA, Michael Brown (a former supervisor of horse show judges in Colorado!) will always be remembered by Bush's praise, "Hekuva job, Brownie!" Barbara Bush had her famous "Marie Antoinette moment" during her visit to the Houston Astrodome, where thousands of refugees from the storm were given shelter. She said "And so many people in the arena here, you know, were underprivileged anyway, so this is working very well for them." Like mother, like son.

September 28, 2005. Tom DeLay is indicted on conspiracy charges.

January 7, 2006. Tom DeLay announces that he will not return to his position as House Majority Leader. In September, 2005, DeLay was indicted on charges of conspiracy and money laundering. Corporate contributions to TRMPAC were laundered through the Republican National Committee and given to GOP candidates in Texas.

January, 2008. DeLay is still awaiting trial. He attacked John McCain in a luncheon speech to RAMS (Republicans Assuring Mutual Support). This is the same guy who said to three young boys, lying on cots after being evacuated to Reliant Park in Houston after Hurricane Katrina, "Now tell me the truth boys, is this kind of fun?" He suggested that this was like being in camp. Strike three for compassionate conservatism! Barbara Bush redux. Don't forget that in 1999 Dubya (W.) Bush was interviewed about Karla Faye Tucker, a murderer who was due to be executed on his orders, though many celebrities had begged him to spare her.

(Bush to Tucker Carlson, the interviewer): "He (Larry King) asked her real difficult questions, like, 'What would you say to Governor Bush?'" (Carlson:) "What was her answer, I wonder?" "Please," Bush whimpers, his lips pursed in mock desperation, "Don't kill me." Though Bush denied ever saying this, Laura Bush later reprimanded him for mocking Karla Faye Tucker. This reinforces Paul Krugman's Op-Ed observation: "...modern movement conservatism attracts a certain personality type...If you think ridicule is an appropriate response to other peoples' woes, you fit right in" (*New York Times*, October 5, 2007).

March 29, 2006. Jack Abramoff, the Washington, D.C. "super-lobbyist," pleads guilty to conspiracy, fraud, and tax evasion. His plea bargain with the Justice Department prosecutors gets him five years and twelve months. His testimony casts a shadow on at least a half-dozen Republican senators and GOP representatives.

Some of the Republicans who have received campaign funds (or gifts) from Abramoff or his clients, many of whom have already given his questionable contributions back to various charities, are Senators John Thune (S. Dakota), Conrad Burns (Montana), Mitch McConnell (Kentucky), George Allen (Virginia), and Representatives Bill Ney (Ohio), John Doolittle (California), J. Dennis Hastert (Illinois, House Speaker), Jo Ann Davis (Virginia), and Tom Delay (Texas).

May 16, 2006. The Senate rejects Bush's Comprehensive Immigration Bill as too lenient on illegal immigrants. (How did Bush get on the side of the angels, and apparent compassion? Perhaps his wealthier supporters want nannies for their kids and gardeners for their estates, as well as peons to pick crops and pick the flesh off carcasses at Armour & Co.?)

Bush says he wants to protect our borders, but also does not want to discriminate against people (that is, immigrants). The bill would allow some twelve million illegal immigrants eventual citizenship, after paying a fine, back taxes, and learning English. They would also have to return to their home countries and reapply for entry. (This assumes that they have money to travel.)

The right wing views illegal immigrants as "lawbreakers" and says it cannot accept "amnesty" (citizenship) for the lawless. As the plan is compromised to make it more palatable to the anti-immigrant faction, it veers away from eventual citizenship and focuses on prevention of terrorism! The administration now plans to use six thousand National Guard troops in short rotations to supplant the twelve thousand Border Patrol agents.

June 12, 2007. Bush tries to persuade GOP senators to back his immigration bill, but most are reluctant. Only 45% of Republicans approve of Bush's handling of immigration. This is a new low.

Bowing to pressure from the GOP base, Bush and Congress change the bill's emphasis to fence-building. Some 700 miles of fence are to be built to keep out illegals and terrorists.

February 14, 2008. Conflicts over eminent domain break out along the border as the government (Homeland Security Department) seizes private land. (What happened to private property rights?)

McCain, Hillary, Obama, and Ted Kennedy all support Bush's comprehensive immigration bill.

September 2006. There has been a resurgence of the Taliban since their defeat in 2001. They now have sophisticated weapons, purchased with money from opium poppy sales. The U.S. and coalition troops number only seventeen thousand, and can barely defend a large country against a guerilla force that often has the sympathy of the populace. Security, even in Kabul, is minimal.

The invasion of Iraq had the consequence of limiting the U.S. forces in Afghanistan and the funds to support them. The coalition has been hampered by diminishing contributions from NATO states. Afghanistan and neighboring Pakistan hold the main forces of al-Qaeda, and provide a training ground in the mountainous tribal areas that lie between the two countries. It is here that Osama bin Laden still operates as the putative head of al-Qaeda. Terrorists from this training center have been sent all over the world, most recently (2008) to Spain. The resurgence of the Taliban and al-Qaeda has taken place after the virtual destruction of the Taliban in 2001. This has happened on Bush's watch, because of his obsession with Iraq to the detriment of other trouble spots. In early 2009, the Taliban has taken control of areas of Pakistan, threatening the capital, Islamabad.

September 29, 2005. John G. Roberts Jr. is seated as Chief Justice of the U.S. Supreme Court. On June 31, 2006, Samuel Alito is seated as Associate Justice. These appointments by Bush have pushed the center of the court far to the right. This is partly because Anthony Kennedy, considered a "moderate conservative," has rather consistently voted with the conservative bloc of four. When Sandra Day O'Connor was the "swing vote," she did not favor right or left. The judges, their political leanings and their birth dates are given below:

Conservative: John G. Roberts Jr., born 1955; Antonin Scalia, born 1936; Clarence Thomas, born 1948; Samuel Alito, born 1950. *Moderate Conservative*: Anthony M. Kennedy, born 1936. *Liberal*: John Paul Stevens, born 1920; Ruth B. Ginsburg, born 1933; Steven G. Breyer, born 1938; David H. Souter, born 1939. Fortunately, Justice Stevens did not die or retire before the end of Bush's second term, or we would have had a very strong conservative majority on the court for many years to come, since these are lifetime appointments. Perhaps more than any other action taken by G.W. Bush, his packing the Supreme Court will have the greatest and most lasting effect on the political climate of our country. (Stevens delivered the oath of office to V.P. Biden on January 20, 2009.)

August 6, 2009. The Senate voted to confirm Sonia Sotomayor as Associate Justice of the Supreme Court, to replace David Souter. She is 56, and is the first Hispanic and the third woman to sit on the court. Appointed by Obama, she is a liberal replacing a liberal.

January 10, 2007. Start of the "Surge," adding 20,000 troops to the U.S. forces in Iraq. This move eventually helped reduce violence and mortality levels in Iraq. General Eric Shinseki, former Army Chief of Staff and wounded Vietnam veteran, recommended adding several hundred thousand troops in 2003, just before the invasion of Iraq. His views clashed with those of Rumsfeld, Secretary of Defense, and he was retired. Obama has appointed him Secretary of Veterans Affairs.

June 2007. The court upheld a federal anti-abortion law, cut back on the free-speech rights of public school students, strictly enforced procedural requirements for bringing and appealing cases, and limited school districts' ability to use racially conscious measures to achieve or preserve integration.

2007–2008. During Bush's watch the value of the dollar has fallen sharply. It is now around $2 against the British pound, and around $1.50 to the euro. (The pound fell sharply in 2009.) This means that those countries can buy American goods on the cheap.

While this is fine for U.S. exports, it is very hard on consumers who buy imports. Not only are foreign cars and electronics getting much more expensive, but much imported food is climbing in price. If foreign governments and businesses see their investments (denominated in U.S. dollars) falling in value, they will soon change over to euros or pounds or other more stable currencies. China holds huge amounts of U.S. Treasury and other bonds, which makes it our virtual banker. It may not want to stay in that position if the dollar tanks further.

January 2007. Bush tries to privatize Medicare and partially succeeds. Through the "Medicare Advantage" program the Government pays 12% more than it costs to treat people with the identical procedures than it costs on standard Medicare. This is a free bonus to insurance companies. In addition, the "donut hole" in the Medicare Plan D (in 2008) forces patients to pay 100% of drug costs once the retail costs of their drugs reach $2,510. The "hole" continues until you reach $5,726 in retail drug costs, at which point you enter the "catastrophic" area. There you only pay 5% of costs. The donut hole is a huge giveaway to the insurance companies. They also typically raise their premiums, deductibles, and drug costs after the first year of enrollment.

2007–2008. With globalization, changes in the U.S. economy seem to have a direct effect on the worldwide economy. Rather than a disconnect between Asian and U.S. markets, the current slide in our stock market has shaken Hong Kong, China, Japan, and the rest of Asia. There has been great volatility all around. The usual retreat of U.S. investors to foreign investments during a recession is no longer the rule. Foreign investors, in turn, are now wary of dollar-denominated funds.

November 12, 2007. Losses in the billions due to defaults among bundled subprime mortgages and other complex investment instruments are not limited to the United States. Worldwide losses ("write-downs") may reach as much as four hundred billion. When financial instruments become so arcane that even economists aren't aware of the risks involved, what chance has the average investor?

December 19, 2007. Not until 2007 did Bush sign the Clean Energy Act. The administration was loath to regulate Detroit's "Big Three." In 2004 the average miles per gallon for passenger cars and light trucks (pickups, vans, and SUVs) was 24.6. This had dropped from the 1987 best average of 26.2 mpg achieved, due to the popularity of SUVs.

The CAFÉ (corporate average fuel economy) required for all companies' fleets was 20 mpg in 2003, and crept up to 21.0 in 2005, 21.6 in 2006, and 22.2 for model year 2007. This slow rate of increase in fuel economy standards has been criticized by the EPA and environmentalists. Global warming and air pollution are low priorities for the GOP.

For 2018 the overall target will be 38 mpg. But for Detroit cars only, the target will be 33 mpg! Bush plans well ahead to favor the Republican base of manufacturers.

2008. Subprime loans were first bundled and securitized around 1990. Since then they were sold by Wall St. and bought by investors who did not realize the risk involved, or who were aware of the risk but attracted by the profits involved. In 2005 the subprime loans were at their peak. In five years of the Bush administration, nothing was done to investigate or control these often illegal loans, with low initial rates. Alan Greenspan ignored the warning signs, and the SEC did nothing. Then when the "teaser" rates (often 1%) expired, homeowners couldn't pay the new higher rates (7% and more). With the burst of the housing bubble, the value of their houses was now often less than the amount of their mortgages. So, in 2008–09 we saw millions of foreclosures. The Obama government is providing massive infusions of money to banks, cutting the prime rate to near zero, and extending the low teaser rates.

In 2005, the peak of the sub-prime loans, Wall Street sold 508 billion dollars worth of loans...In 2007 the bubble burst.

December 27, 2007. In 2007, financial firms took more than eighty billion dollars in write downs. A Goldman Sachs Group Inc. analyst doubled its forecast for fourth-quarter write-downs at Citigroup Inc., Merrill Lynch & Co. and J.P. Morgan Chase & Co. to $33.6 billion. Forecasters say there is more to come in 2008.

February, 2008. In addition to the bursting of the housing bubble, the United States is in a severe credit crunch. We have maxed out on our credit cards, bought cars on credit, and received cheap credit (until the rates went up after the initial teaser rates) by borrowing against our houses. When our houses lost their inflated value, many of us were left with properties worth less than the mortgage money we owed. This lack of credit regulation can be laid at the door of Alan Greenspan, but it is also part of a general lack of regulation, in fact active *de*regulation during the Bush administration. Millions of families now face foreclosure. Many will walk away, leaving their homes to deteriorate and thus lower adjacent property values. Since homes are the biggest lifetime investment for most families, this is a tragic collapse of the American Dream.

December 27, 2007. Benazir Bhutto, former Prime Minister of Pakistan, is assassinated by a suicide bomber. Condoleeza Rice had brokered a power-sharing agreement between Bhutto and President Pervez Musharraf, encouraging Bhutto to return to her country. This attempt to bolster Musharraf and save our Pakistan policy has failed catastrophically. There has been severe criticism of the lack of security for Bhutto provided by Musharraf, and the United States. Bhutto's death has caused nationwide rioting by her supporters.

Chaos in a nuclear-armed country of 160 million is a grave threat to U.S. and world security. Pakistan has been at war with India, another nuclear power, twice in the recent past. It is also the key to controlling the Taliban in the tribal areas bordering Afghanistan. President Obama has said he will send troops to the tribal areas between Pakistan and Afghanistan, and bolster the troop levels inside Afghanistan to control the resurgence of the Taliban.

Bhutto's husband, Asif Ali Zardari and her nineteen-year-old son, Bilawal Zardari, are appointed co-chairman and chairman of the Pakistan People's Party, upon Bhutto's death.

January 30, 2008. Attorney General Michael Mukasey (appointed by Bush to replace A.G. Alberto Gonzales, who was forced to resign because of his politicizing of the firing of U.S. attorneys), refuses before the U.S. Senate to say whether waterboarding is torture or not. Waterboarding consists of strapping the victim down and pouring water on a cloth covering his face. The result is near-drowning and suffocation. In 2006 the CIA banned waterboarding.

February 8, 2008. Attorney General Mukasey said he could not investigate or prosecute people for actions (waterboarding) that had been authorized earlier.

February 13, 2008. The Senate compromises, and accepts the "recession" emergency bill proposed by the House (pushed by Nancy Pelosi) and signed by Bush (on this date) to give tax rebates of $600 to singles and $1,200 to couples, with an extra $300 for each child. The entire stimulus bill will cost $168 billion, and the cost of rebates (within that bill) to individuals and couples will cost $117 billion. Of course, this will greatly increase the budget deficit.

Singles with income higher than $75,000 and couples with incomes higher than $150,000 will get smaller rebates. The top limits for rebates are $87,000 (singles) and $174,000 (couples). Those who get too little income to pay taxes, but get at least $3,000, will get rebates of $300 (singles) and $600 (couples).This is assumed to cover the elderly and veterans.

To help avoid foreclosure, the FHA (Federal Housing Administration) loan limit is raised to $729,000, and mortgage caps for Fannie Mae and Freddie Mac are also raised. Tax breaks are given to business to promote investment in factories and equipment.

Senate Democrats led by Harry Reid tried to add extended benefits for the unemployed and heating aid for the poor, but these were dropped in the compromise bill. It is interesting to see what was left out as well as what was included. While the Democrats used these items they were "forced" to drop in order to gain future political points, especially in the cold Northeast and pockets of high unemployment like Detroit and Ohio, the Recession Emergency Bill clearly only gives money to those who already have some money. This is in keeping with the GOP ethos.

February 21, 2008. Obama and Hillary Clinton had another debate at the University of Texas at Austin. While there were few attacks, Hillary's bringing up an accusation of plagiarism brought forth boos from the audience. She said "Lifting whole passages from someone else's speeches is not 'change you can believe in.' It's change you can Xerox." (Obama's platform book is called *Change You Can Believe In.*) Obama responded by saying that he often shared language with his colleague, Massachusetts Governor Patrick Deval, and suggested that "We shouldn't spend time tearing each other down. We should spend time lifting the country up." This response brought cheers from the audience.

Hillary ended by saying it was an honor to be on stage with Obama, and they shook hands. Jeffrey Toobin commented afterward that he thought her final speech was Hillary's valedictory. It is commonly assumed that if she doesn't win in Texas and Ohio on March 4, she will have lost the race. The contest for the presidency has apparently narrowed to John McCain and Barack Obama.

2000–2008. Our national debt has risen from $6 trillion in 2000 to $9 trillion in 2008. While the GOP has always claimed to be fiscally conservative, that changed radically with Bush II. Instead of spending on social supports, Bush has spent extravagantly on war, while cutting taxes for the very rich.

2001–2008. There has been sharp inflation on Bush's watch. In 2001 crude oil was $26/ barrel In 2008 it varies between $80 and $100/ barrel. Actually when adjusted for inflation, crude oil is not much different from the high U.S. prices in the early eighties. But this is no comfort to the homeowner who is paying at the rate of $3.00–$4.00 per gallon. In the last quarter of 2008, the price of crude oil drops below $50 per barrel. There is also a worldwide shortage of commodities. There are predictions of depletion of oil (in four years) and coal (in twelve years). Water and metals are also in short supply. Metals (iron, steel, nickel, zinc, and copper) are showing price rises. China is using more crude oil, and has become an importer of commodities and raw materials. It is now the primary exporter of cell phones and radios, and also exports refrigerators, air conditioners, televisions and video cameras. This requires large amounts of metal.

Cooking oil, rice, wheat, and soybean prices have risen rapidly. Price caps and government stockpiling of these items is occurring in Asia to avoid shortages. Bush's failure to fully fund new energy sources and to support stricter emission controls and tougher fuel efficiency standards has not only put his country at risk. It has missed the chance for the United States to be a leader in worldwide conservation. Our refusal to sign off against global warming gives China and India an excuse to avoid adequate controls for their burgeoning populations. In a closed system each change affects all other elements. Thus the use of corn for making ethanol produces a shortage of corn planted for food. Historians may look back on these eight Bush years as the start of the economic apocalypse.

March 4, 2008. The race is not over. Hillary wins Ohio, Texas, and Rhode Island, while Obama wins Vermont. By winning two big states she revives her chances for the nomination. Obama, however, is still ahead in delegates.

McCain, meanwhile, bests Mike Huckabee, and wins the Republican nomination.

Some Democratic pundits say that their two candidates now seem to be savaging each other. They fear that this may weaken the winner in the eventual race against McCain. Other talking heads say that the more combative campaigning may hold the interest of the public, and give the Democrats more exposure in the media than McCain.

March 23, 2008. U.S. combat death toll in Iraq rises to four thousand.

June 18, 2008. Bush calls for offshore drilling after a twenty-seven-year ban. McCain and Palin inspire a chant of followers at the Republican National Convention of "Drill, baby, drill!" This became a mantra in the GOP campaign. Gasoline was at $4 a gallon, but the recession soon put an end to that price. So many anti-environmental rules and laws were passed during Bush's eight years that I am unable to list them all.

September 15, 2008. Lehman Brothers, investment bankers, files for bankruptcy. The firm had debts of $613 billion, the largest on record. It could not find a buyer to persuade the U.S. government to bail it out. On May 15, 2008, Bear Stearns, another investment banking house, also facing bankruptcy due to toxic bundled subprime mortgage instruments, was bought by J.P. Morgan Chase for a paltry $2 per share.

September 16, 2008. The Federal Reserve loans $85 billion to AIG Insurance Co, deemed "too large to fail."

September 18, 2008. U.S. Treasury fund of $800 billion is announced by Treasury Secretary Henry Paulson. Part of it is to be used to buy back bundled subprime mortgages from banks and other financial institutions. Paulson also announces a ban on short selling, and creation of insurance for money market deposits. (In early 2007, Paulson said that he didn't think subprime mortgages were going to be a big problem. A consistent GOP stand against regulation has been the main cause of the current financial meltdown.)

September 25, 2008. Washington Mutual Bank (WaMu) fails, among others.

September 28, 2008. U.S.–India nuclear pact is approved by the House of Representatives (HR 7081). It is seen as balancing China's nuclear power, but viewed by some as encouraging further nuclear weapons production and development in Pakistan, Iran, North Korea, and other countries. The Senate still must approve. This pact has been in discussion since 2005.

November 20, 2008. The Dow Jones industrial index falls below 8,000 to 7,552, for the first time since 2003. It is down from an all-time high of 14,164 on October 9, 2007. The threat to the auto industry, the loss of liquidity (banks aren't making loans, though given huge bailouts), job loss, and business closings all contribute. (By November 9, 2009, the Dow Jones index had recovered to 10,266, then hovering between 9,000 and 10,000. This was still a long way from the October 9. 2007 all time high of 14,164. Unemployment, in contrast, hit 10%+ in 2009.)

December 4, 2008. Iraq parliament passes law that all U.S. troops must exit by January 1, 2012.

December 14, 2008. An Iraqi TV journalist, Muntadar al-Zaidi, throws his shoes at Bush during his speech in Baghdad. With the first shoe he shouted "This is a goodbye kiss from the Iraqi people, dog." With the second shoe he said "This is for the widows and orphans and all those killed in Iraq." Bush ducked both shoes. Al-Zaidi was beaten, arrested, and jailed incommunicado. Bush said, with his usual inappropriate humor, "If you want the facts, it's a size 10 shoe he threw."

January 3, 2009. Israel invades the Gaza Strip in attempt to destroy Hamas rocket launchers. After twenty-three days, the Palestinian death toll is over 1,300, and the Israeli death toll is thirteen. There is widespread destruction of the Gaza infrastructure.

January 19, 2009. Israel is hastening its withdrawal from Gaza to avoid being there during Obama's inauguration on January 20. It is suggested that this will let Obama focus on the peace effort, rather than on asking Israel to withdraw. Israel then slows the withdrawal, due to small arms and rocket fire.

January 20, 2009. Barack Hussain Obama, age forty-seven, is sworn in as the forty-fourth President of the United States by Chief Justice John G. Roberts. Roberts, at the time of his appointment by Bush, was the third-youngest chief justice ever. He and Samuel Alito, a second Bush appointee, are both well to the right of center, and the court will presumably be in opposition to much of Obama's agenda. Obama is the first African American president in U.S. history. He was a Harvard law professor, as well as being the junior senator from Illinois from January 2005 until his presidency.

Joseph R. Biden Jr., age sixty-six, is also sworn in, but by Associate Justice John Paul Stevens (a liberal). Biden has been a senator from Delaware for thirty-six years. He started as a civil rights lawyer, and is an expert on foreign policy.

Former President Bush and his wife Laura take a helicopter across Washington, D.C., over the heads of the Obama supporters, to Andrews Air Force Base, where he and V.P. Cheney say farewell to staffers. V.P. Cheney attended the inauguration and farewell meeting, although he was in a wheelchair, having injured his back while moving his belongings from his former office.

Some cried for Bush, or felt sorry for him. Not I.

January 22, 2009. President Obama signed executive orders closing the detention camp at Guantánamo Bay, Cuba, within a year; ending the Central Intelligence Agency's secret prisons; and requiring all interrogations to follow the noncoercive methods of the Army Field Manual.

This is a great start, and will raise our moral standing worldwide. Senator Dianne Feinstein of California (Democrat) is asking for a law governing all interrogation, since the President can cancel an executive order at any time.

February and March, 2009. The Dow-Jones Index fell into the 6000s. There is a worldwide financial meltdown. Home foreclosures and unemployment t figures continue to rise. Obama says that he has no choice but to deal with the severe recession, health care, energy, Iraq, and Afghanistan simultaneously. Companies such as AIG and General Motors seem to be failing, despite repeated infusions of bailout money. Unrest grows in developing countries, which are hit harder by the global economic crisis than developed nations. Many critics of the financial rescue plan point out that Timothy Geithner and Larry Summers seem to have no clear plan and are just "dithering." There have been seventeen bank failures in the U.S. in 2009. The status of two large banks, Citigroup and Bank of America, has been lowered, suggesting they might fail in the future.

It looks as if Bush and Cheney have handed Obama a hornet's nest of problems as their eight-year legacy.

April 22, 2009. Obama said it is possible to prosecute the lawyers who wrote the laws justifying torture of terrorists. He stated that this was up to his Attorney General. He reiterated that he would not want the CIA operatives who did the actual torturing to be prosecuted, because they thought they were obeying the law. He also suggested that Congress might set up a special bipartisan review to investigate the problem. An independent commission, modeled on the 9/11 Commission, was also a possibility. This new position is a reversal of Obama's statement of only a week ago, when he said "...we should be looking forward, not backward." He was concerned with the bitter politicization on this issue, which could interfere with his ability to get his agenda enacted. The fact that Senator Arlen Specter of Pennsylvania switched (April 29) from the GOP to the Democrats brought the administration close (fifty-nine votes) to a filibuster-proof majority. Al Franken's confirmation as the Senator from Minnesota gave the Democrats the necessary sixty votes. This ability to bypass a GOP Senate filibuster should make it much easier for Obama to get his agenda approved, if Blue Dog and Reagan Democrats and Senate centrists will help him.

Bibliography

Adverse. "Adverse Childhood Experiences Study: Major Findings." *Centers for Disease Control and Prevention.* http://www/ cdc/gov/NCCDPHP/ACE/links.htm (2005).

Adverse (ACE), Anda, R. F., Nordenberg, D., et al. "Relationship of Childhood Abuse and Household Dysfunction to Many of the Leading Causes of Death in Adults" (The Adverse Childhood Experiences [ACE] Study). *American Journal of Preventative Medicine,* 14(4):245–258, May, 1998.

Alexander. http://www.royalty.nu/Europe/Balkan/Alexander.html

Alterman, E. *What Liberal Media?: The Truth about Bias and the News.* New York: Basic Books, 2003.

Anon. "Government Needs to Borrow...? " *The New York Times,* February 8, 2005, p. 4.

Anon. "Student Favors the Rod and Soon Gets the Ax." *The New York Times,* March 10, 2005.

Anon. "The Poor Need Not Apply." *The New York Times,* December 21, 2005, p. A 38 (editorial section).

Bageant, J. *Deer Hunting with Jesus.* New York: Crown, 2007.

Bakan, D. *Slaughter of the Innocents.* New York: Jossey-Bass, 1971.

Becker, E. *The Denial of Death.* New York: The Free Press, 1973.

Bettelheim, B. "Individual and Mass Behavior in Extreme Situations." *Journal of Abnormal and Social Psychology,* 38:417–452, 1943.

Bouchard, T. J. Jr., et al. "Evidence for the Construct Validity and Heritability of the Wilson-Patterson Conservatism Scale: A Reared Apart Twins Study of Social Attitudes." *Personality and Individual Differences*, 34: 959–969, 2003.

Brickner, R. *Is Germany Incurable?* New York: J. B. Lippincott, 1943.

Brooks, D. "Dollars and Sense." *New York Times*, January 26, 2006, p. A 23.

Burke, K. *Permanence and Change: An Anatomy of Purpose.* New York: New Republic.

Bush, G. W., Jeb, uncle, http://www.guardian.co.uk/usa/story/0,12271,1033904,00.html

Carey, B. "A Shocker: Partisan Thought Is Unconscious." *The New York Times*, January 24, 2006.

Chesterton, G. K. *What's Wrong with the World.* Gloucester, U.K.: Dodo Press. Paperback, April 1994. Original ed. Ignatius Press, 1910.

Child abuse. "Child Maltreatment 2003: Summary of Key Findings." National Clearinghouse on Child Abuse and Neglect Information, http://nccanch.acf.hhs.gov/pubs/factsheets/constats.cfm (2003).

Clinton, H. R. *It Takes a Village.* Touchstone ed. New York: Simon & Schuster, 1996.

Clinton, W. (http://encarta.msn.com/encyclopedia_761564341/Bill_Clinton.html

Clinton, W. (with Dan Rather) "Bill Clinton, His Life." CBS News (excerpts from an interview with Dan Rather on *60 Minutes*). http://www.cbsnews.com/stories/2004/06/01/60minutes/main620619.shtml (2004).

CNN "CNN.com Election Results." http//www.cnn.com/ELECTION/2004/pages/results/US/P/00/epolls.0.html (2004).

Cohen, A. K. *Delinquent Boys: The Culture of the Gang.* Glencoe, IL: The Free Press, 1955.

Contractors, P. "Windfalls of War: Post-War Contractors Ranked by Total Contract Value in Afghanistan and Iraq." Vol.

2005: The Center for Public Integrity. publicintegrity.org/wow/resources.asp (2005).

Curtis, B. "The Anchor Is a Madman." Slate "Assessment." http://www.slate.com/id/2107006 (2004).

DeNavas-Walt, C., Proctor B. D., & Lee, C. H. *Income, Poverty, and Health Insurance Coverage in the United States: 2004* (Vol. 2005): Washington D.C.: U.S. Census Bureau, U.S. Government Printing Office. http://www.census.gov/prod/2005pubs/p60-229.pdf (2005). (See Table 1, Income and Earnings Summary by Selected Characteristics, 2003 and 2004. Median income by age of householder, p. 11.)

Diamond, J. "The Ends of the World as We Know Them." *The New York Times,* January 1, 2005, Op-Ed.

Dowd, M. "Less Spocky, More Rocky." *The New York Times,* September 9, 2009, Op-Ed.

Durkheim, E. *Le Suicide, Etude de Sociologie* Paris: Alcan, 1897. Translated by J. Spaulding & G. Simpson, New York: Free Press, 1951.

Eisenhower, D. D. (1960). "Public Papers of the Presidents, Dwight D. Eisenhower." Washington, D.C.: U.S. Government Report, 1960.

Frank, T. *What's The Matter with Kansas?: How Conservatives Won the Heart of America.* New York: Henry Holt & Co, 2004.

Franke-Ruta, G. "Remapping the Cultural Debate." *The American Prospect Online Edition* http://www.prospect.org/web/page.ww?section=root8name=ViewWeb&articleId=10844 (2006).

Franken, A. *Lies (And the Lying Liars Who Tell Them): A Fair and Balanced Look at the Right.* New York: Dutton (Penguin Group), 2003.

Franken, A. *The Truth.* New York: Dutton (Penguin Group), 2005.

Freud, S. *Collected Papers.* Translated by A. Strachey & J. Strachey. London: Hogarth, 1900.

Freud, S. "Civilisation and Its Discontents." (In *Civilisation, War and Death* ed.). London: The Hogarth Press. Translated by Joan Riviere (written 1929, rev. ed 1953).

Freud, S. *The Future of an Illusion.* New York: Doubleday Anchor Books, 1957.

Fromm, E. *Escape from Freedom.* New York: Holt, Rinehart & Winston, 1941.

Genghis Khan, http://www.accd.edu/sac/history/keller/Mongols/empsub1.html

Gersten, J. C., Langner, T. S., Eisenberg, J. G., & Orzeck, L. "Child Behavior and Life Events: Undesirable Change or Change per se?" In B. P. Dohrenwend & Dohrenwend, B. S. (Eds.), *Stressful Life Events: Their Nature and Effects.* New York: John Wiley & Sons, 1974, pp. 159–170.

Gersten, J. C., Langner, T. S., Eisenberg, J. G., Sincha-Fagan, O., & McCarthy, E. D. "Stability and Change in Types of Behavioral Disturbance in Children and Adolescents." *Journal of Abnormal Child Psychology,* 4(2):111–127, 1976.

Gladwell, M. *The Tipping Point.* London: Little, Brown & Co., 2002.

Goldhagen, D. *Hitler's Willing Executioners.* New York: Knopf, 1996.

Greenspan, A. "Greenspan Testifies: Our Political language Just Changed."http://blogs.forbes.com/trailwatch/2008/10/greenspan-testi.html

Gruen, A. *The Insanity of Normality: Realism as Sickness: Toward Understanding Human Destructiveness.* Translated by Hildegarde & Hunter Hannum. New York: Grove Weidenfeld, 1992.

Helton, G. B., & Oakland, T. D. "Teachers' Attitudinal Responses to Differing Characteristics of Elementary School Students." *Journal of Educational Psychology,* 69:261–265, 1977.

Herbert, R. "Feed the Billionaires, Starve the Students." *The New York Times,* November 15, 2004, Op-Ed.

Herbert, R. "Torture, American Style." *The New York Times,* February 11, 2005, Op-Ed.

Herrnstein, R., & Murray, C. *The Bell Curve.* New York: Free Press, 1994.

Hitler, A. http://en.wikipedia.org/wiki/Adolf_Hitler#Childhood

Hitler, P. http://www.adolfhitler.dk/paula/Default.html

Hughes, C. C., Tremblay, M., Rapoport, R. N., & Leighton, A.H. *People of Cove and Woodlot*, Vol. II. New York: Basic Books, 1992.

Inglehart, R., et al. *Human Values and Beliefs: A Cross Cultural Sourcebook*. Ann Arbor, MI: University of Michigan Press, 1999.

James, O. "So George, How Do You Feel about Your Mom and Dad?" *The Guardian*, September 2, 2003.

Jensen, A. "How Much Can We Boost I.Q. and Scholastic Achievement?" *Harvard Educational Review*, 39:1–123, 1976.

Jill. "Brilliant at Breakfast: If Brooks is Right, then Americans Are Idiots." Vol. 2006. http://briliantatbreakfast.blogspot. com2006/01/if-brooks-is-right-then-americans-are. html?fta=y (2006).

John, O. P., Robins, R. W., & Pervin, L. A. (Eds.). *Handbook of Personality*. New York: Guilford Press, 2008.

Kenworthy, L. "Consider the Evidence; Bread, Peace and the 2008 Election." *Kenworthy's Home Page*, February 10, 2008.

Kessler, R. C. U., & Bedirhan T. "Prevalence, Severity, and Unmet Need for Treatment of Mental Disorders in the World Health Organization World Mental Health Surveys." *JAMA*, 291(21):2851–2590, May 2, 2004.

Klein, N. "The Shock Doctrine." *The Guardian* (U.K.), September 8, 2007 (extract).

Kohut, A., et al. *The Pew Report: Beyond Red and Blue*, http//people-press.org/reports/display.php3?ReportID=242 (2005).

Kohut, A. H. "Stuck in Second." *The New York Times*, August 9. 2005, Op-Ed.

Krugman, P. "Kansas on My Mind." *The New York Times*, February 25, 2005, Op-Ed.

Krugman, P. "On Being Partisan." *The New York Times*, January 26, 2007, Op-Ed.

Krugman, P. "Don't Blame Bush." *The New York Times*, May 18, 2007, Op-Ed.

Krugman, P. "Conservatives Are Such Jokers." *The New York Times*, October 5, 2007, Op-Ed.

Krugman, P. "Forgive and Forget." *The New York Times*, January 16, 2009, Op-Ed.

Labarre, W. "Social Cynosure and Social Structure." *Journal of Personality*, 14(3):169–183, 1946.

Lakoff, G. "Metaphor, Morality and Politics, or Why Conservatives Have Left Liberals in the Dust." http://www.wwcd.org/ issues/Lakoff,html#STRICT (1995, original. publication date).

Lakoff, G. *Moral Politics: How Liberals and Conservatives Think.* Paperback. 2nd ed. Chicago: The University of Chicago Press, 2002.

Landau, M. J., et al. (2004). "Deliver Us From Evil: The Effects of Mortality Salience and Reminders of 9/11 on Support for President George W. Bush." *Personality and Social Psychology Bulletin*, 30:1136–1150, September, 2004.

Langner, T. S. "A Twenty-two Item Screening Score of Psychiatric Symptoms Indicating Impairment." *Journal of Health and Human Behavior*, 3: 269–276, Winter, 1962.

Langner, T. S. *Choices for Living: Coping with Fear of Dying.* New York: Kluwer Academic/Plenum Publishers, 2002.

Langner, T. S., Gersten, J. C., Greene, E. L., Eisenberg, J. G., Herson, J. H., & McCarthy, E. D. "Treatment of Psychological Disorders among Urban Children." *Journal of Consulting and Clinical Psychology*, 42(2):170–179, 1974.

Langner, T. S., Gersten, J. C., McCarthy, E. D., Eisenberg, J. G., Greene, E. L., Herson, J. H., & Jameson, J. D. "A Screening Inventory for Assessing Psychiatric Impairment in Children Six to Eighteen." *Journal of Consulting and Clinical Psychology*, 44(2):286–296, 1976.

Langner, T. S., & Michael, S. T. Life *Stress and Mental Health: The Midtown Manhattan Study*, Vol. II. Glencoe, IL: The Free Press of Glencoe, IL and Macmillan, 1963.

Lasch, Christopher. *The Culture of Narcissism.* New York: Norton, 1979.

Lasswell, H. *Psychopathology and Politics.* (paper, 1977 ed.). Chicago: The University of Chicago Press, 1930.

Lawrence, J. A. "Letter to the Editor." *The New York Times*, January 25, 2005.

Leighton, A. H. *My Name Is Legion.* New York: Basic Books, 1959.

Leonhardt, D. "All Worked Up and Wondering Why." *The New York Times*, July 31, 2005, p. 1, Week in Review.

Lifton, R. J. *The Broken Connection.* New York: Simon & Schuster, 1959.

Lincoln, A. (1904). *Lincoln's Yarns and Stories.* A. C. McClure (Ed.). New York: Henry Neil, 1901.

Lincoln, A. "Speech at Edwardsville, Illinois," September 11, 1958. Reprinted in *Collected Works of Abraham Lincoln*, Vol. 3, p. 95. Rutgers University Press, 1953, 1990.

Mamet, D. *House of Games.* Co-author and director, film, 1987.

Maslow, A. (1962). *Toward a Psychology of Being.* New York: Van Nostrand (John Wiley & Sons, 1998).

McCarthy, E. D., Langner, T. S., Gersten, J. C., Eisenberg, J. G., & Orzeck, L. "The Effects of Television on Children and Adolescents: Violence and Behavior Disorders." *Journal of Communication*, 25(4):71–85, 1975.

Mead, M. *And Keep Your Powder Dry.* New York: William Morrow, 1942.

Miller, A. *Prisoners of Childhood.* Translated by Hildegarde & Hunter Hannum. New York: Farrar, Strauss & Giroux, 1981.

Miller, A. *For Your Own Good: Hidden Cruelty in Child Rearing and the Roots of Violence.* Translated by Hildegarde & Hunter Hannum, New York: Farrar, Strauss, & Giroux (2nd ed., 1983; paperback, 1984).

Miller, A. *Thou Shalt Not Be Aware: Society's Betrayal of the Child.* Translated by Hildegarde & Hunter Hannum. New York: New American Library, (1984 paperback).

Miller, M. C. *Fooled Again.* New York: Basic Books, 2005.

Moyers, B. "There Is No Tomorrow." *The Star Tribune*, January 30, 2005.

Muirhead, J. R. *Left and Right: A Defense of Party Spirit.* (A work in progress?). Leland Stanford University Board of Trustees, 2009

Napoleon. http://library.thinkquest.org/C0110901/standard/early. html

Niewert, D. "The Rise of Pseudo-Fascism." http://dniewert. blogspot.com (2004).

Obama, B. *Change We Can Believe In.* New York: Three Rivers Press, 2008.

O'Donnell, E. "Twigs Bent Left or Right." *Harvard Magazine,* 108(3):34–39, 2006.

Oxley, D. R, Smith, K. B., et al., "Political Attitudes Vary with Psychological Traits." *Science,* 321(5896):1667–1670, 2008.

Parenting. (2004). "Using Evidence-based Parenting Programs to Advance CDC Efforts in Child Maltreatment." cdc.gov/ ncipc/pub-res/parenting/default.htm (2004).

Parr, L. A., Waller, B. M., & Fugate, J. "Emotional Communication in Primates: Implications for Neurobiology." *Current Opinion in Neurobiology,* 15:716–720, 2008.

Penke, L, Dennisen, J., & Miller, G. "The Evolutionary Genetics of Personality." *European Journal of Personality,* 21(5):589–637, 2007.

Pinker, S. "My Genome, My Self." *The New York Times,* January 11, 2009, pp. 26–29, 46, 50.

Popular Mechanics, December, 2008. http://www. popularmechanics.com/technology/military_law/4295077. html

Prince, M. (1906). *The Dissociation of a Personality.* (2nd ed., 1969, is reprint of 1906 original ed.). Westport, CT: Greenwood Press, 1969.

Rand, A. http://en.wikipedia.org/wiki/Ayn_Rand#Atlas_Shrugged (1957).

Rand, A. *The Fountainhead.* Indianapolis, IN: Bobbs-Merrill, 1943.

Rassman, J. "Shame on Swift Boat Vets for Bush." *The Wall St. Journal,* August 10, 2004, editorial page.

Rentfrow, P. J., Gosling, S. D., & Potter, J. "A Theory of the Emergence, Persistence, and Expression of Geographic Variation in Psychological Characteristics." *Perspectives on Psychological Science,* 35:339–369, 2008.

Revkin, A. C. "A New Measure of Well-Being from a Happy Little Kingdom." *The New York Times*, October 4, 2005, pp. F-1, F-6.

Ridge, T., with Bloom, L. *The Test of Our Times*. New York: Thomas Duane Books.

Rieber, R. W. *Manufacturing Social Distress: Psychopathy in Everyday Life*. New York: Plenum Press, 1997.

Rose, S. "Talking about Social Class: Are the Economic Interests of the Majority of Americans with the Democratic Party?" http://www.emergingdemocraticmajorityweblog.com/rose/rose/html (2005).

Safire, W. "Goodbye to Privacy." *The New York Times*, April 10, 2005, Book Review.

Schemo, D. J. "A Bush Brother Spreads His Vision of Computerized TeachingPrograms."http://www.nytimes.com/2007/05/30/nyregion/30education.html (2007).

Schmitt, E. T. S. "New Name for War on Terror Reflects Wider U.S. Campaign." *The New York Times*, July 7, 2005, p. A7.

Schreiber, F. R. *Sybil*. Chicago: H. Regnery, 1973. (also published by Warner Books and by Allen Lane, division of Penguin Books, London, 1973.)

Sowell, T. *A Conflict of Visions: Ideological Origins of Political Struggles*. New York: William Morrow, 1987.

Srole, L., Langner, T. S., Michael, S. T., Opler, M. K., & Rennie, T. A. C. *Mental Health in the Metropolis*, Vol. I. New York: McGraw-Hill, 1962.

Stalin, J. http://en.wikipedia.org/wiki/Joseph_Stalin#Childhood_and_early_years

Steinfels, P. "Beliefs." *The New York Times*, January 29, 2005.

Stern, F. "National Socialism as Temptation." 1985, source unknown.

Stern, F. "Acceptance Speech, Leo Baeck Medal." New York: Leo Baeck Institute. http://www.lbi.org/fritzstern.html (2005).

Stouffer, S. A., et al. *The American Soldier: Adjustment During Army Life*. Princeton, NJ: Princeton University Press, 1949.

Teixeira, R. "Values to the Left of Me, Values to the Right of Me, and Nary a Strategy in Sight." Center for American Progress, Vol. 2006. http://www.motherjones.com/commentary/columns/2006/01/values.html.

Thompson, D. http://www.capitolhillblue.com/artman/publish/article 7218.shtml (August 15, 2005).

Toennies, F. *Gemeinschaft and Gesellschaft* (Community and Society) Edited and translated by Charles P. Loomis (Original ed. 1887). New York: Harper & Row, 1957, 1963.

Turnbull, C. M. *The Mountain People.* New York: Simon & Schuster, 1972.

Wallis, J. "God's Politics: Why the Right Gets It Wrong, and the Left Doesn't Get It." *The New York Times*, August 4, 2005, Op-Ed.

Weber, M. *The Protestant Ethic and the Spirit of Capitalism.* New York: Scribner's Press, 1958.

Wolf, N. *The End of America.* White River Junction, VT: Chelsea Green Publishing, 2007.

Williams, W., & Pellegrino, D. "Gatekeeping and Student Role." *Journal of Educational Research*, 68:366–370, July, 1975.

Winnicott, D. W. (1960). "Ego Distortion in Terms of True and False Self," in *The Maturational Process and the Facilitating Environment: Studies in the Theory of Emotional Development.* New York: International UP, 1965, pp. 140–152.

Index

H

Hannity, Sean 112
happiness by countries 156
Harris, Katherine xxxvii, 54, 200, 238
Hearst, Patty 64
Herbert, Bob 5, 45, 48, 49
Hispanics xx, xxiii, xxxii, xlvii, xlviii, 50, 83, 97, 157, 210, 238
Hitler, Adolf 28, 41, 77, 154, 213
Hobbesian view xxiv, 93
Hobbes, Thomas 99
homogeneity xxxv, 111, 205, 206, 211
homosexuality xxxiv, 11, 19, 88, 101, 102, 120, 140, 141, 147, 175
human nature, view of 8, 9, 211
humiliation 28, 30, 77, 100, 108, 109, 159, 212
Hurricane Katrina xlvii, 12, 37, 46, 81, 92, 112, 119, 124, 125, 144, 170, 173, 178, 203, 246, 247
Hussein, Saddam xxxiii, 52, 58, 81, 120, 169, 191, 203, 228, 242, 243
hypervigilance xlv, 210

I

idealism 13, 211
ideal types xxi, 3, 14, 94, 95, 116, 117, 119, 122, 174, 211
identification upward xxv, xxix, 230
identification with the aggressor 64
Ik tribe 3
immigrants xxii, xxiii, xxvii, xxix, xlvii, 12, 13, 140, 141, 150, 152, 157, 173, 248
imperceptivity 206
Inglehart, Ronald 156, 265
instrumental values xlvi, 12, 13, 206, 211
introspection xlii, 63
introspective xli, xlvi
Iraq xii, xiii, xvii, xxiv, xxxi, xxxiii, xxxvi, xxxvii, xli, xlii, xlv, l, 1, 3, 12, 19, 21, 24, 37, 38, 40, 42, 46, 50, 52, 65, 81, 87, 89, 92, 97, 100, 107, 110, 111, 112, 114, 120, 124, 126, 127, 133, 136, 138, 139, 140, 141, 148, 150, 151, 153, 154, 159, 162, 164, 165, 167, 169, 173, 178, 189, 190, 191, 192, 200, 203, 204, 210, 212, 215, 216, 218, 225, 232, 236, 241, 242, 243, 249, 250, 256, 257, 258, 259, 262
irony 12, 211
isolation of leaders 128

J

Jackson, Michael 108
Jaffe, Joseph xvii
Jefferson, Thomas 201, 217
Johnson, Lyndon 9, 23, 183

K

Kassirer, Susan xvii
Kennedy, Anthony 249
Kennedy, John F. 32
Kennedy, Ted 114, 241, 249
Kenworthy, Lane xxxv
Kerry, John xli, xlii, 6, 8, 13, 22, 51, 52, 53, 59, 111, 242, 245
Kessler, Ronald C. xxxiv, 187, 190, 265
Khan, Genghis 26, 28, 32, 37, 41, 213, 264
Klein, Naomi xxxi, xxxii
Kohut, Andrew 138, 165
Koran 237
Krugman, Paul xxi, xlvi, 2, 4, 19, 49, 58, 200, 202, 247

L

LaBarre, Weston 118, 266
labile parenting xxii
laissez-faire model 96

Lakoff, George P. 116, 119, 266
Landau, Mark J. 225, 266
Langner, Lisa xvii
Langner, Thomas S. 186, 264, 266, 267, 269
Lasch, Christopher xlvi, 5
Lazarus, Andrew xvii
Leighton, Alexander xxxii, 82
Leno, Jay 12
Leonhardt, David 158, 267
Letterman, David 12
Lewinsky, Monica 51, 108, 245
Libby, I. Lewis 40
liberal xxii, xxiv, xxxi, xxxix, xl, xliii, xlv, xlviii, 6, 7, 8, 11, 19, 21, 22, 42, 50, 51, 59, 116, 122, 141, 150, 166, 180, 205, 218, 225, 233, 235, 250, 258, 261
liberals xxi, xxii, xxxix, xli, xlii, xliii, xliv, xlv, xlvi, 3, 13, 54, 55, 58, 60, 64, 65, 114, 116, 117, 120, 125, 137, 141, 143, 144, 150, 151, 199, 200, 202, 218, 226, 236, 266
lies xxviii, 46, 83, 136, 159, 205, 220, 221, 227, 233, 234, 263
Limbaugh, Rush 112
Lincoln, Abraham 38, 130, 167, 243, 267
locus of control xlii, xliii, 20, 197, 211
loneliness 90, 98
longing for authority 83
longing for community 93, 129, 183, 214
loss of identity xiii, 77, 78, 85, 90, 184
loss of love and affection xiii, 90, 184
loss of self esteem 184
loss of social supports xiii, 79, 91, 184
loss over control of life events xiii, 80, 184
Luria, Alexander R. xxxi
lying xxvi, xxxiii, 29, 45, 46, 84, 144, 189, 200, 215, 247, 263

M

Madoff, Bernie xliv, 96
Maher, Bill 12, 114
Main Street xxxiv, 200
Mamet, David xliii
Manichaean worldview 12, 39, 120
McCain, John xxix, xli, xlvii, l, 5, 48, 53, 63, 210, 212, 213, 214, 247, 255
McCarthy, Elizabeth D. 264, 266, 267
Mead, Margaret 10
Medicare Plan D 235, 244, 251
mental disorder xx, xxi, xxxii, xxxiii, xxxiv, 43, 44, 82, 156, 171, 182, 184, 185, 187, 188, 189, 209, 210, 215, 265
mentoring 193, 196
middle class xii, xx, xxiv, xxv, xxvii, xxviii, xxxviii, l, 1, 36, 46, 47, 58, 60, 75, 117, 119, 159, 170, 171, 172, 175, 176, 178, 209, 213, 215, 230, 232, 237
Midtown Manhattan Study xiv, 184, 186, 188, 266
military over-extension 123
Miller, Alice xiii, xxv, 28, 30, 77, 103, 108, 109, 118, 120, 122, 153, 171, 195
minorities xi, xx, xxi, xxii, xxiii, xxix, xxxv, xxxvii, xli, xlvii, 12, 14, 50, 60, 83, 85, 116, 120, 121, 141, 148, 150, 153, 154, 173, 183, 199, 210, 213, 215, 229, 230
mirror neurons xlvii
Miss Beauchamp 62
moralism 206
moral realism 19, 21
mortality salience xlvi, 225, 266
mother's physical and emotional illness 71

violence xxii, xxv, xxvi, xxxix, 26, 32, 49, 63, 66, 73, 100, 102, 104, 108, 111, 112, 113, 153, 159, 234, 250, 267

W

waffling 6, 45, 111, 151, 178, 206, 229
Wallis, Jim 162
war xii, xiii, xvii, xxiii, xxiv, xxix, xxx, xxxi, xxxii, xxxvi, xxxvii, xxxix, xli, xlii, xlv, l, 1, 2, 19, 24, 28, 31, 33, 35, 38, 40, 42, 43, 46, 47, 48, 49, 50, 52, 65, 77, 78, 80, 81, 84, 87, 89, 91, 92, 96, 97, 107, 108, 109, 110, 111, 113, 123, 124, 126, 127, 130, 133, 138, 139, 140, 141, 148, 151, 153, 155, 159, 160, 163, 164, 165, 166, 167, 169, 170, 177, 178, 181, 184, 189, 190, 191, 199, 200, 204, 206, 207, 210, 212, 213, 215, 216, 218, 225, 236, 237, 242, 243, 245, 253, 255, 262, 263, 269
wars xii, 8, 19, 24, 35, 46, 49, 92, 95, 127, 135, 159, 161
Washington, D.C. xii, xxx, xlii, 41, 51, 56, 164, 201, 202, 203, 237, 241, 248, 257, 258, 263
Washington, George xiii, 190, 213
weapons of mass destruction xiii, xxxiii, 1, 40, 46, 52, 81, 133, 153, 159, 203, 216, 225, 228, 241, 242, 243
Weber, Max 3, 11, 78, 117, 118, 119, 200
Welfare xii, xv, xxvi, xxvii, 7, 11, 22, 34, 46, 66, 74, 75, 79, 91, 119, 139, 166, 175, 212
white males 120
whites xxiii, xxiv, xxxvi, 50, 145, 148
W.H.O. survey xxxiv, 215
Williams and Pellegrino 106
Wilson, Joseph C. IV 128, 203, 243

Winkler, Robin xvii
Winnicott, Donald 103
WMD's xxxiii, xxxiv, xli, 40, 46, 52, 114, 177, 178, 181, 191, 216, 229, 242
Wolf, Naomi 114
women xiv, xxiii, 19, 34, 50, 83, 88, 90, 100, 107, 108, 116, 121, 128, 140, 141, 147, 149, 151, 158, 233, 236
working class xx, xxii, xxiii, xxiv, xxv, xxvi, xxvii, xxix, xxxv, l, 1, 3, 36, 58, 65, 159, 175, 183, 189, 209, 215, 237
worldly asceticism 11
World Mental Health Survey 187, 265
World Trade Center xxxi, 45, 133, 240

Z

zero-sum culture 98